Essential Music Theory

Answers 1-8

Mark Sarnecki

San Marco Publications

Elementary Music Theory © 2023 by San Marco Publications. All rights reserved.

All right reserved. No part of this book may be reproduced in any form or by electronic or mechanical means including Information storage and retrieval systems without permission in writing from the author.

ISNB: 1-896499-43-0

Contents

Level 1:	1
Level 2:	28
Level 3:	51
Level 4:	82
Level 5:	110
Level 6:	153
Level 7:	187
Level 8:	231

Level 1

Page 8, No. 1

F D B A E E
G F C A B D
E D C B A G
F E A F C D

Page 10, No. 1

B G E D A A
G F C A B D
A G F E D C
A G C A E F

Page 12, No. 1

B C A G B C
B C B D D E
D A F B D C
C D E D E C
A D B B F G

Page 13, No. 2

Page 13, No. 3

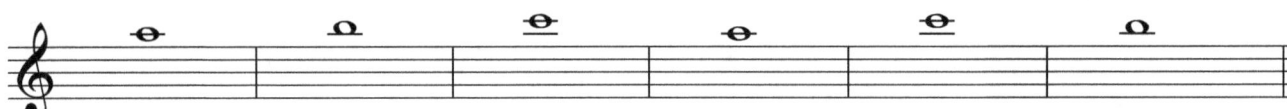

Page 13, No. 4

Page 13, No. 5

Page 13, No. 6

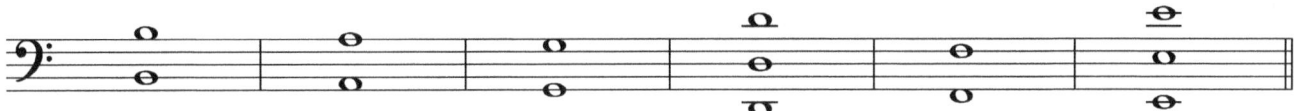

Page 14, No. 1

F C F B A D E C
E D B F G A C C

Page 14, No. 2

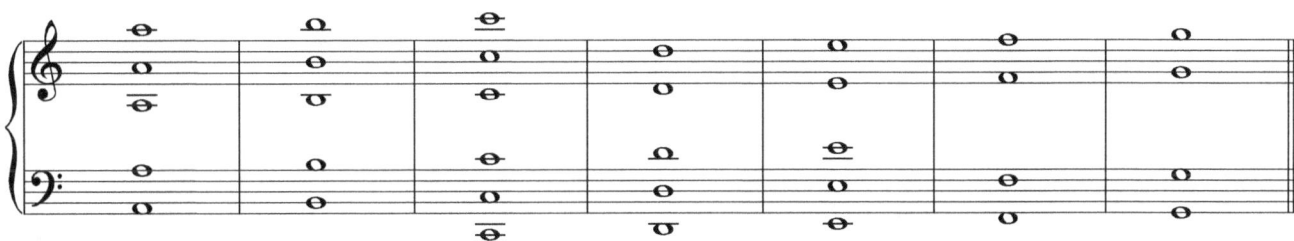

Page 15, No. 3

C B F E D A
B G D C F E

Page 16, other choices are possible

©San Marco Publications 2022   Level 1

Page 21, No. 1

quarter	eighth
half	eighth
whole	dotted half

Page 21, No. 2

1	1
2	4
1/2	3

Page 22, No. 3

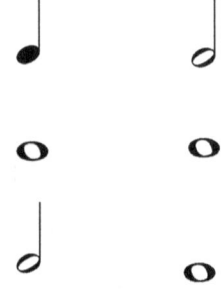

Page 23, No. 1

Page 26, No. 5

quarter note	eighth rest
half rest	whole rest
whole note	eighth note
quarter rest	half note

Page 27, No. 6

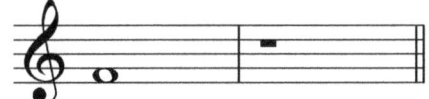

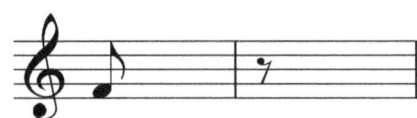

Page 27, No. 7

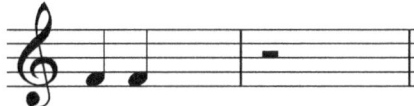   

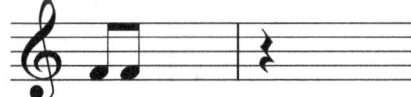   

Page 29, No. 1

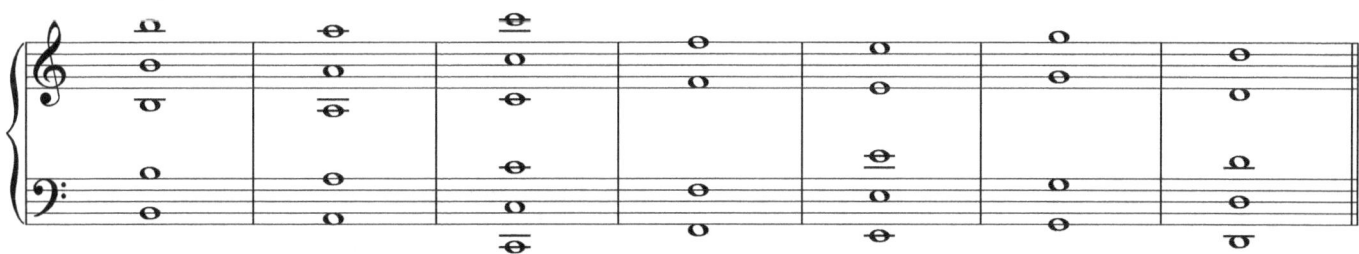

Page 29, No. 2

F   E   A   D   C   G   A   B   G
4   1   2   1/2 1/2 1   1/2 2   1/2

©San Marco Publications 2022   4   Level 1

Page 29, No. 3

Page 30, No. 4

p	piano	soft
mp	mezzo piano	moderately soft
mf	mezzo forte	moderately loud
f	forte	loud

Page 30, No. 5

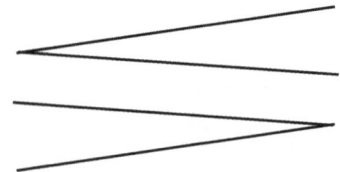

Page 33, No. 1

Page 34, No. 1

©San Marco Publications 2022   Level 1

Page 34, No. 1, continued

Page 35, No. 2

2/4, 4/4, 2/4, 4/4, 3/4

Page 35, No. 3

Page 36, No. 4

Page 36, No. 5

Page 38, No. 1

Page 41, No. 1, other answers are possible

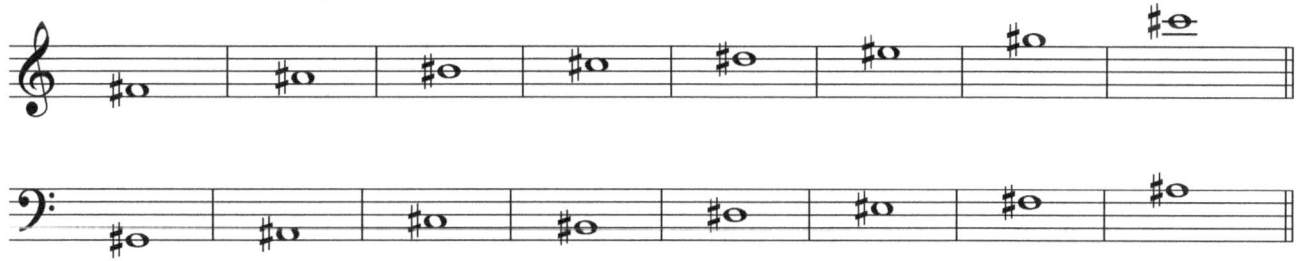

Page 42, No. 2, other answers are possible

Page 44, No. 3

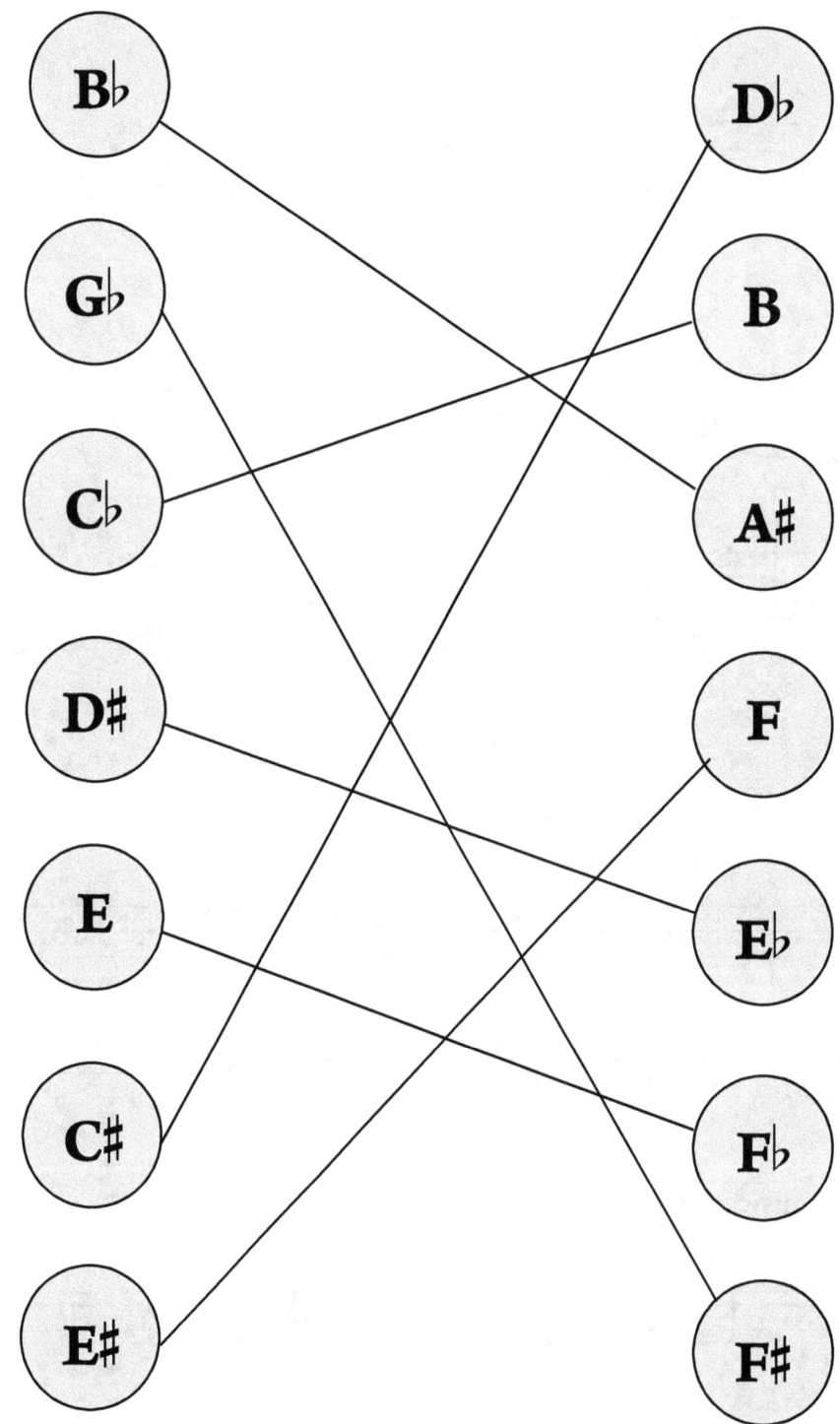

Page 46, No. 1

F♯ E F♯ C♯ D A B♭ E♭ E F♯ E D

A♭ C E♭ A G♯ E G B B♭ D B♭ F♯

Page 46, No. 2, other options are possible

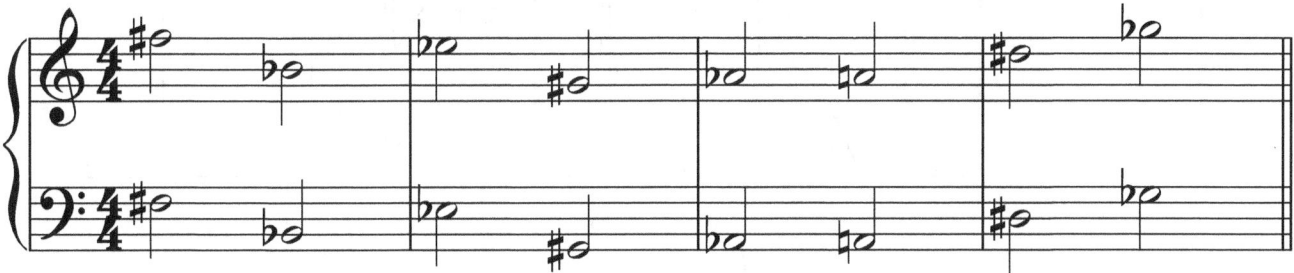

Page 46, No. 3, other options are possible

Page 47, No. 4

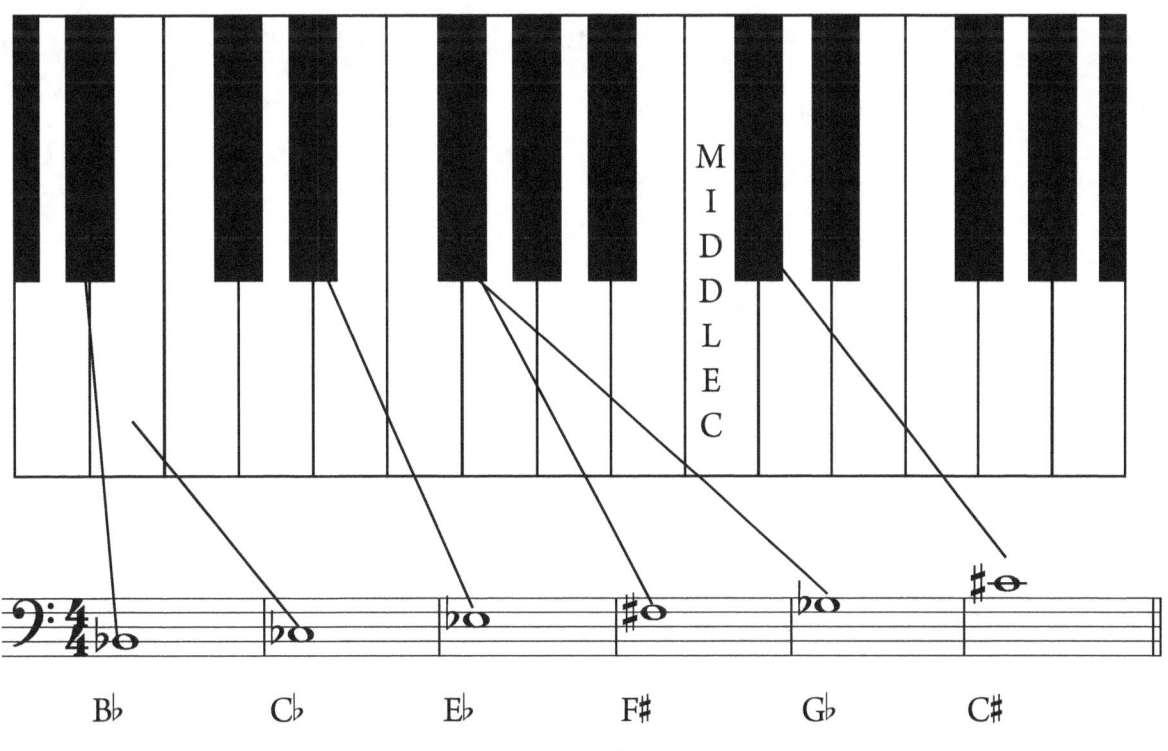

B♭   C♭   E♭   F♯   G♭   C♯

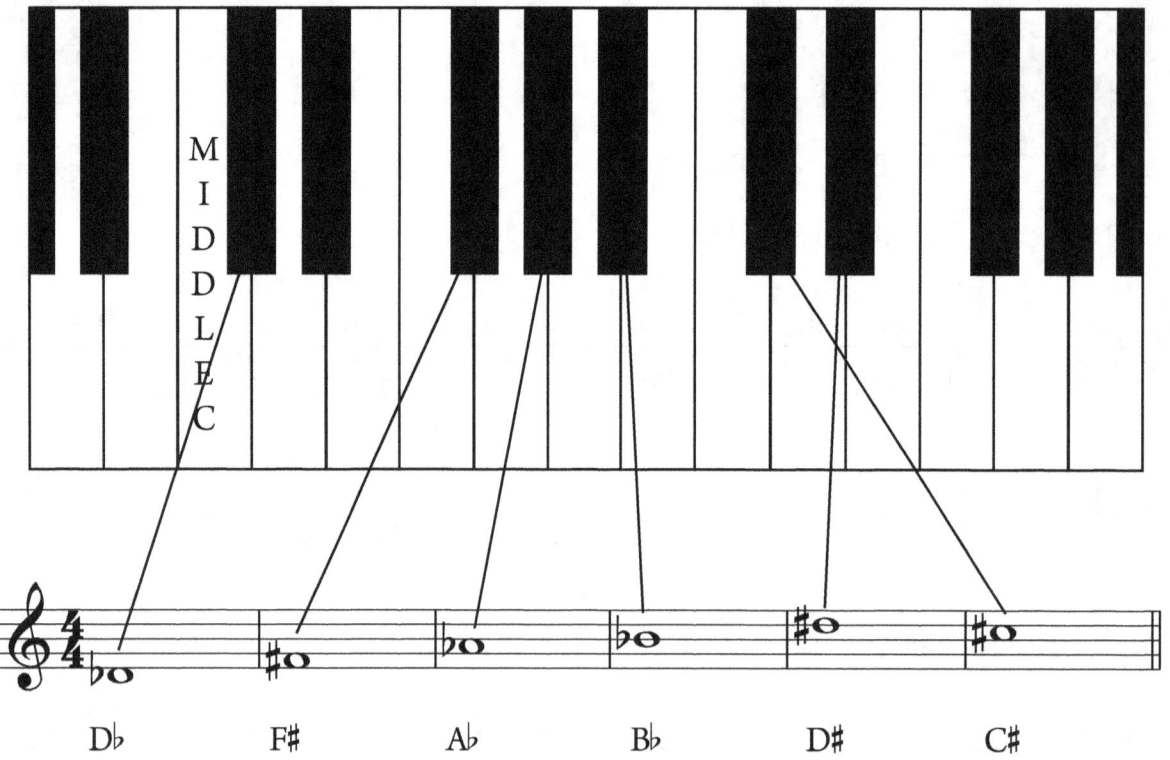

Page 48, No. 5

A whole step	A half step	A whole step	A whole step
A half step	A half step	A half step	A whole step
A whole step	A half step	A half step	A whole step
A half step	A whole step	A half step	A half step

Page 48, No. 6 (other options are possible)

Page 49, No. 7 (other options are possible)

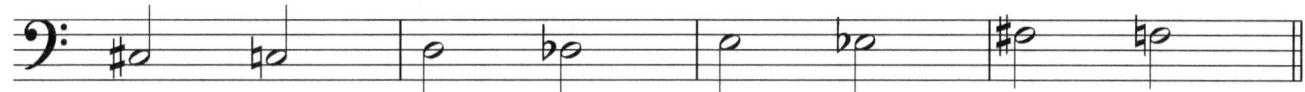

Page 49, No. 8

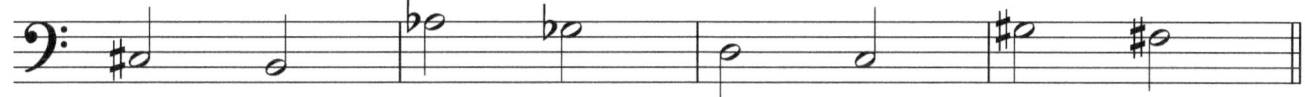

Page 49, No. 9

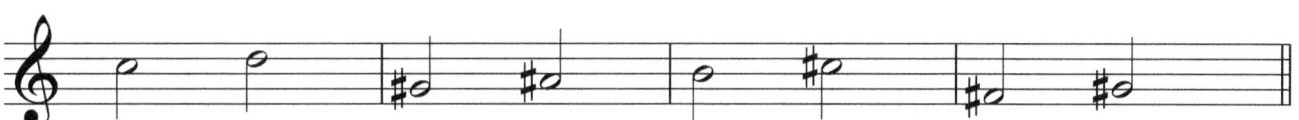
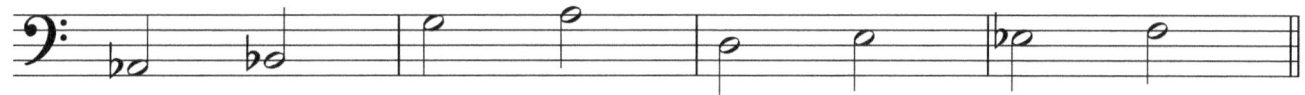

Page 51, No. 1

5 7 2 1 3 7 3 8

4 2 8 6 5 6 2 1

1 8 2 3 6 6 4 5

8 5 2 1 8 3 8 7

Page 52, No. 2

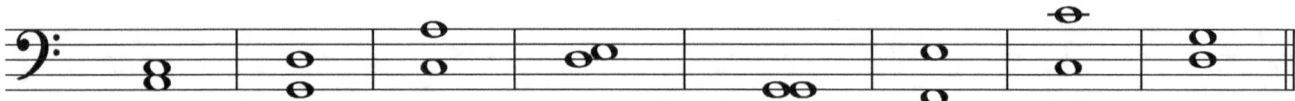

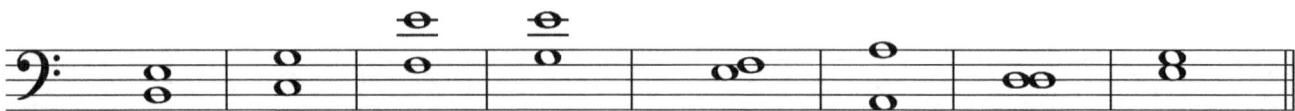

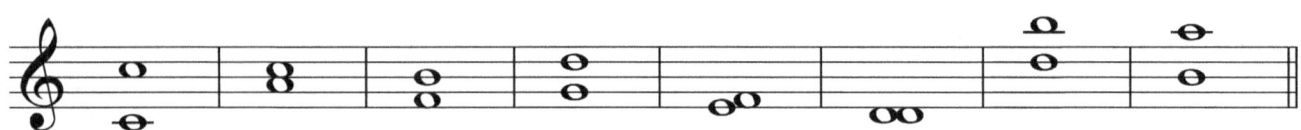

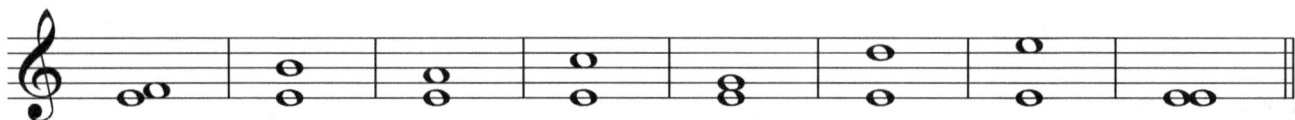

Page 53, No. 3

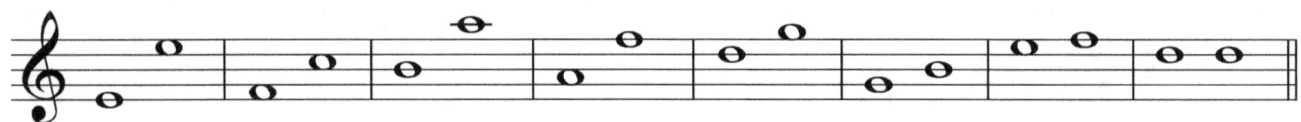

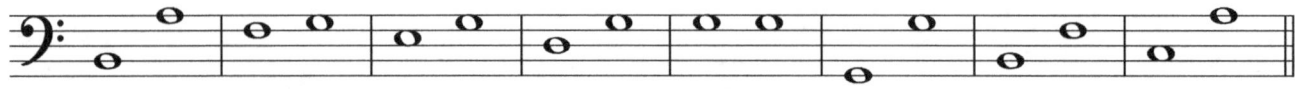

Page 58, No. 1

piano	soft
forte	loud
crescendo	becoming louder
mezzo forte	moderately loud
descrescendo	becoming softer
tie	curved line between two of the same notes meaning to hold for the combined value of both notes
accent	a stressed note
slur	curved line meaning to play the notes smoothly
mezzo piano	moderately soft
staccato	dot on a note meaning play the note short and detached
diminuendo	becoming softer

Page 59

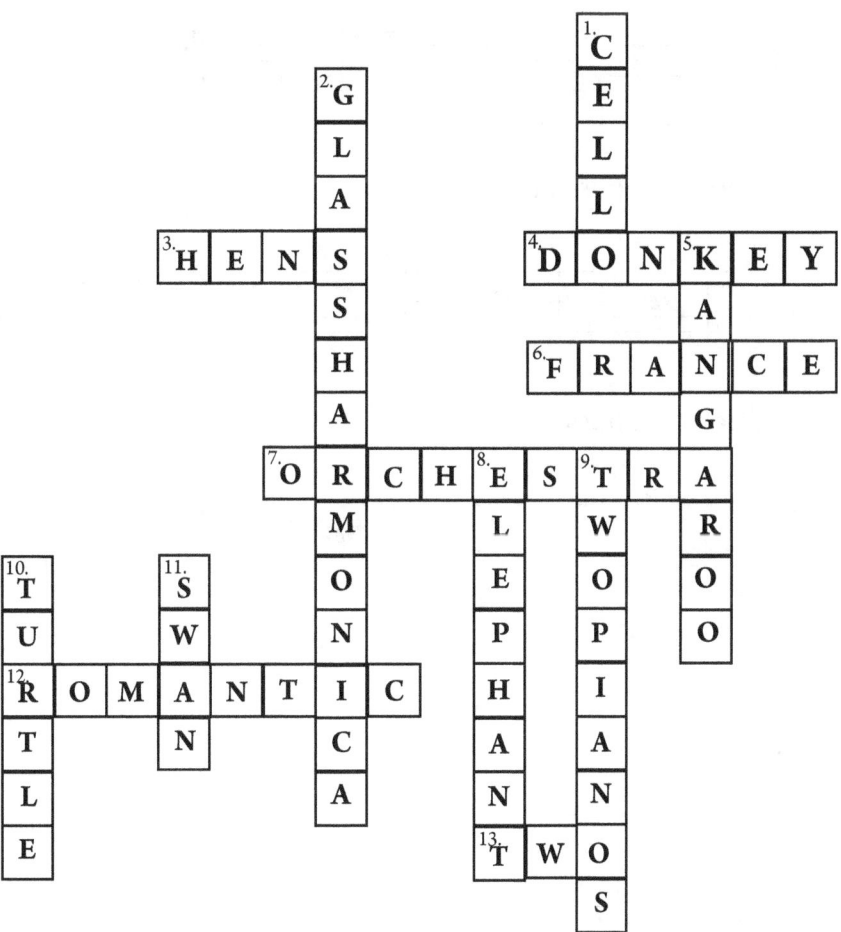

Page 60, No. 1 (Review)

4/4

2/4

Page 60, No. 2

Page 60, No. 3

Page 61, No. 4 (other options are possible)

Page 61, No. 5 (other options are possible)

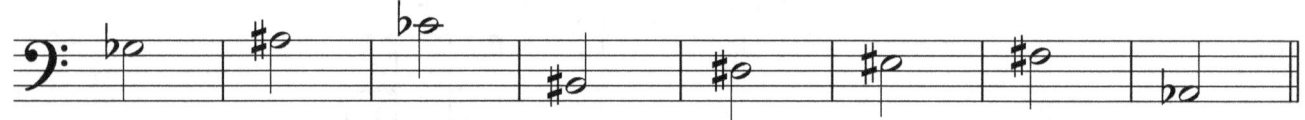

Page 61, No. 6

3 7 4 2 5 6 1 8

Page 61, No. 7

Page 62, No. 8

a. ☑Conductor
b. ☑Maracas
c. ☑French Horn
d. ☑France
e. ☑3
f. ☑2 pianos
g. ☑Wolf
h. ☑Glass Harmonic
i. ☑Cello
j. ☑Program Music

Page 64, No. 1

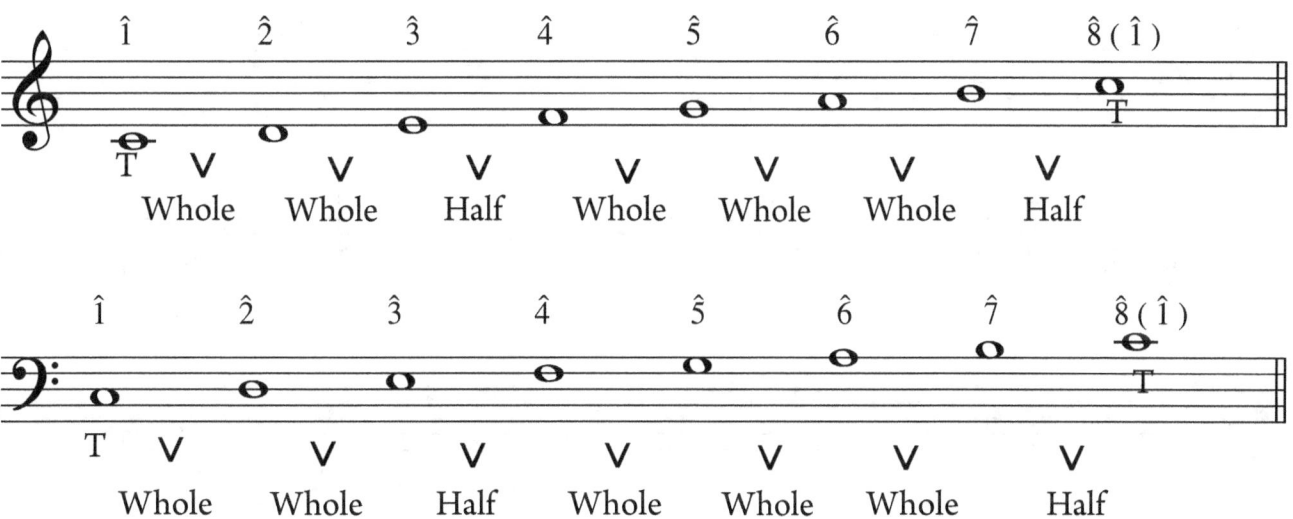

Page 65, No. 2

Page 65, No. 3

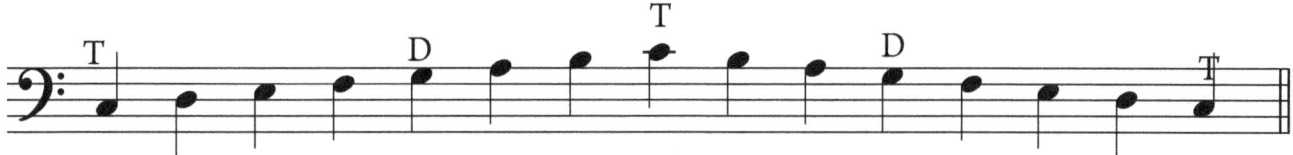

Page 66, No. 4

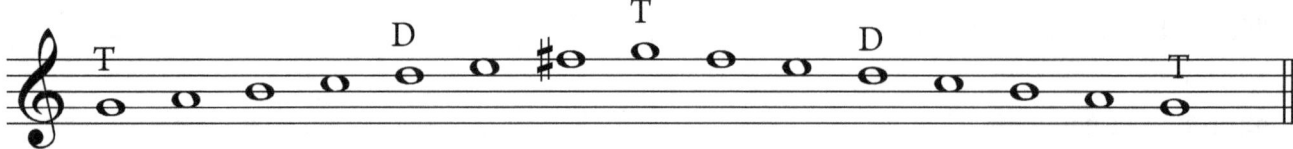

Page 67, No. 5

Page 68, No. 6

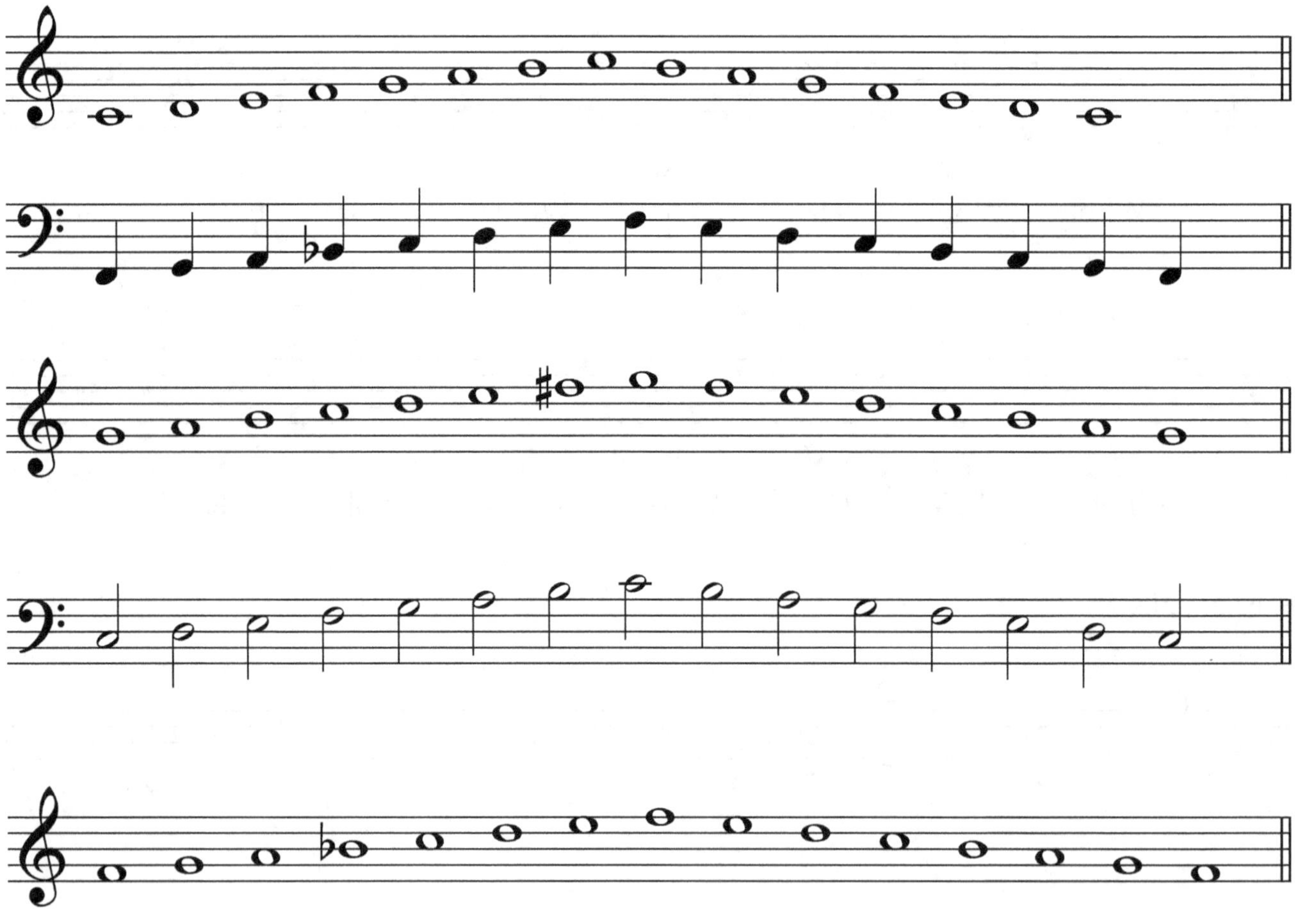

Page 69, No. 7

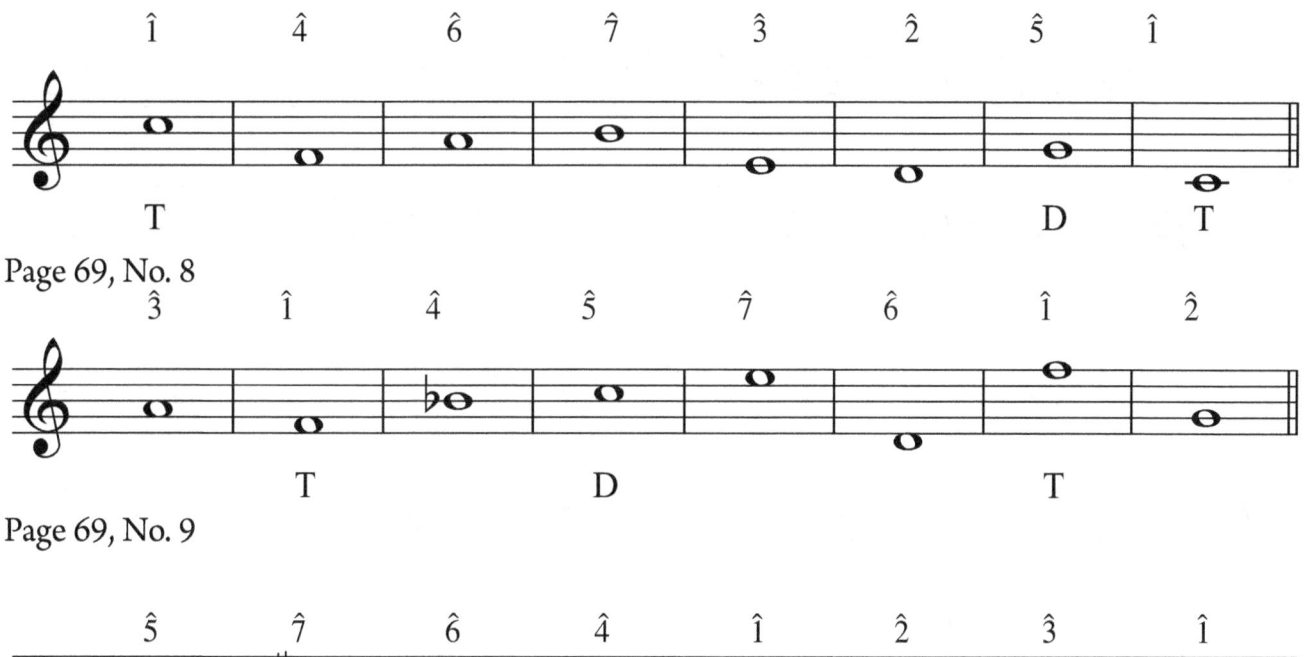

Page 69, No. 8

Page 69, No. 9

Page 71, No. 1

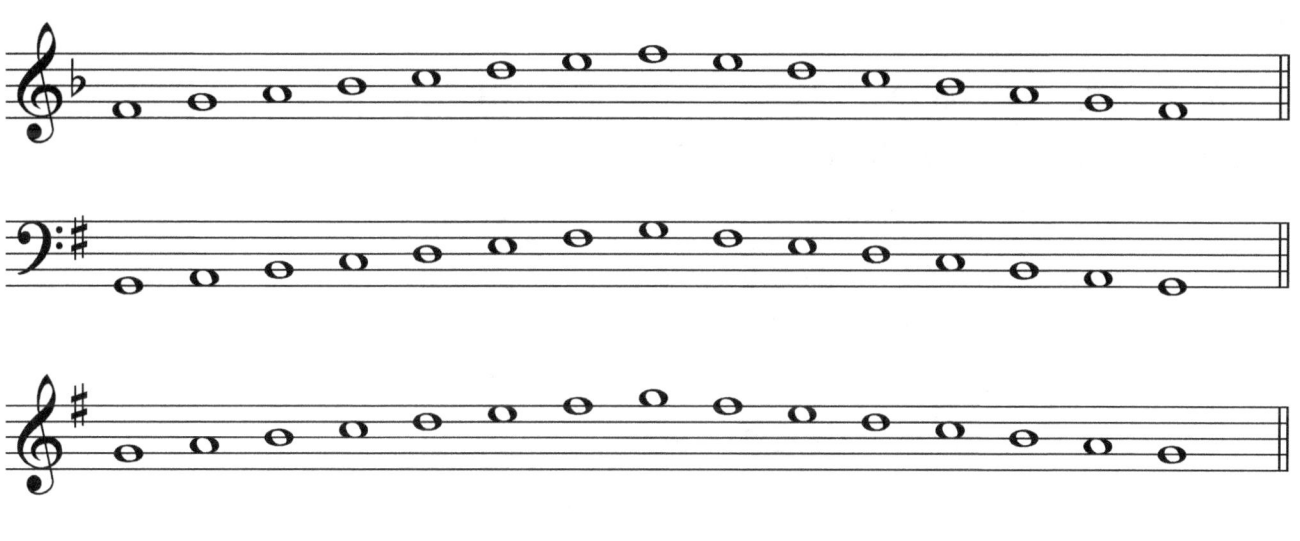

Page 72, No. 1

Page 73, No. 1

F major
G major
C major
F major

Page 77

1. Where was Prokofiev born? — **Russia**
2. At what age did Prokofiev begin composing? — **five**
3. In what musical era did he compose? — **Modern**
4. Peter and the Wolf is written for narrator and — **orchestra**
5. What type of music is Peter and the Wolf? — **Program**
6. Name 4 animals in Peter and the Wolf. — **Wolf, duck, cat, bird**
7. What instruments are used to portray Peter? — **strings**
8. What instrument is used to portray the grandfather? — **bassooon**
9. What instument is used to portray the duck? — **oboe**

©San Marco Publications 2022 — Level 1

Page 78, No. 1

k) tempo
i) crescendo
e) moderato
c) piano
g) forte
j) andante
l) ritardando
f) mezzo piano
h) allegro
d) diminuendo
b) lento
a) mezzo forte

a) moderately loud
b) slow
c) soft
d) becoming softer
e) a moderate tempo
f) moderately soft
g) loud
h) fast
i) becoming louder
j) moderately slow; walking pace
k) speed at which music is performed
l) slowing down gradually

Page 80, No. 1

Page 83, No. 1

Root: C	Root: F	Root: G	Root: A
Third: E	Third: A	Third: B	Third: C
Fifth: G	Fifth: C	Fifth: D	Fifth: E

Page 84, No. 2

F major	G major	C major	C major
F major	G major	G major	F major
A minor	C major	F major	G major
A minor	G major	F major	C major

Page 84, No. 3

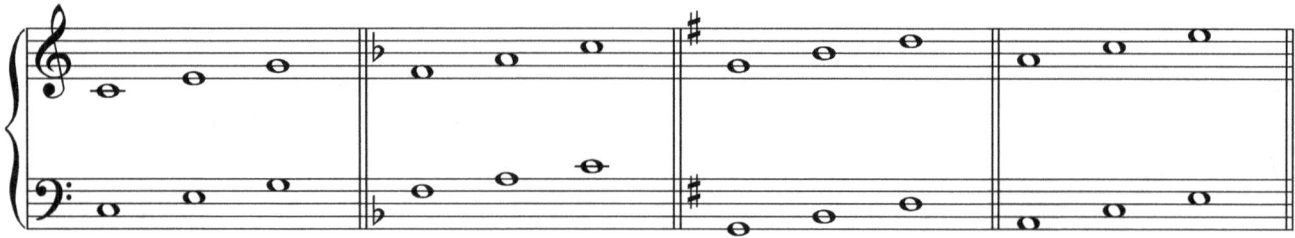

Page 85, No. 4

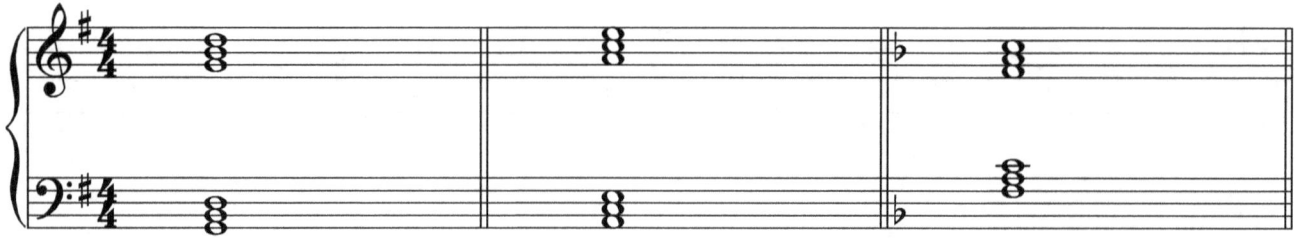

Page 85, No. 5

Triad	Root	3rd	5th
F major	F	A	C
G major	G	B	D
C major	C	E	G
A minor	A	C	E

Page 85, No. 6

Antonin Dvorak
Sonatina

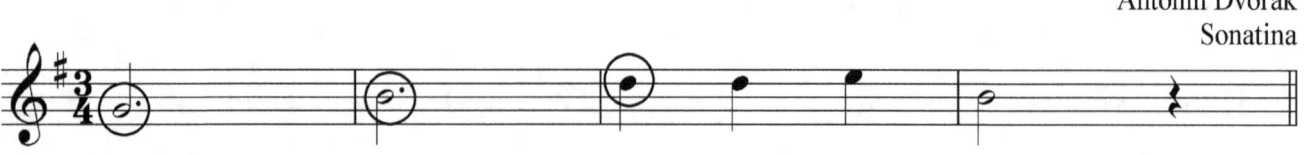

key: G major

Wolfgang Amadeus Mozart
Dissonant Quartet

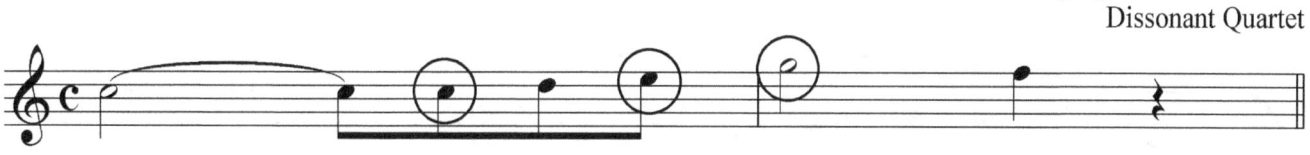

key: C major

Johann Sebastian Bach
Invention No. 8

key: F major

Page 87, No.1

English Folk Song

key: F major

Norwegian Folk Song

key: C major

Page 89, No.1 (other options are possible)

Page 89, No. 2 (other options are possible)

Page 89, No.3

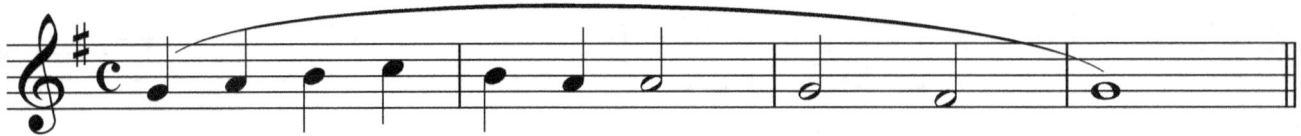

Page 90, No. 1

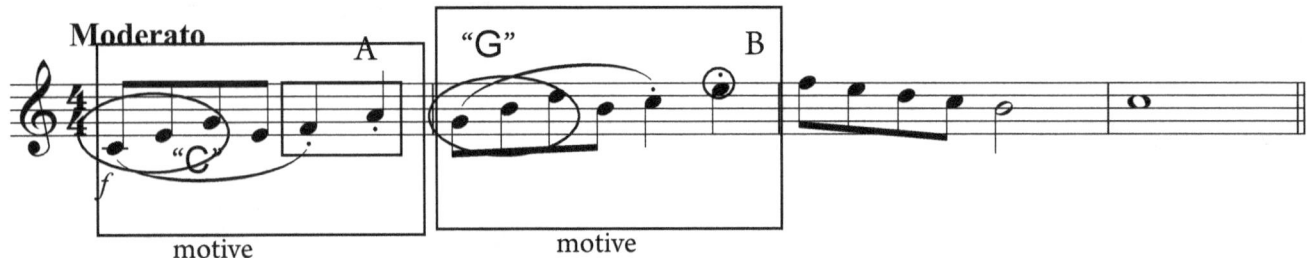

a. Add the correct time signature directly on the music.

b. Name the key of this piece. C major

c. Name the interval at A. 3rd

d. Find and circle a C major triad. Label it "C."

e. Find and circle a G major triad. Label it "G."

f. Define **Moderato**. at a moderate speed

g. Name and define the sign at letter B. staccato, play short and detached

h. Find a motive and draw a square around each time it occurs.

i. How many slurs are in this piece?   2

Page 91

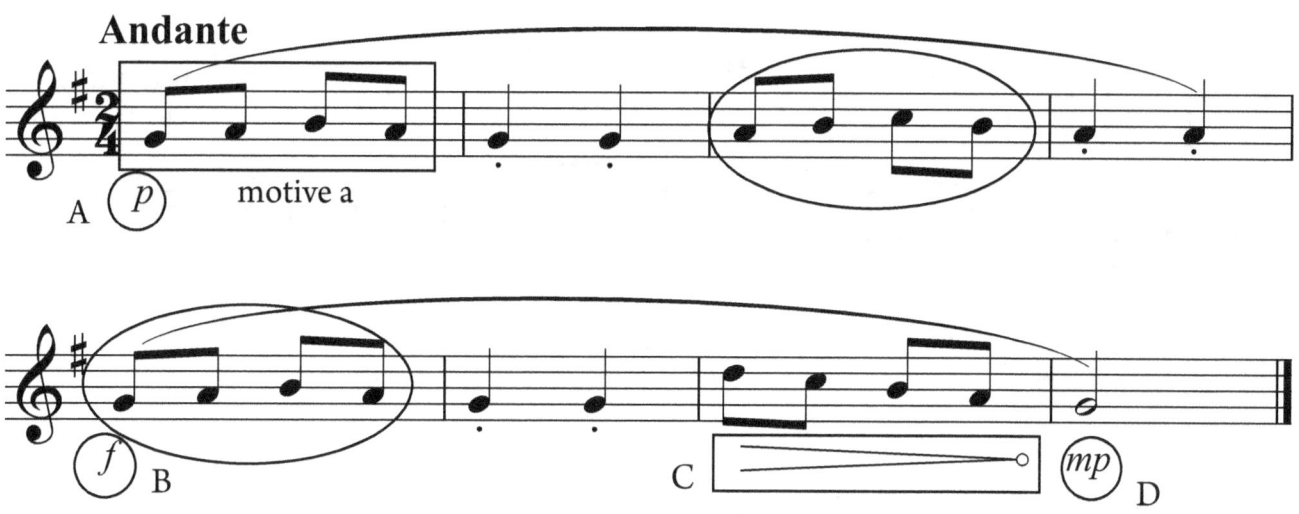

a. Add the correct time signature directly on the music.

b. Name the key of this piece. G major

c. Circle each time motive "a" appears in this piece.

d. How many phrases are in this piece? 2.

e. On which scale degree does phrase two end? $\hat{1}$

f. Define **Andante**. moderately slow, at a walking pace

g. Name and define the sign at letter A. piano, play soft

h. Name and define the sign at letter B. forte, play loud

i. Name and define the sign at letter C. decrescendo, becoming softer

j. Name and define the sign at letter D. mezzo piano, play moderately soft

Page 92

Bagatelle

Anton Diabelli
(1781 - 1858)

a. What is the title of this piece? Bagatelle

b. Who is the composer? Anton Diabelli

c. Name the key of this piece G major

d. Add the time signature directly on the music.

e. How many phrases are in this piece? 1.

f. On which scale degree does the melody this piece begin? $\hat{5}$

g. Define *Allegro*. fast

h. Name the interval at A. 3rd

i. Name the interval at B. 4th

j. This piece is played:

    ☑loud   ☐soft

©San Marco Publications 2022   Level 1

Page 93, No. 1

Page 93, No. 2

Page 93, No. 3

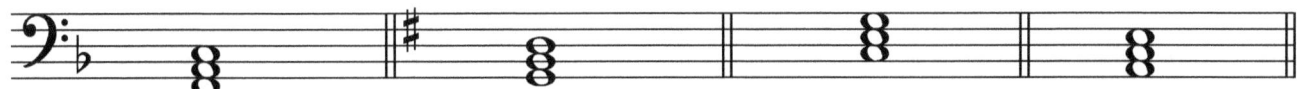

Page 94, No. 4

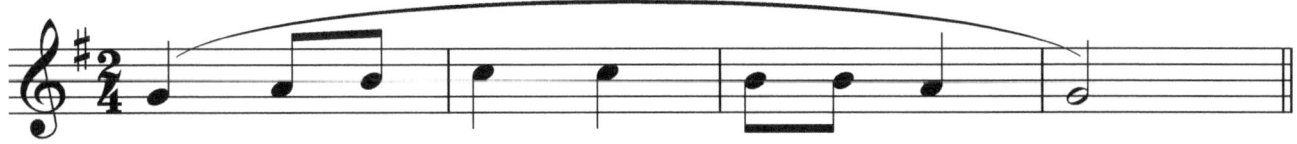

Page 94, No. 5

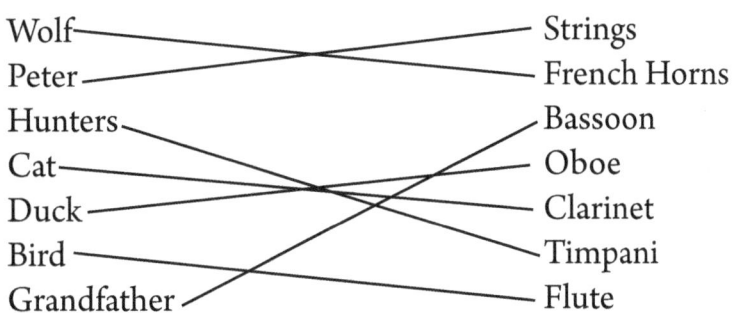

©San Marco Publications 2022   26   Level 1

Page 95, No. 6

a. F
b. F
c. T
d. T
e. F
f. T
g. T

Page 95, No. 7

a. rit
b. dim
c. cresc
d. decresc
e. mp
f. ff

Level 2

Page 3, No. 1

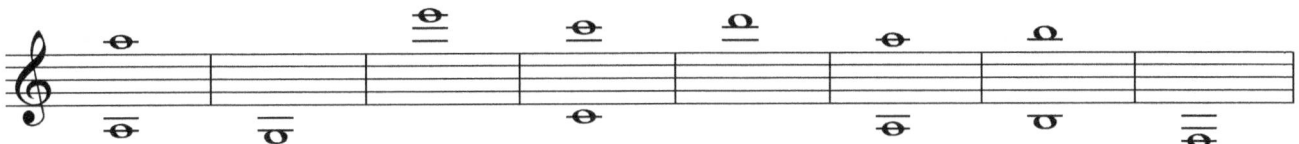

Page 3, No. 2

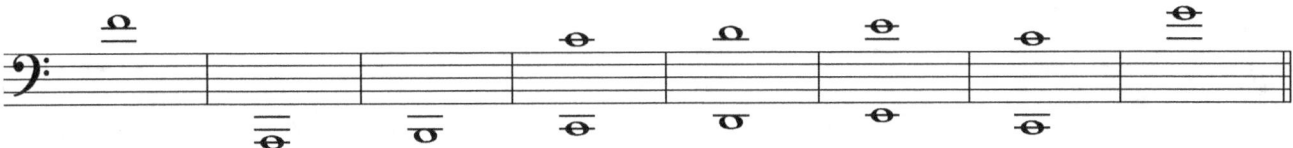

Page 3, No. 3

A C# G B♭ D E B A

B C# D♭ B F G F G

Page 3, No. 4

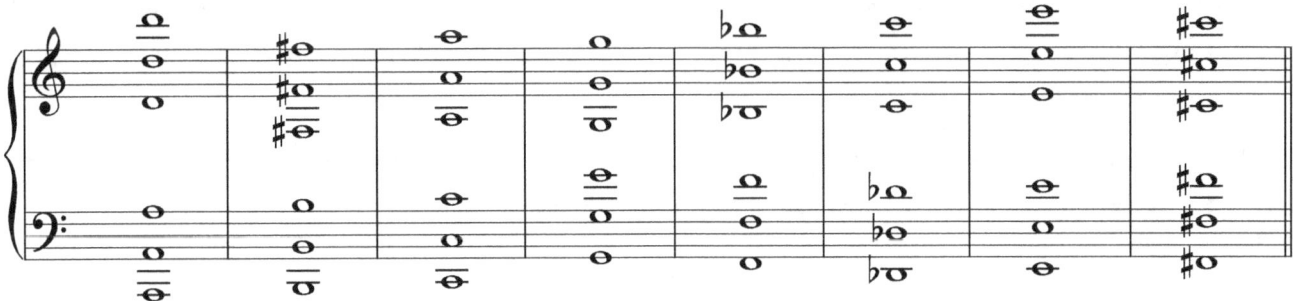

Page 4, No. 1

Page 4, No. 2

Page 5, No. 1

Page 8, No. 1

Page 8, No. 2

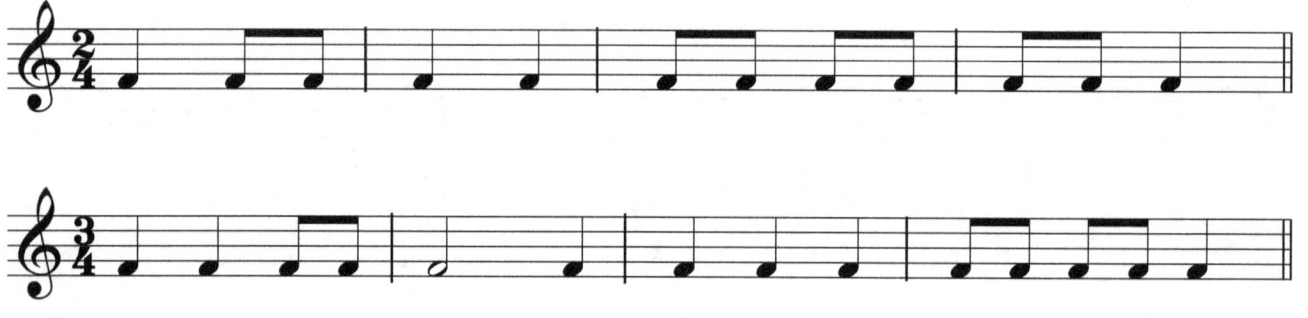

Page 10, No. 1

Page 11, No. 2

Page 12, No. 1

Page 12, No. 2

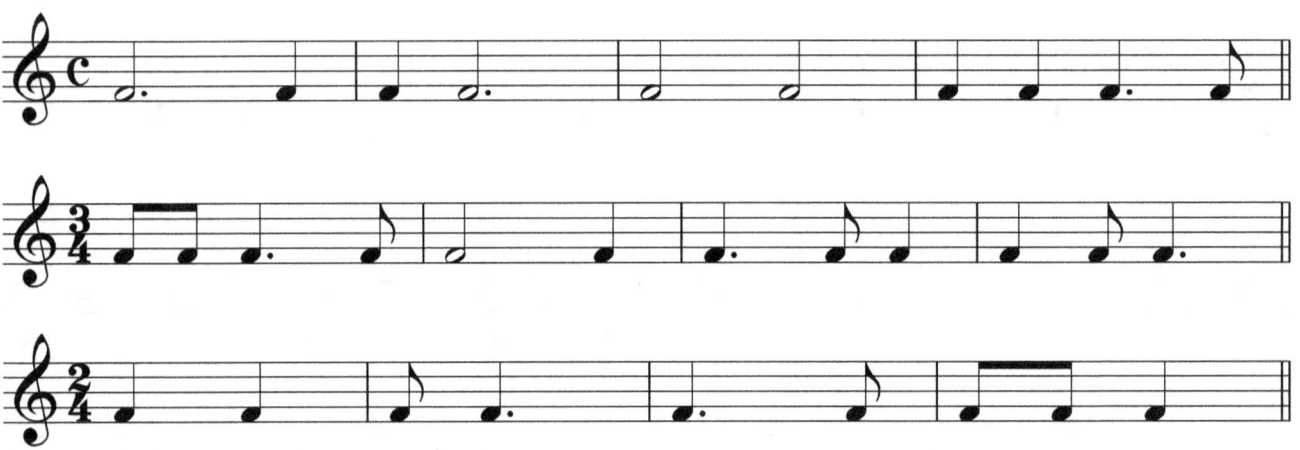

Page 16, No. 1

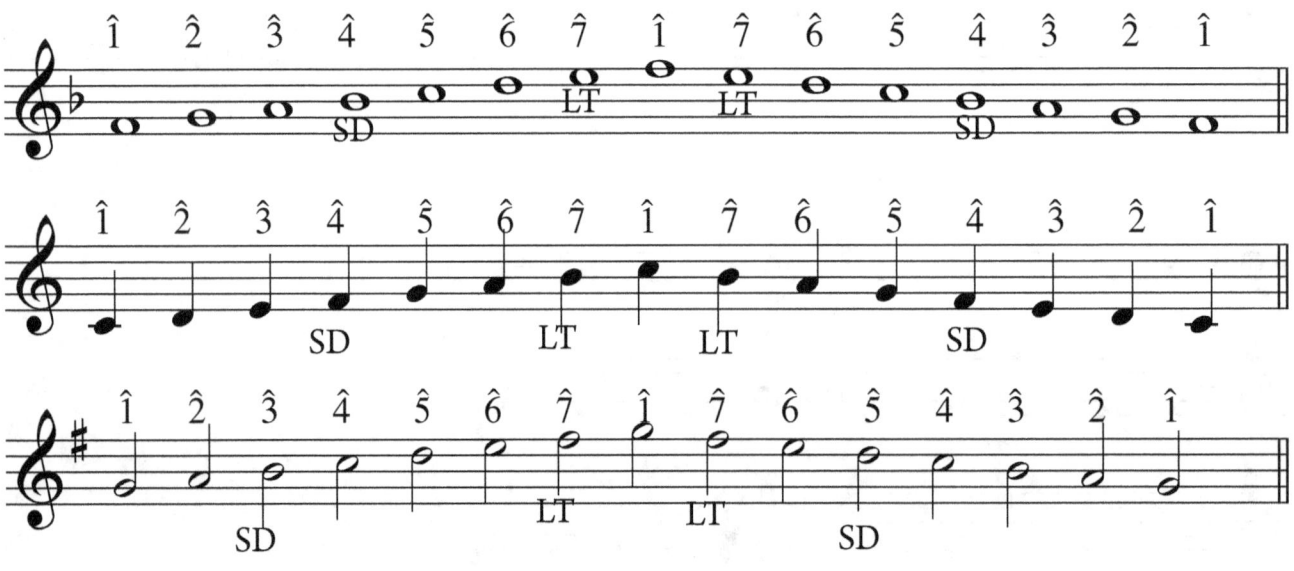

Page 16, No. 2

Page 17, No. 3

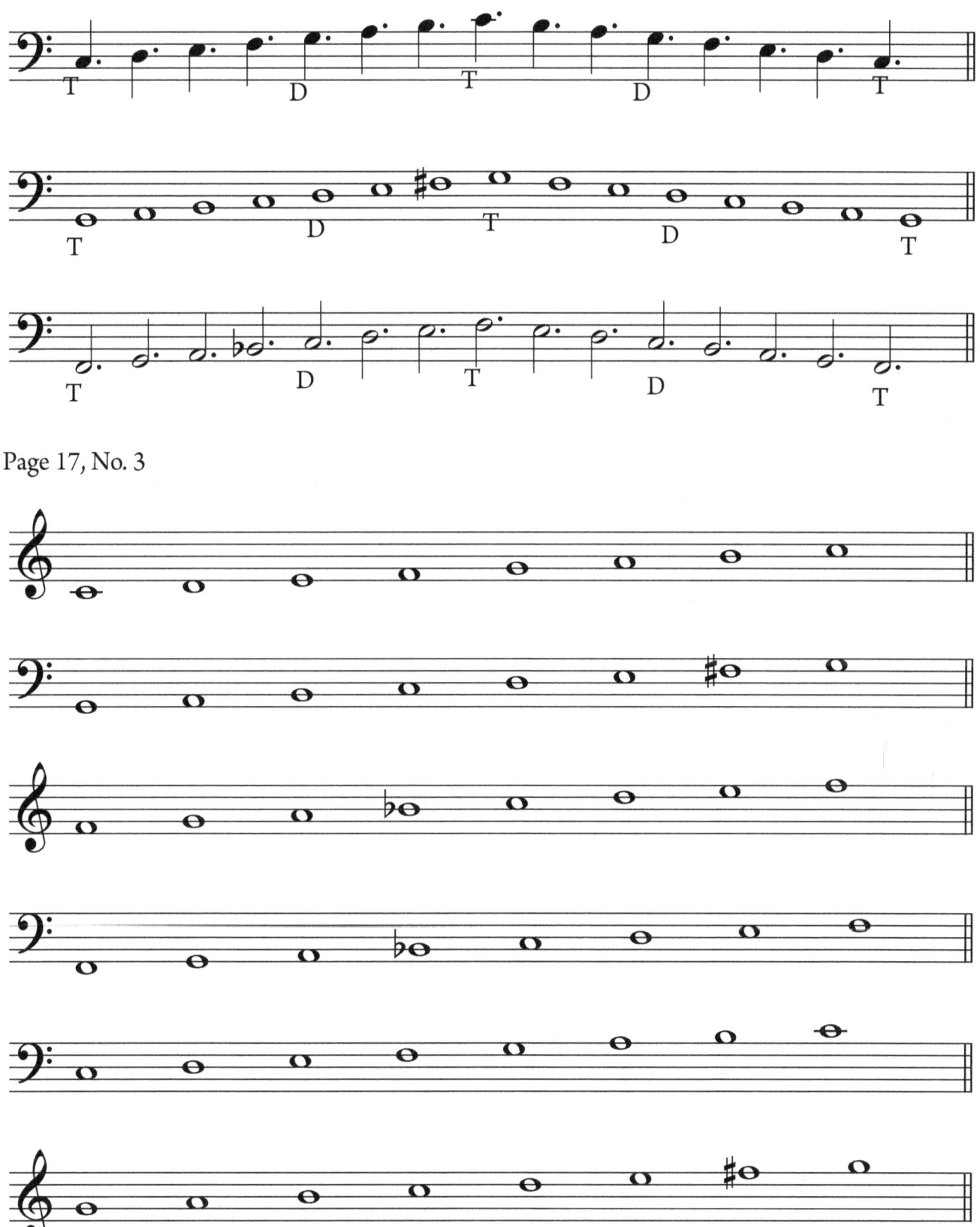

Page 18, No. 4

1 2 7 3 5 4
1 6 7 5 6
5 1 4 2 7
1 7 6 4 2

Page 19, No. 5

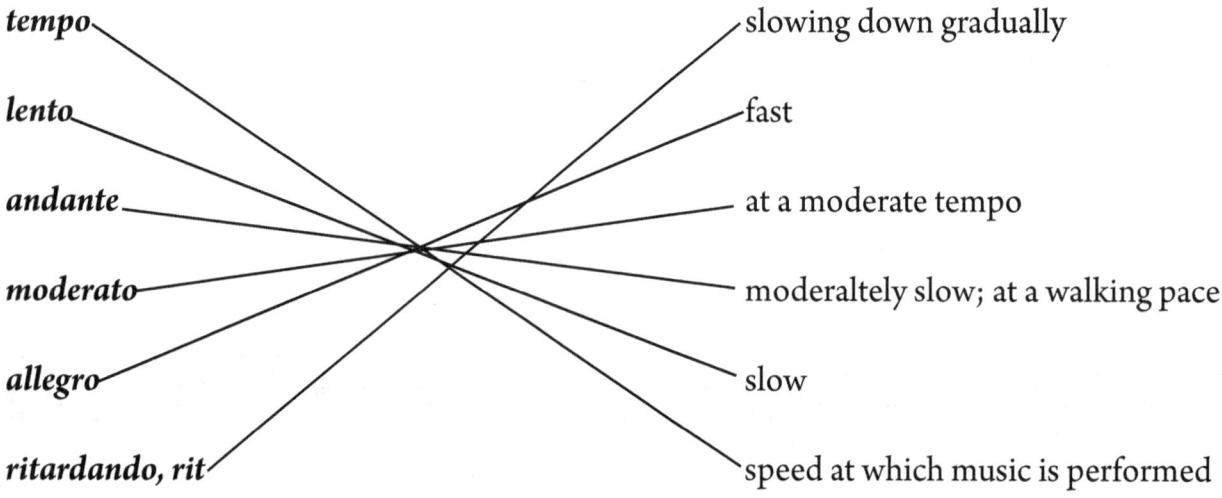

tempo — speed at which music is performed
lento — slow
andante — moderately slow; at a walking pace
moderato — at a moderate tempo
allegro — fast
ritardando, rit — slowing down gradually

Page 20, No. 1 (Review 1)

E B D A C B G F
C D D E E G B A

Page 20, No. 2

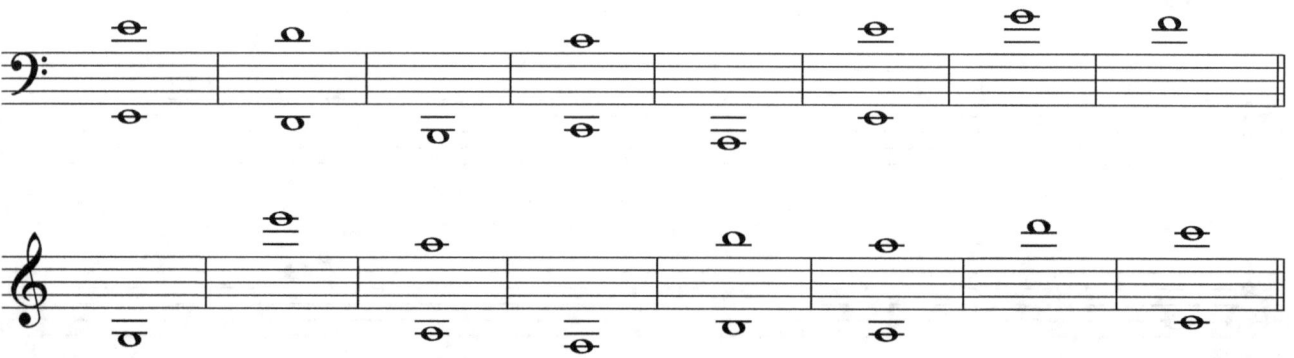

Page 21, No. 3

Page 21, No. 4

Page 22, No. 5

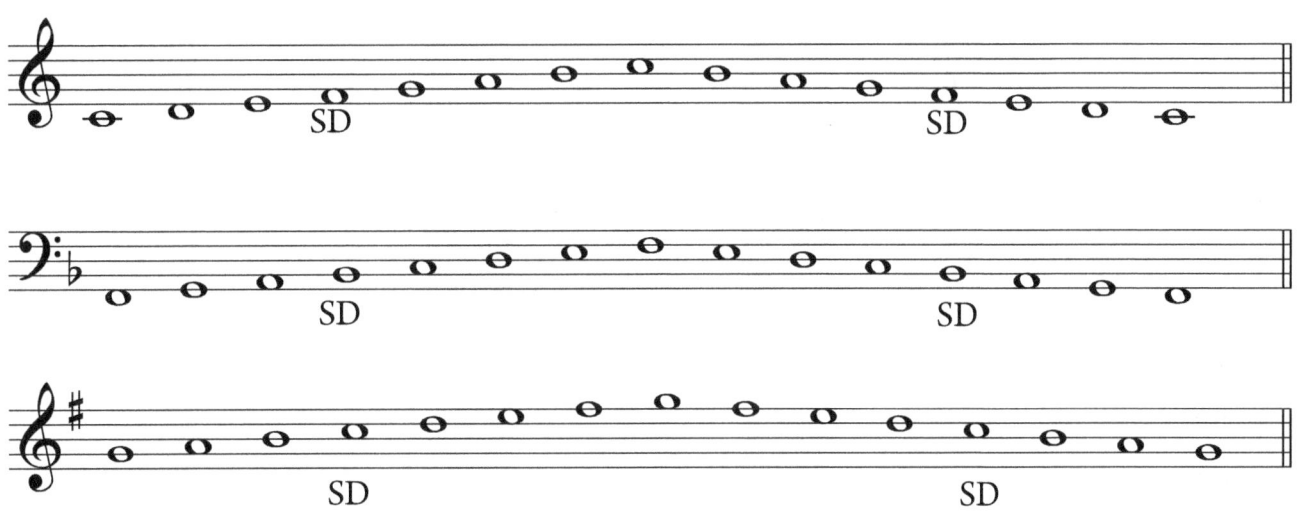

Page 22, No. 6

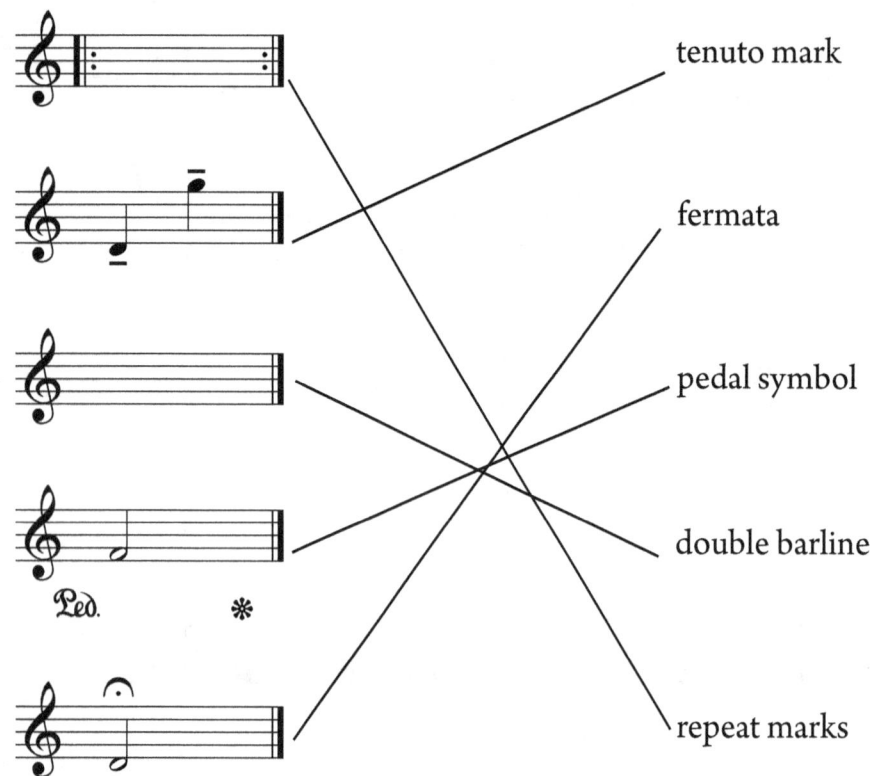

Page 23, No. 7

tempo	speed at which music is performed
lento	slow
moderato	at a moderate tempo
rallentando, rall.	slowing down
a tempo	return to the original tempo
allegretto	fairly fast, not as fast as allegro
andante	moderate, walking pace
presto	very fast
allegro	fast
ritardando, rit	slowing down gradually

Page 27, No. 1

A minor

E minor

D minor

Page 27, No. 2

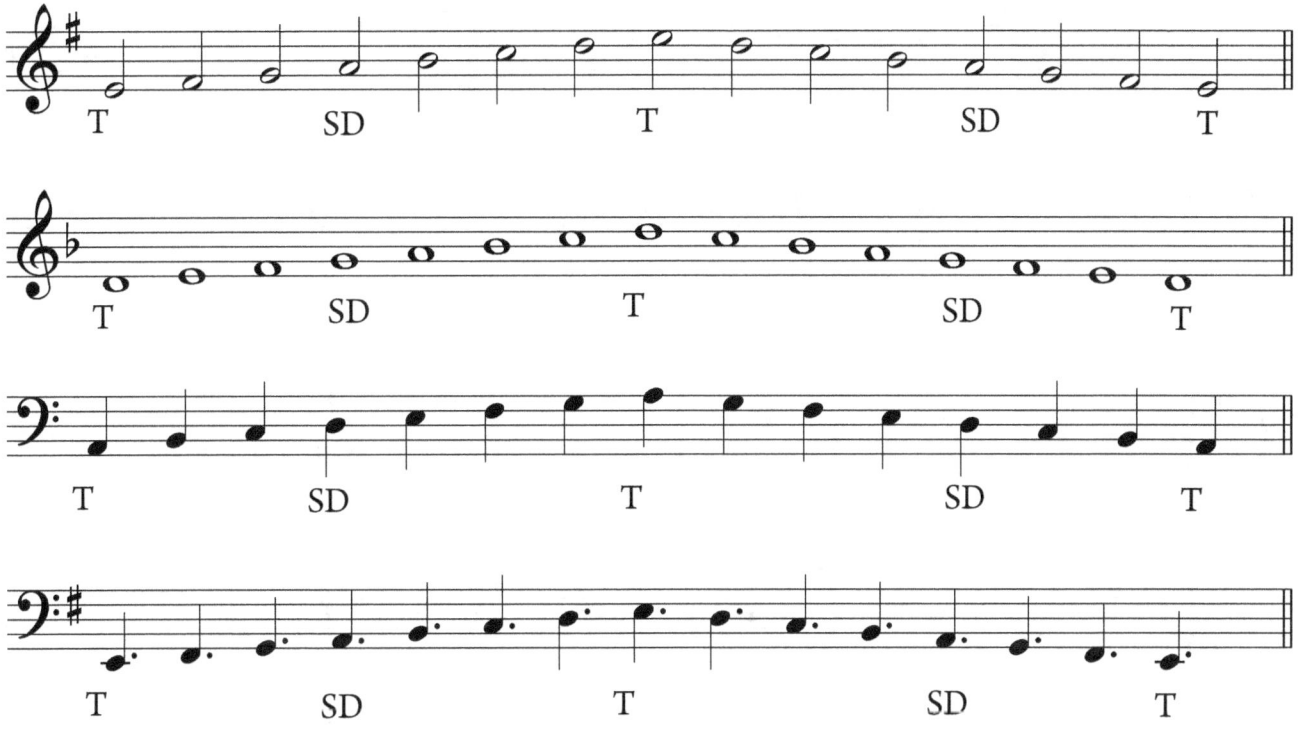

Page 29, No. 1

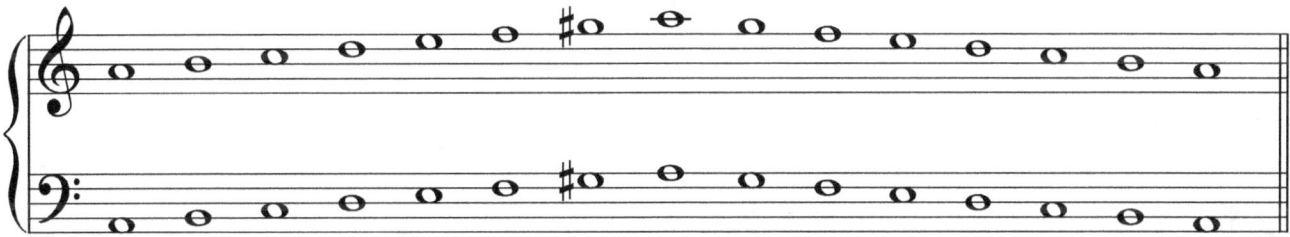

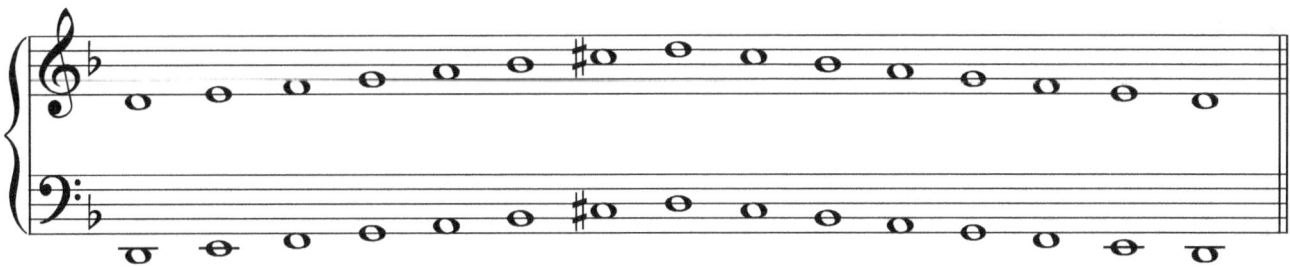

Page 30, No. 2

Page 31, No. 3

Page 33, No. 1

Page 33, No. 2

Page 34, No. 1

Page 34, No. 2

Page 35, No. 1

Page 35, No. 2

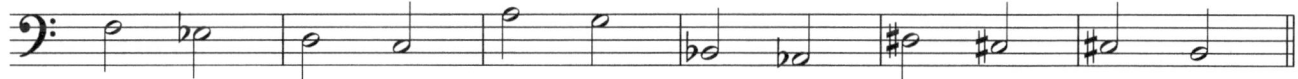

Page 36, No. 1

Page 36, No. 2

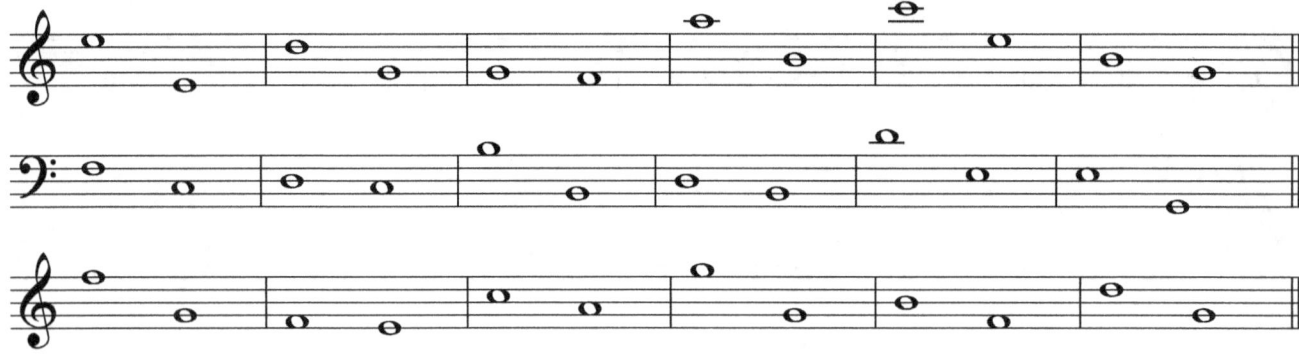

Page 37, No. 3

4 5 3 8 6 7 6 2

7 5 3 2 1 4 5 6

2 4 8 3 1 8 5 5

8 2 5 1 3 7 4 4

Page 40, No. 1

a. Austria
b. His father
c. classical
d. french horn
e. movements
f. rondo
g. piano
h. 12
i. theme
j. Twinkle Twinkle, Baa Baa Black Sheep, Alphabet Song

Page 44, No. 1

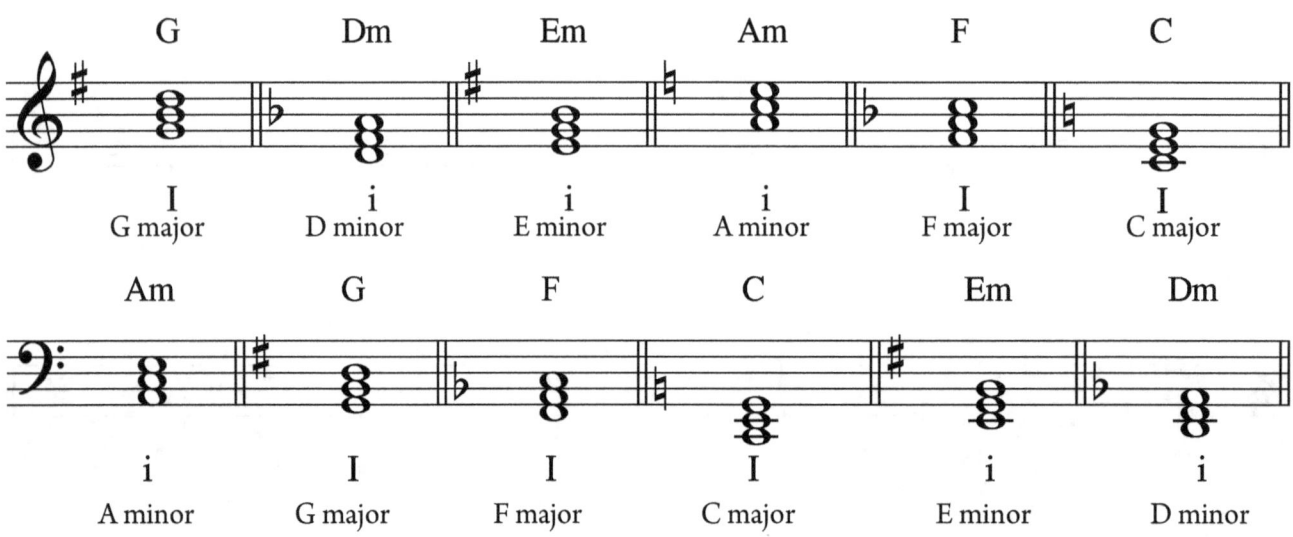

Page 44, No. 2 (naturals are optional, but not necessary after double bar)

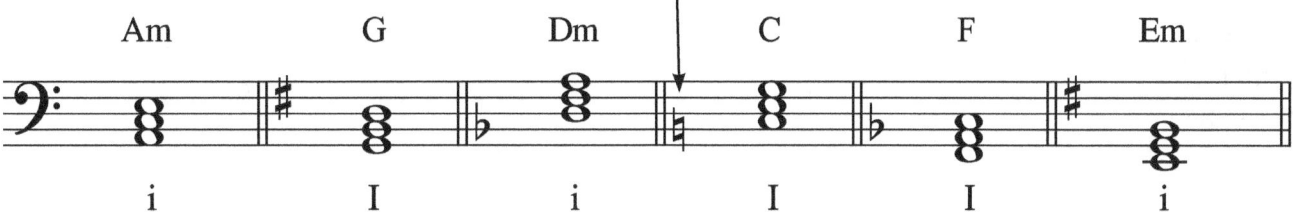

Page 45, No. 3

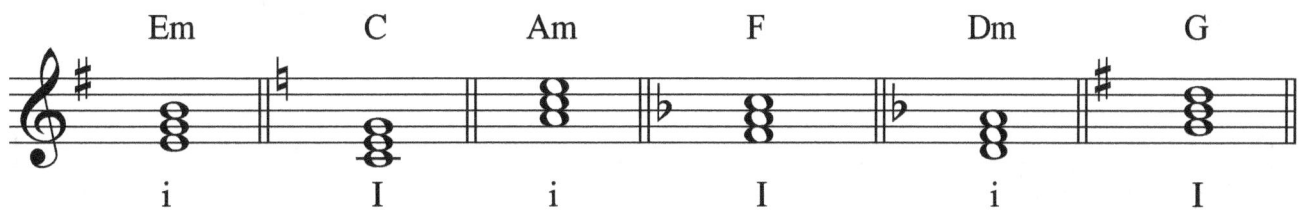

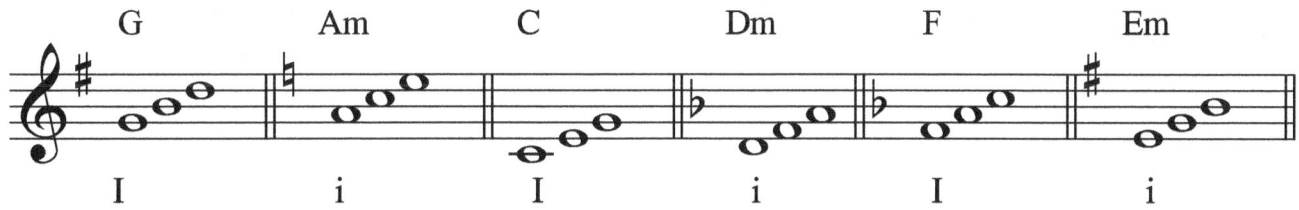

Page 45, No. 4

chord symbol:	**C**	chord symbol:	**Dm**	chord symbol:	**G**
key:	**C major**	key:	**D minor**	key:	**G major**
root:	**C**	root:	**D**	root:	**G**
3rd:	**E**	3rd:	**F**	3rd:	**B**
5th:	**G**	5th:	**A**	5th:	**D**
chord symbol:	**Em**	chord symbol:	**Am**	chord symbol:	**F**
key:	**E minor**	key:	**A minor**	key:	**F major**
root:	**E**	root:	**A**	root:	**F**
3rd:	**G**	3rd:	**C**	3rd:	**A**
5th:	**B**	5th:	**E**	5th:	**C**

Page 47, No. 1 (Review 2)

C major
F major
G major

Page 47, No. 2

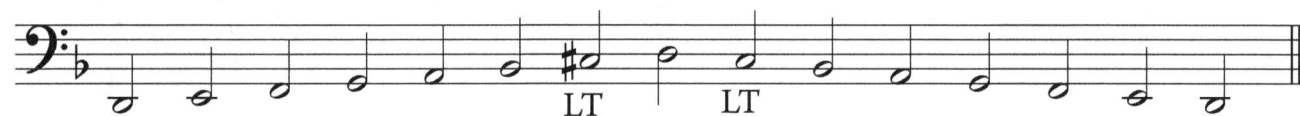

Page 48, No. 3

H H H W W H

W W H H W W

Page 48, No. 4

5 6 2 1 3 8 7 4

8 4 1 6 5 7 3 6

1 3 2 8 7 6 4 5

Page 49, No. 5

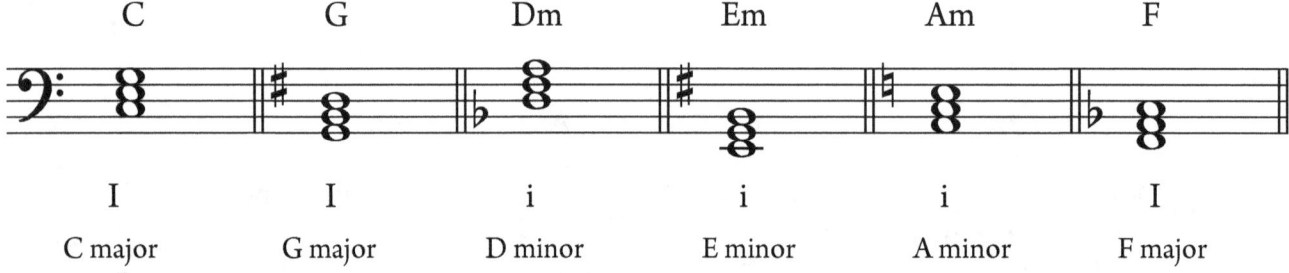

Page 49, No. 6

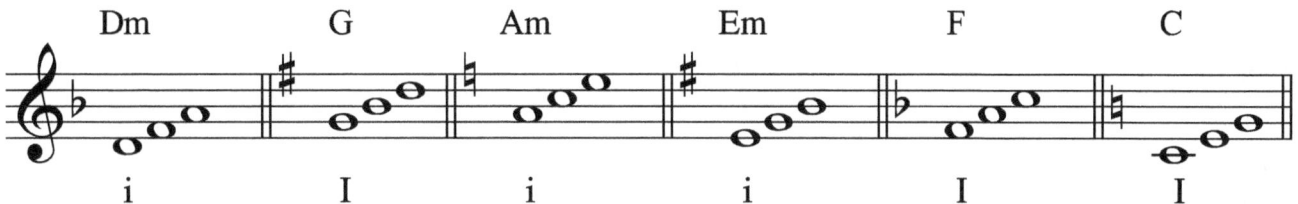

Page 49, No. 7

poco — little

molto — much very

fine — the end

da capo, D.C. — from the beginning

D.C. al fine — repeat from the beginning and end at fine

Page 50, No. 8

a. In what country was Mozart born? **Austria**

b. Name one instrument Mozart played. **piano, violin**

c. How old was Mozart when he wrote his first opera?

☐ 5   ☑ 12   ☐ 7

d. Who was Mozart's first teacher? **His father**

e. What is the solo instrument in Mozarts horn concerto? **French horn**

f. For which instument are the variations "Ah vous dirai-je, Maman" written? **Piano**

g. How many variations are there in "Ah vous dirai-je, Maman?" **Twelve**

h. Name one popular childrens song based on this theme. **Twinkle, Twinkle Baa Baa Black Sheep, Alphabet Song**

Page 53, No. 1

G major
F major
A minor
C major
E minor
D minor
G major

Page 54

1. Fairly fast, slower than allegro — allegretto
2. Very loud — fortissimo
3. Little — poco
4. Much, very — molto
5. The end — fine
6. Very fast — presto
7. Very soft — pianissimo
8. At a moderate tempo — moderato
9. Soft — piano
10. Moderately loud — mezzo piano
11. Loud — forte
12. Becoming louder — crescendo
13. Play smoothly — legato
14. Play short and detached — staccato

Page 56, No. 1

F major	$\hat{2}$	unstable
C major	$\hat{1}$	stable
G major	$\hat{3}$	stable

Page 57, No. 1

F major

C major

G major

Page 59, No. 1 (other options are possible)

Page 59, No. 2 (other options are possible)

Page 59, No. 3 (other options are possible)

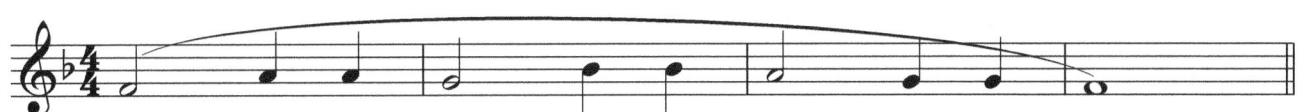

© San Marco Publications 2022   Level 2

Page 60, No. 4 (other options are possible)

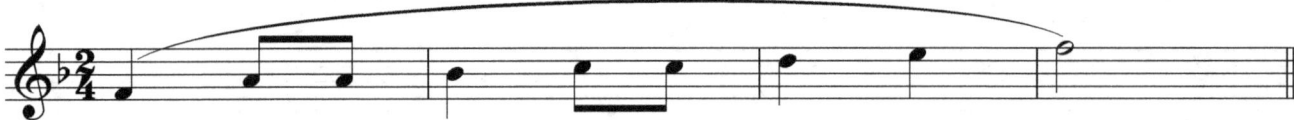

Page 60, No. 5 (other options are possible)

Page 60, No. 6

Page 61, No. 1

a. Add the correct time signature directly on the music.

b. Name the key of this piece. **F major**

c. Circle a complete F major scale in this piece.

d. Draw a phrase mark over the phrase.

e. On which scale degree does this phrase end? $\hat{1}$

f. Is this a stable degree? **yes**

g. Define *Allegro*. **fast**

h. Explain the sign at letter A. **fortissimo, very loud**

i. Explain the sign at letter B. **fermata, pause**

j. Label all the leading tones **LT.**

Page 62

a. Add the correct time signature directly on the music.

b. Name the key of this piece. **G major**

c. Circle each time motive "a" appears in this piece.

d. There are two phrases. Draw a phrase mark over each phrase.

e. On which scale degree does this phrase one end? $\hat{2}$

f. Is this a stable degree? **no**

g. Define *Presto*. **very fast**

h. Explain the sign at letter A. **mezzo piano, moderately soft**

i. Explain the sign at letter B. **pianissimo, very soft**

j. Name and define the sign at letter C. **staccato, play short and detached**

Page 63

Allegro in C

Alexander Reinagle
(1756 - 1809)

a. Give the title of this piece. **Allegro in C**

b. Add the correct time signature directly on the music.

c. Name the key of this piece. **C major**

d. Name the composer of this piece. **Alexander Reinagle**

e. When did he live? **1756- 1809**

f. There are two phrases. Draw a phrase mark over each phrase.

g. On which scale degree does phrase two end? **î**

h. Is this a stable degree? **yes**

i. Define *Molto allegro*. **Very fast**

j. Name and define the sign at A. **forte, loud**

k. Name the interval at B. **3rd**

© San Marco Publications 2022   Level 2

Page 64, No. 1 (Review 3)

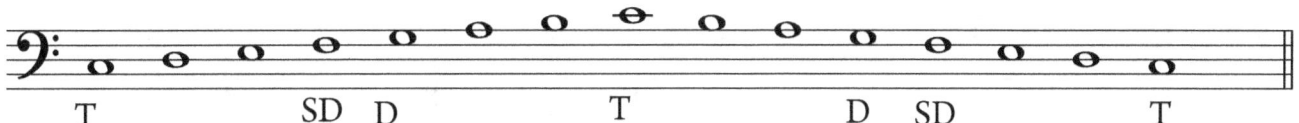

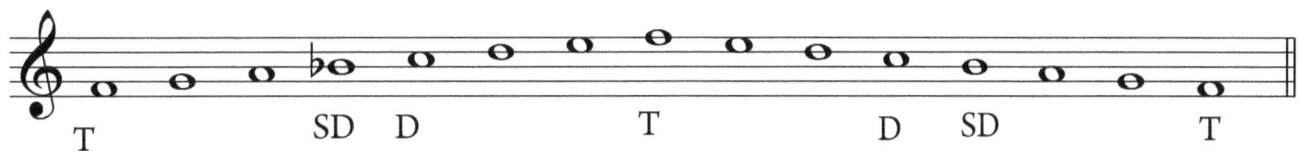

Page 64, No. 2

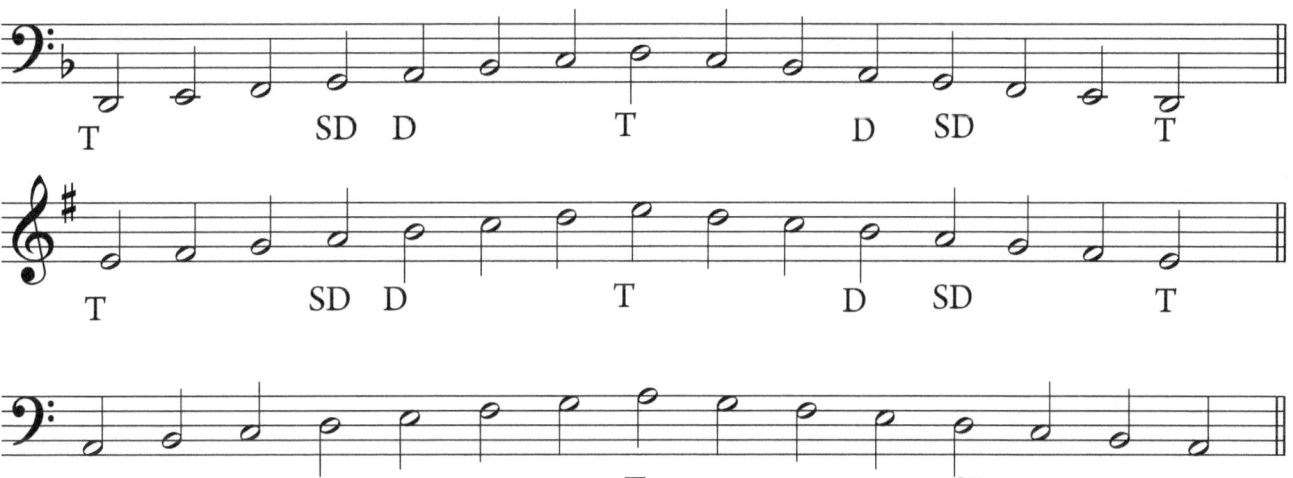

Page 65, No. 3

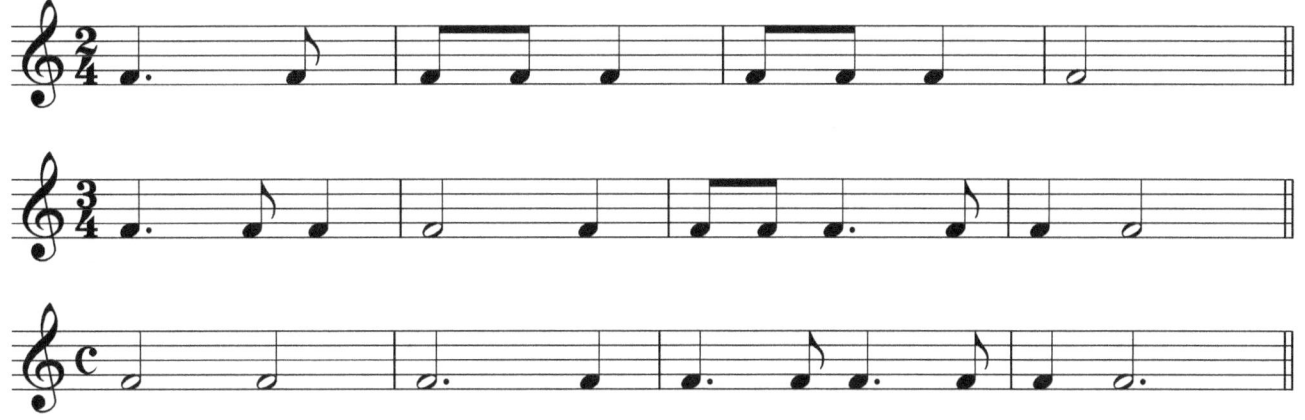

Page 65, No. 4

4/4   3/4   2/4

Page 66, No. 5

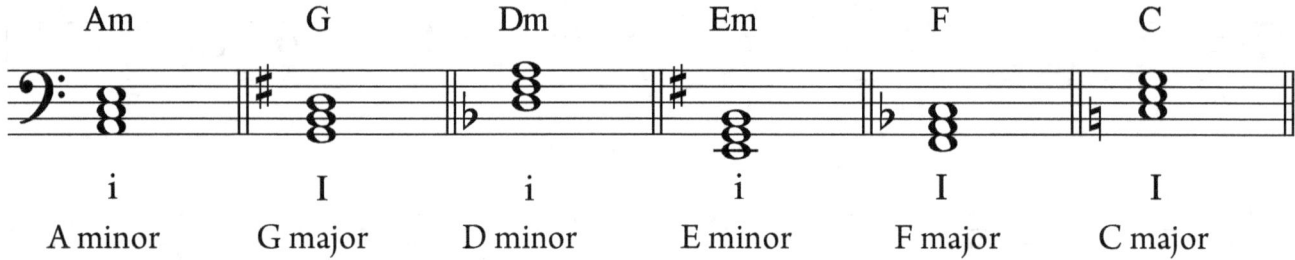

Page 66, No. 6

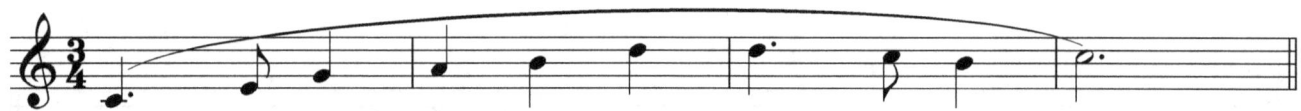

Page 66, No. 7

f, a, b, e, d, g, c

Page 67, No. 8

Study Op.125, No. 3

Anton Diabelli
(1781 - 1858)

a. Add the correct time signature directly on the music.

b. Name the key of this piece. **C major**

c. Name the composer of this piece. **Anton Diabelli**

d. Draw a phrase mark over each phrase.

e. On what scale degree does phrase one end? $\hat{2}$ Is this stable or unstable? **unstable**

f. On what degree does phrase two end? $\hat{1}$ Is this stable or unstable? **stable**

g. Define *Allegretto*. **Fairly fast, not as fast as allegro**

h. Name the triad at letter A. **C major**

i. Explain the sign at letter B. **Repeat sign, repeat from the beginning.**

Level 3

Page 2, No. 1

F♯ G♭	A♯ B♭	F E♯
B♭ A♯	B C♭	G♭ F♯
C♯ D♭	G♯ A♭	D♭ C♯
D♯ E♭	C B♯	A♭ G♯
E♯ F	B♭ A♯	E♭ D♯

Page 3, No. 2

Page 4, No. 1

Page 5, No. 1

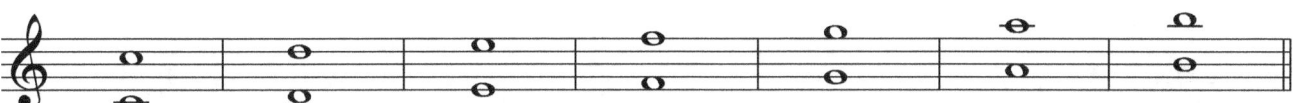

Page 5, No. 2

Page 6, No. 1

Page 6, No. 2

Page 6, No. 3

Page 9, No. 1

© San Marco Publications 2022   Level 3

Page 9, No. 2

Page 10, No. 1

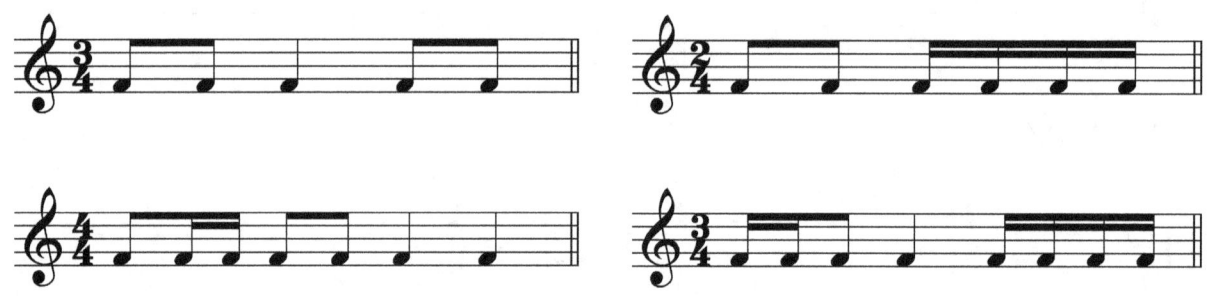

Page 11, No. 2

a) 2
b) 2
c) 2
d) 4
e) 2

Page 11, No. 3

Page 12, No. 4

3/4	3/4
2/4	2/4
4/4	4/4
3/4	4/4
2/4	3/4

Page 12, No. 5

Page 14, No. 1

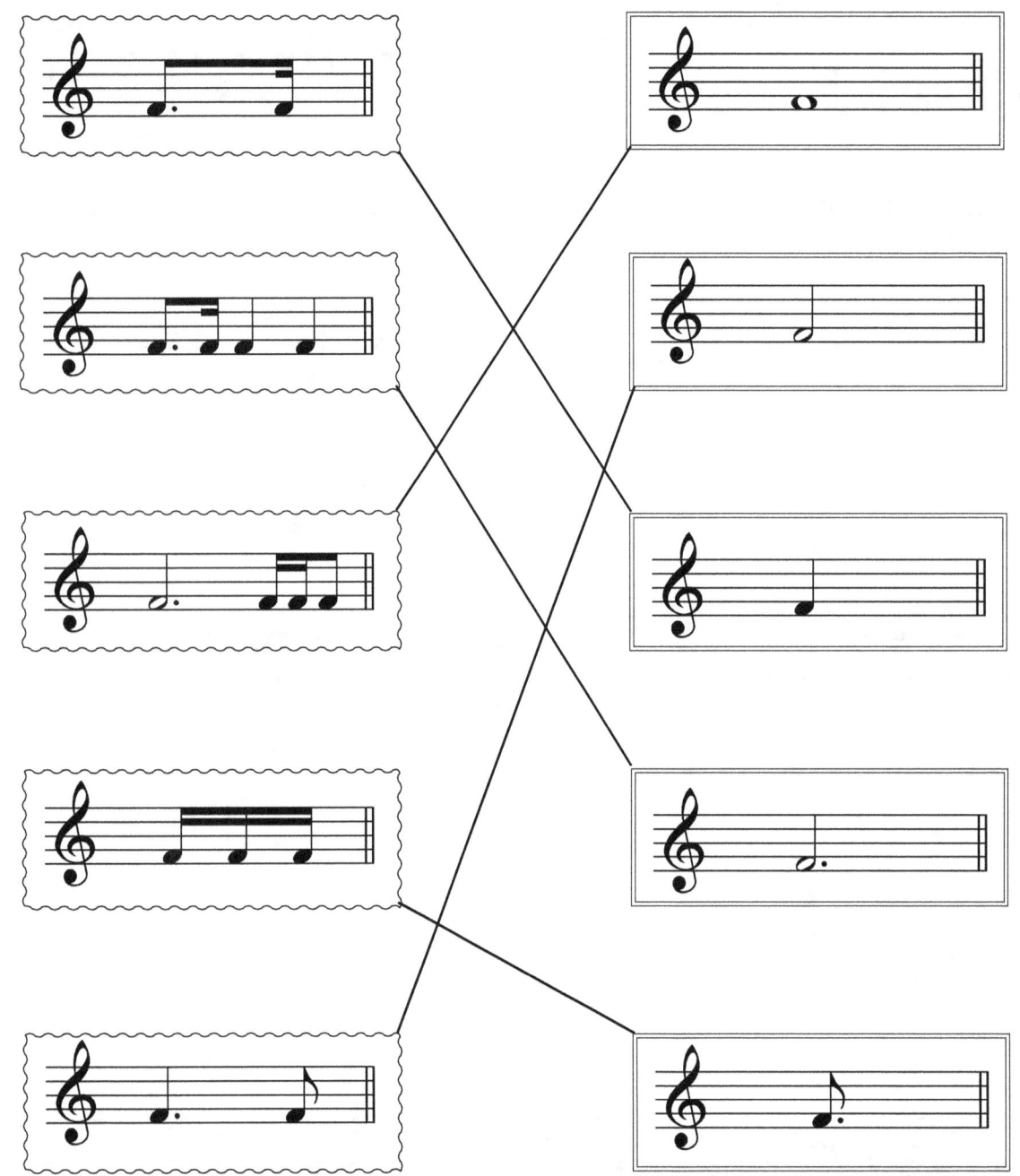

Page 15, No. 2

Page 17, No. 1

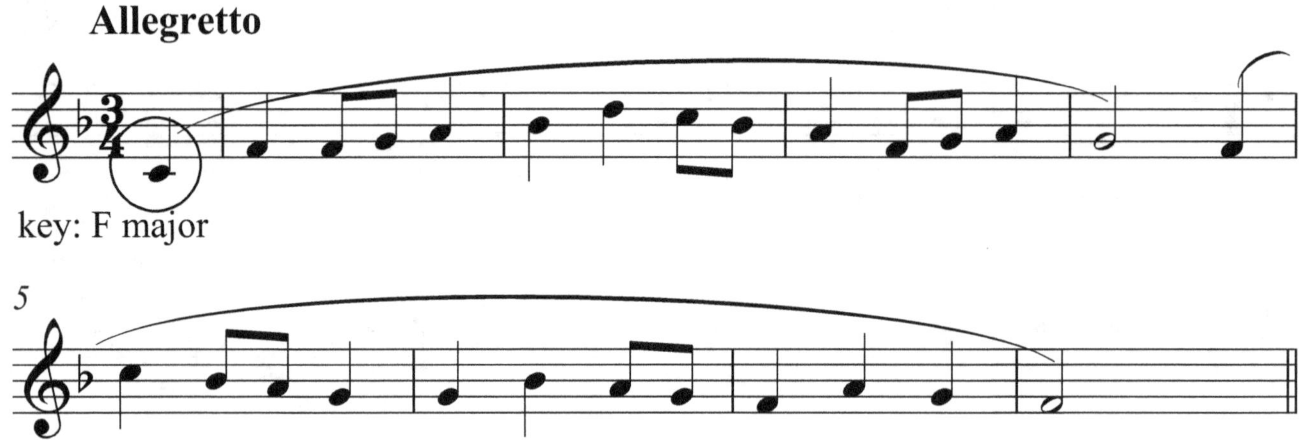
Allegretto
key: F major
5

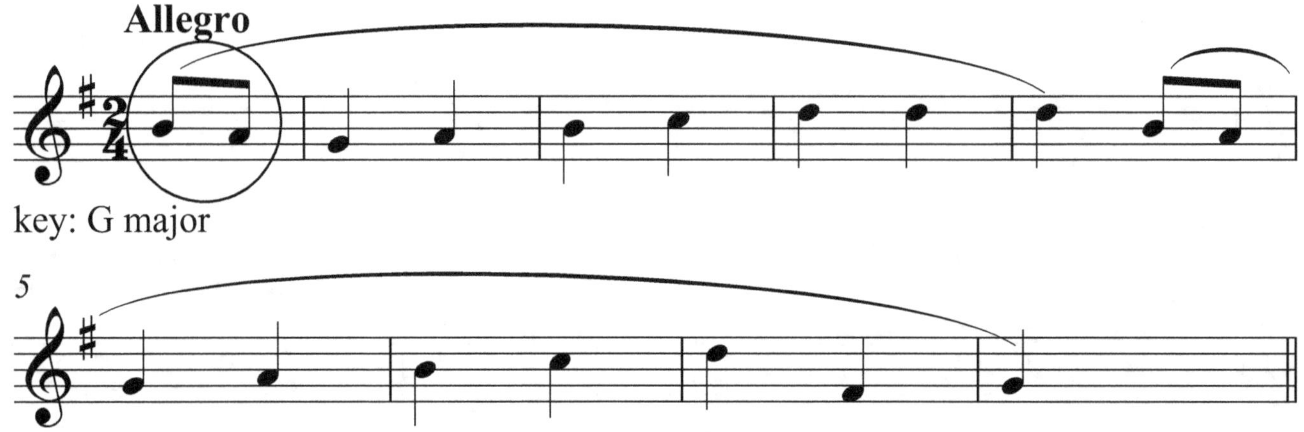
Allegro
key: G major
5

Page 20, No. 1

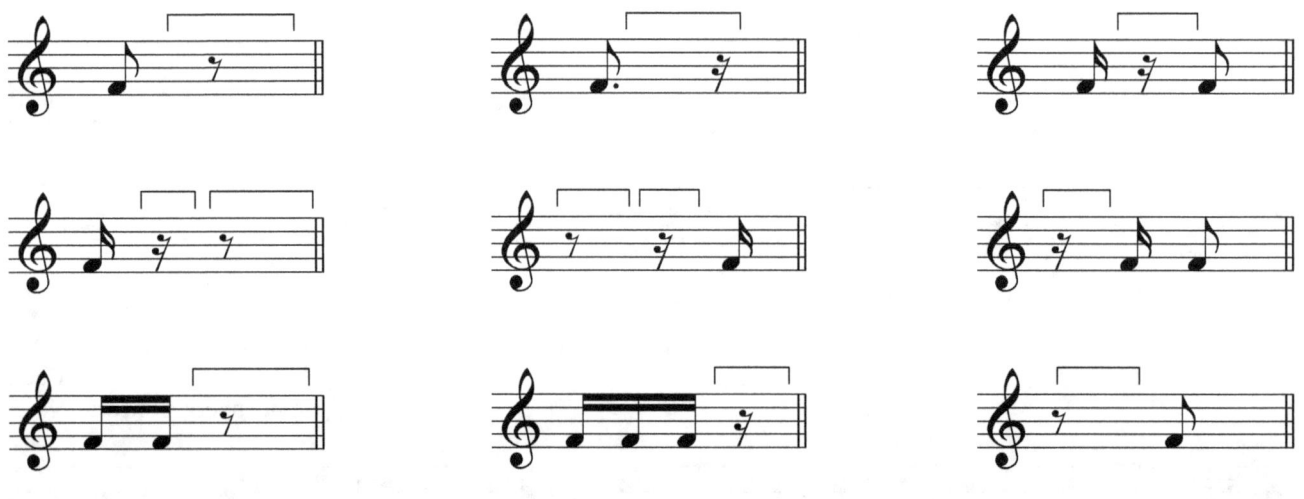

Page 20, No. 2

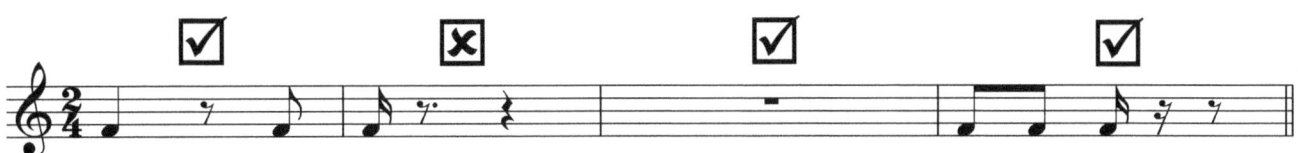

Page 21, No. 3

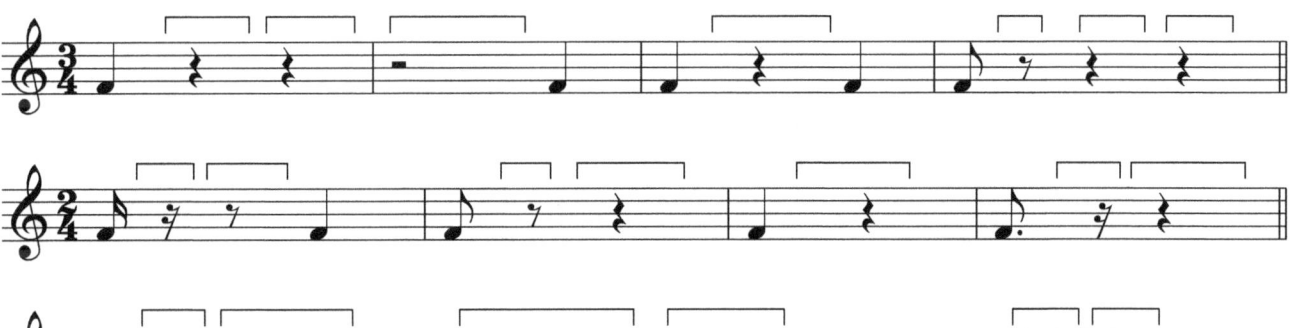

Page 21, No. 4

Page 23, No. 1

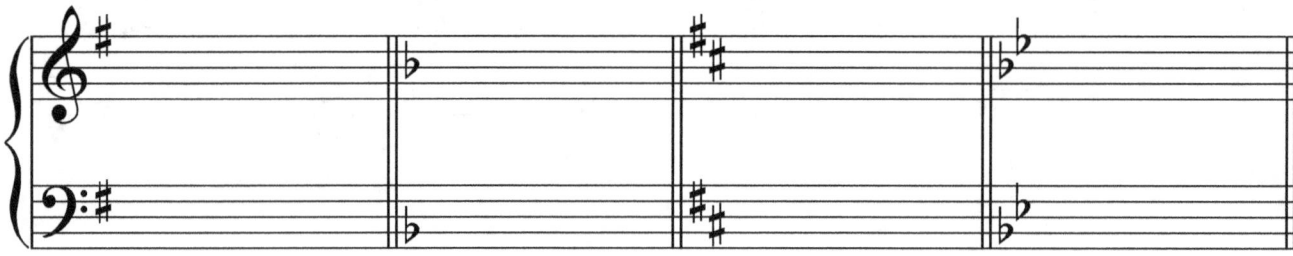

Page 24, No. 1

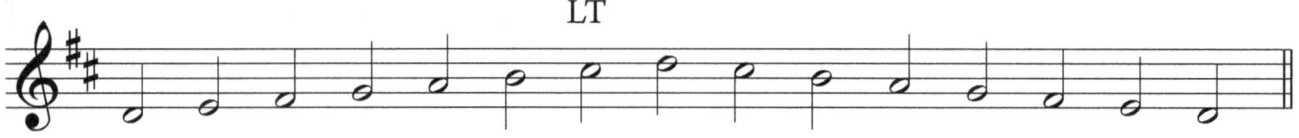

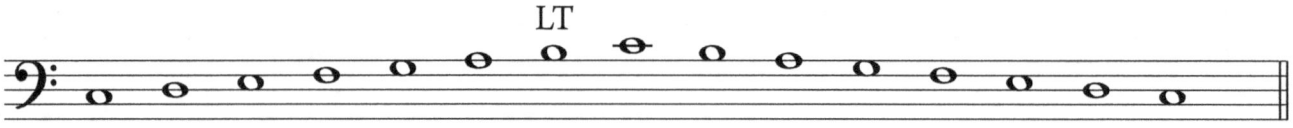

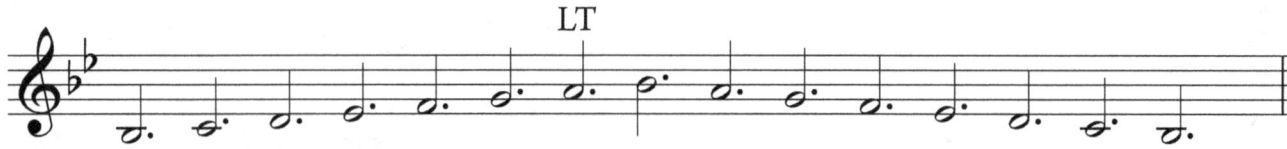

Level 3

Page 25, No. 2

B♭ major

D major

F major

G major

C major

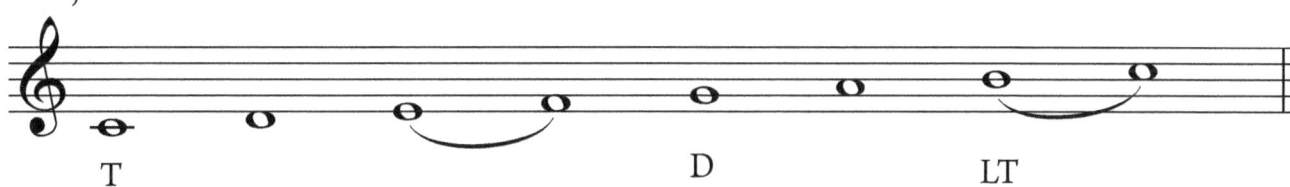

Page 26, No. 3

C major   B♭ major   D major   G major   F major

Page 26, No. 4

B♭ major

G major

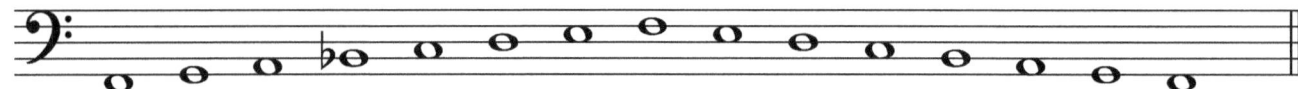

F major

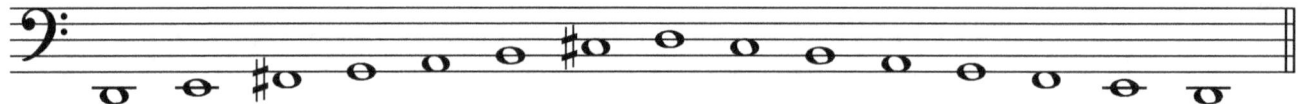

D major

Page 27, No. 5

E
D
E♭
D
B

Page 27, No. 6

Page 30, No. 1 Review 1

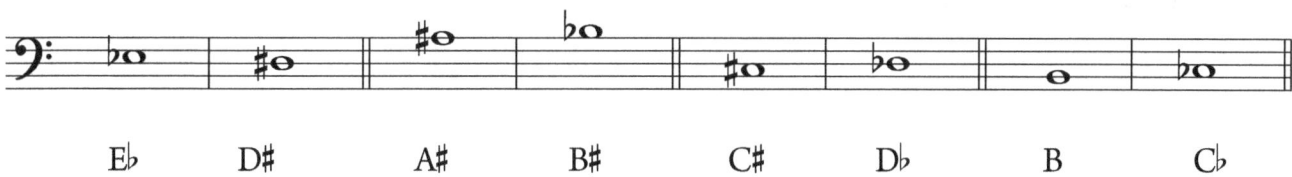

Page 30, No. 2

Page 30, No. 3

Page 31, No. 4

3/4
2/4
4/4
3/4

Page 31, No. 5

Page 32, No. 6

Page 32, No. 7

Page 32, No. 8

G major

Page 33, No. 9

a) Baroque
b) Johann Sebastian
c) Germany
d) Violin and Harpsichord
e) 20
f) Carl Phillip Emmanuel Bach, Johann Christian Bach
g) ☑ organist   ☑ cantor   ☐ pianist   ☑ composer   ☐ farmer   ☑ teacher
h) Felix Mendelssohn
i) 1750

Page 33, No. 10

d
c
e
a
b

Page 36, No. 1

    D major **B minor**   B minor **D major**

    E minor **G major**   A minor **C major**

    C major **A minor**   G major **E minor**

    F major **D minor**   D minor **F major**

Page 36, No. 2

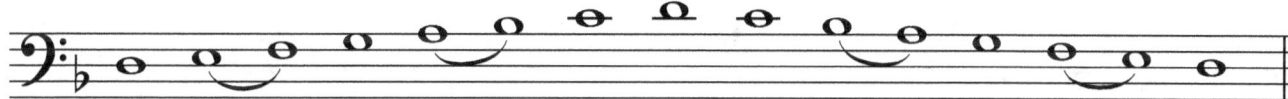

Page 38, No. 1

G minor

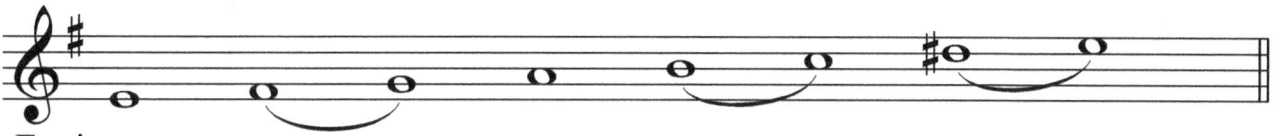
E minor

D minor

A minor

E minor

G minor

Page 39, No. 2

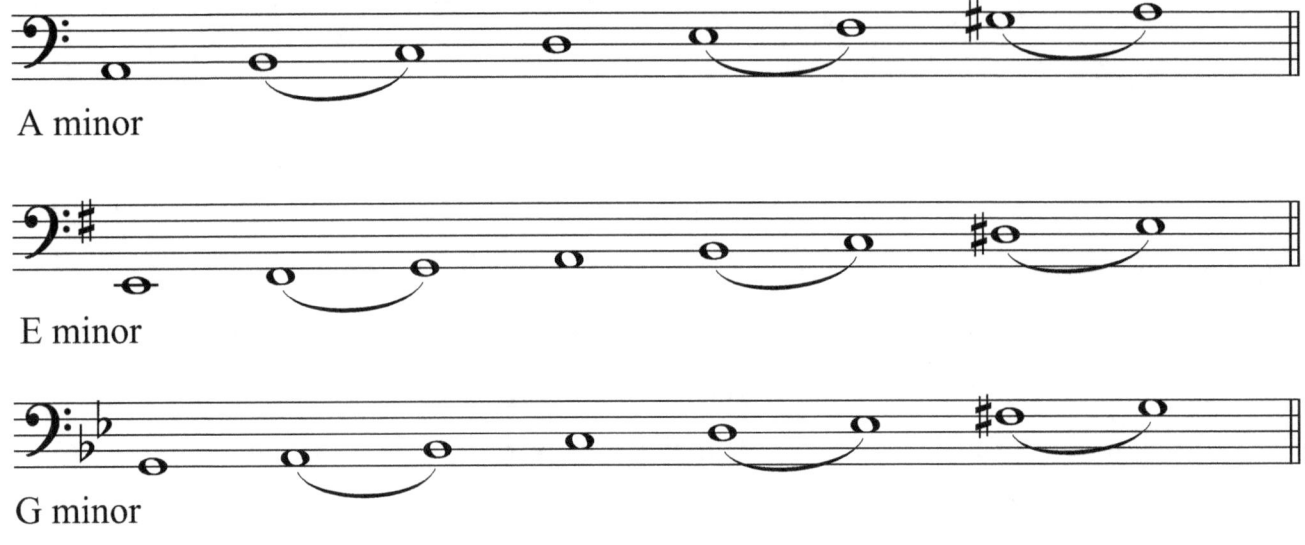

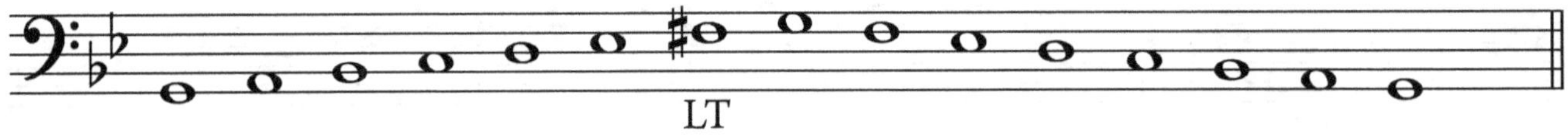

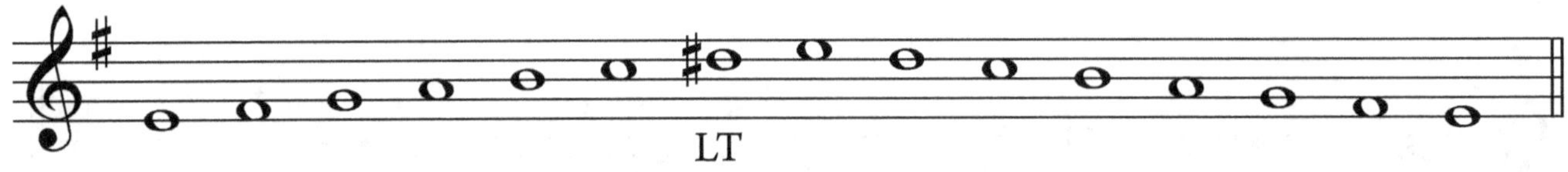

Page 41, No. 1

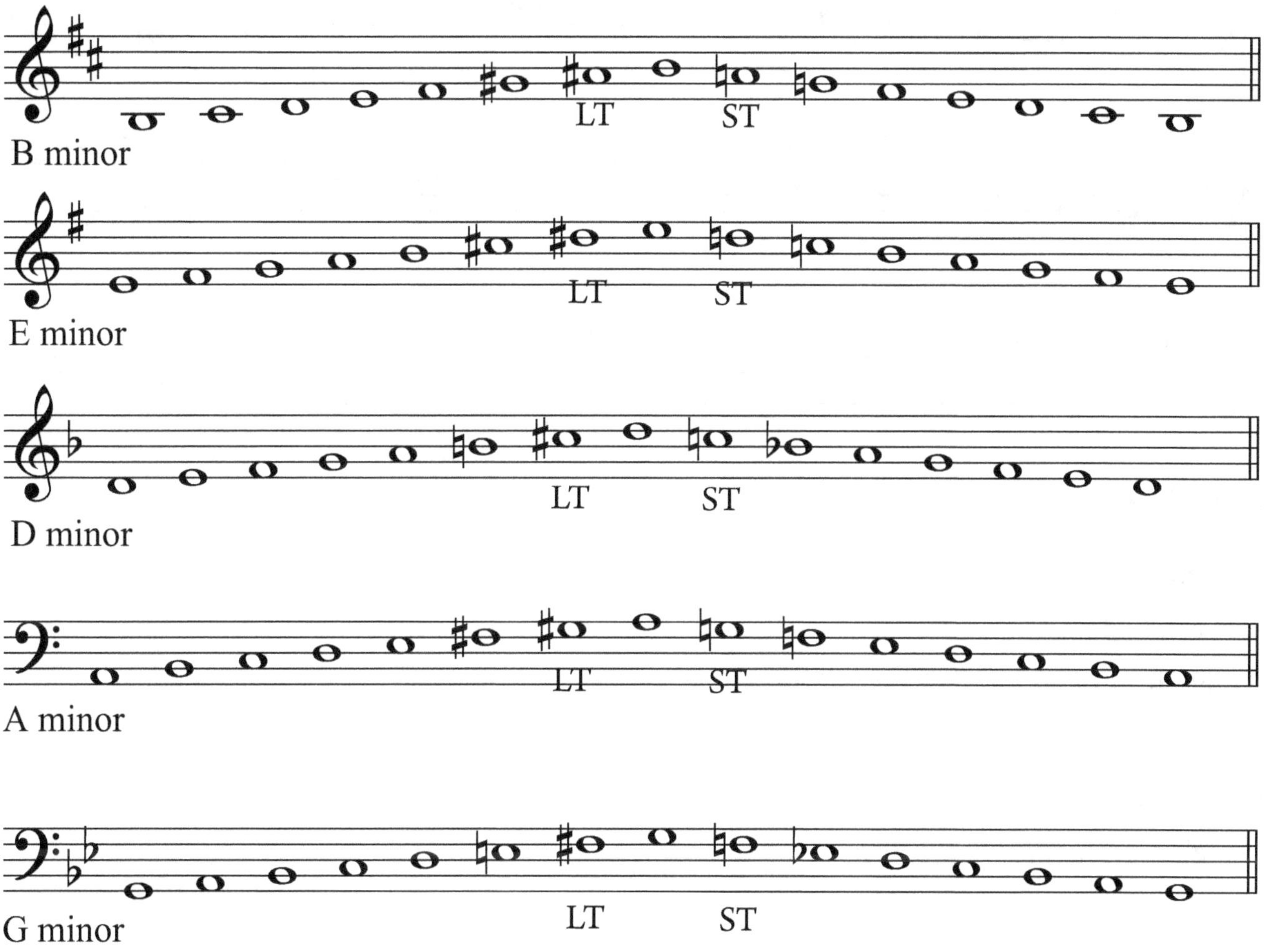

B minor

E minor

D minor

A minor

G minor

Page 42, No. 2

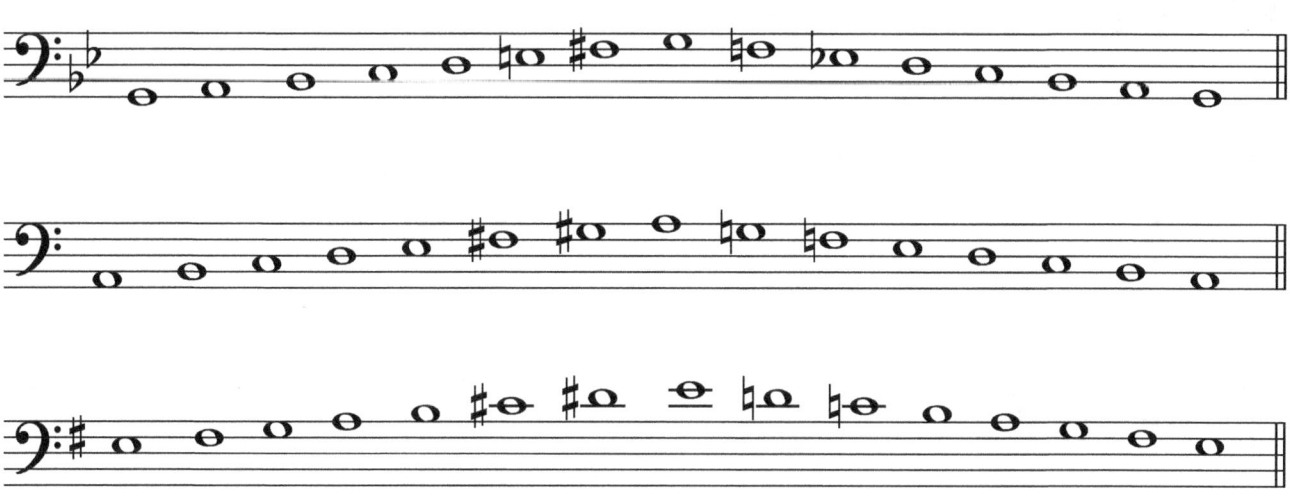

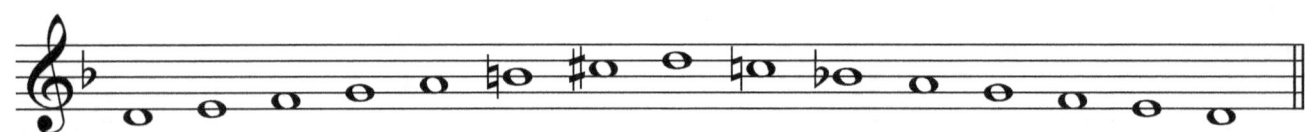

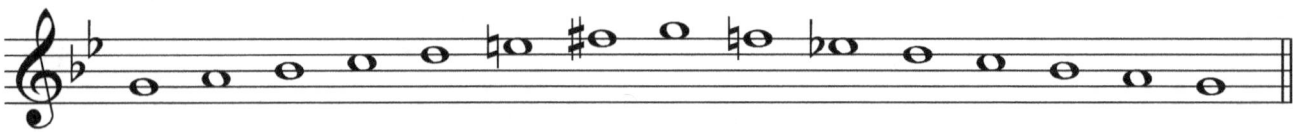

Page 43, No. 3

A harmonic minor

G natural minor

E melodic minor

D harmonic minor

B melodic minor

G melodic minor

Page 44, No. 4

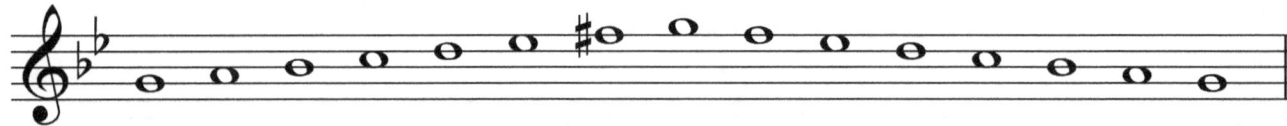

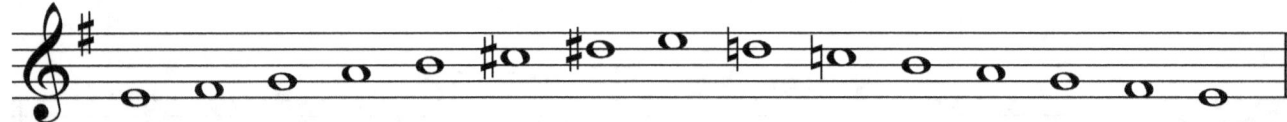

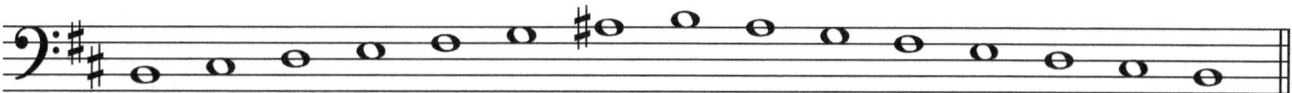

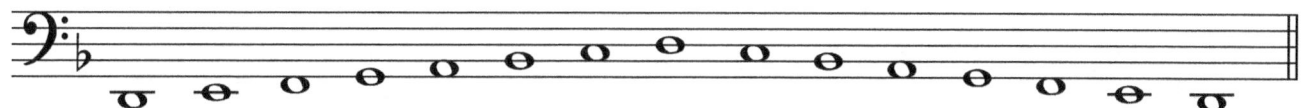

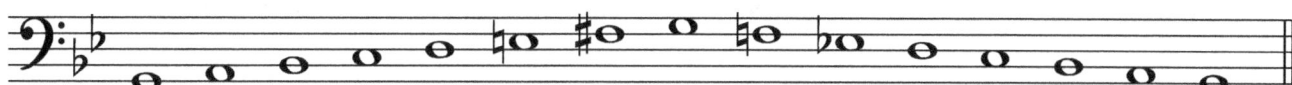

Page 45, No. 1

5 3 8 2 1 6
7 6 4 2 5 4

Page 46, No. 1

Page 47, No. 2

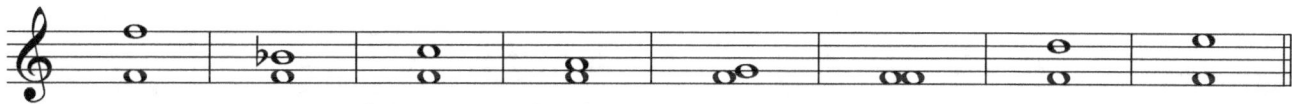

Page 47, No. 3

Page 47, No. 4

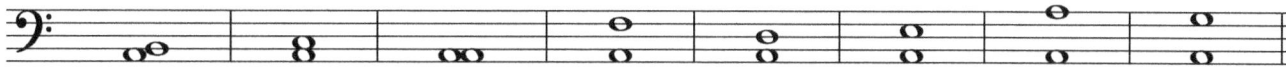

Page 47, No. 5

Page 50, No. 1

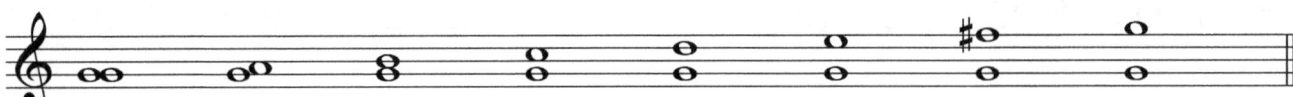

Page 50, No. 2

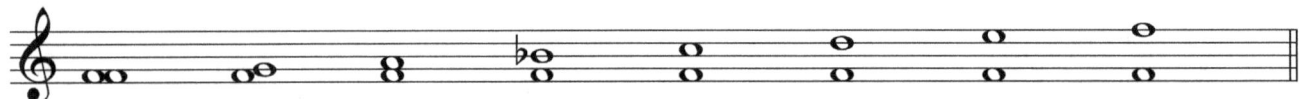

Page 50, No. 3

maj 6   per 4   maj 7   per 8   maj 2   per 4

maj 7   maj 3   per 4   per 5   per 8   per 1

Page 51, No. 4

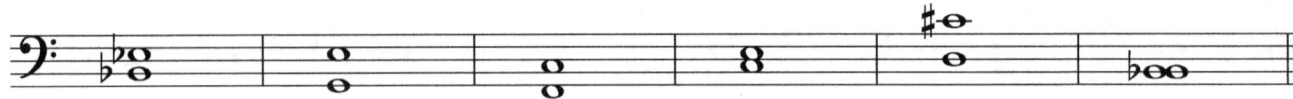

Page 51, No. 5

Page 52, No. 1

Page 52, No. 2

min 3   min 3   maj 3   min 3   maj 3
maj 3   min 3   maj 3   maj 3   min 3

Page 53, No. 3

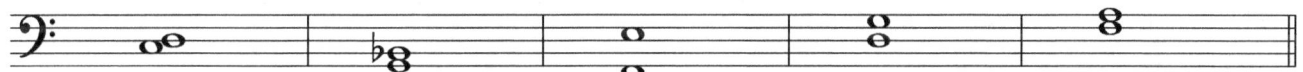

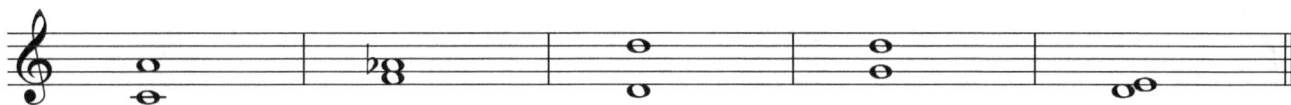

Page 53, No. 4

min 3   per 5   maj 2   maj 7   per 5
maj 3   min 3   per 8   maj 6   maj 7
min 3   per 4   maj 7   min 3   maj 6

Page 55, No. 1

Page 56, No. 2

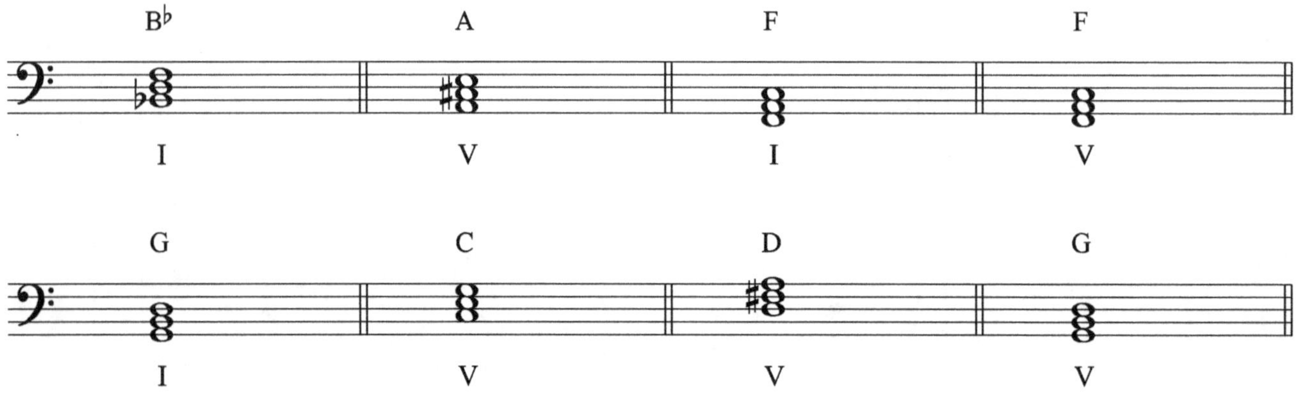

Page 57, No. 1

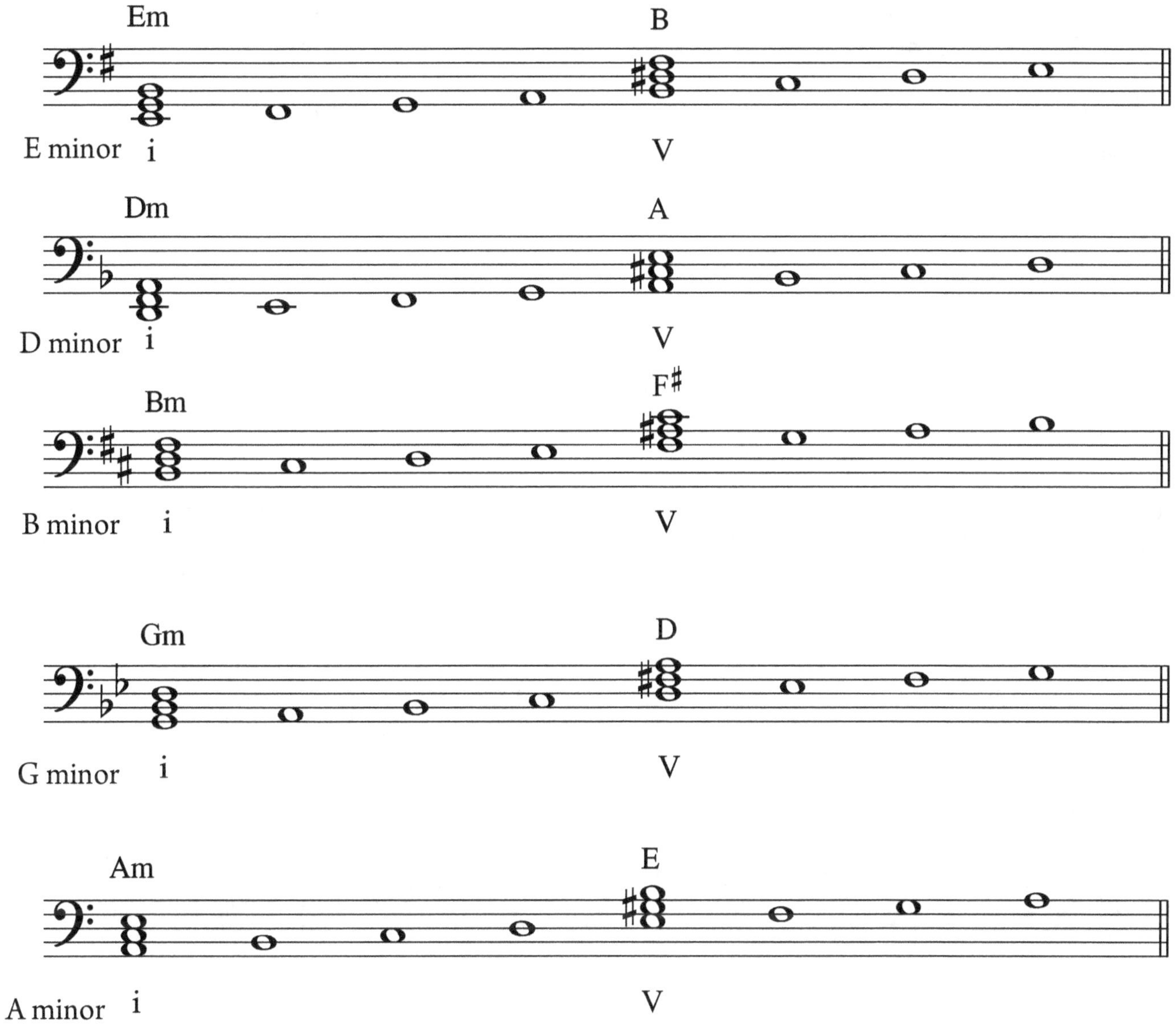

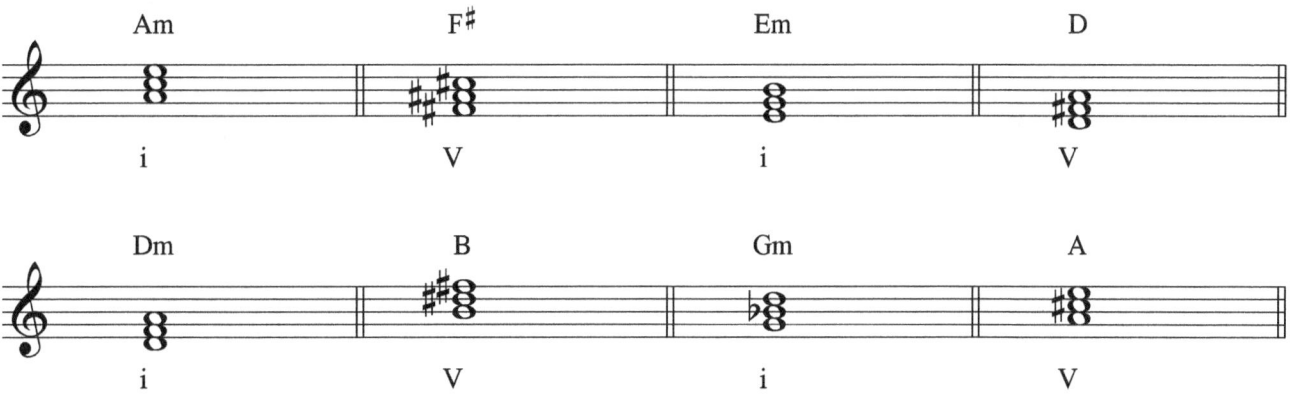

Page 58, No. 3

tonic	dominant	tonic	tonic
A minor i	D minor V	B minor i	E minor i
dominant	dominant	dominant	dominant
G minor V	E minor V	A minor V	B minor V

Page 61, No. 1   Review 2

per 4   maj 7   maj 3   per 5   maj 2   maj 6

per 8   per 1   maj 3   per 5   per 4   maj 6

Page 61, No. 2

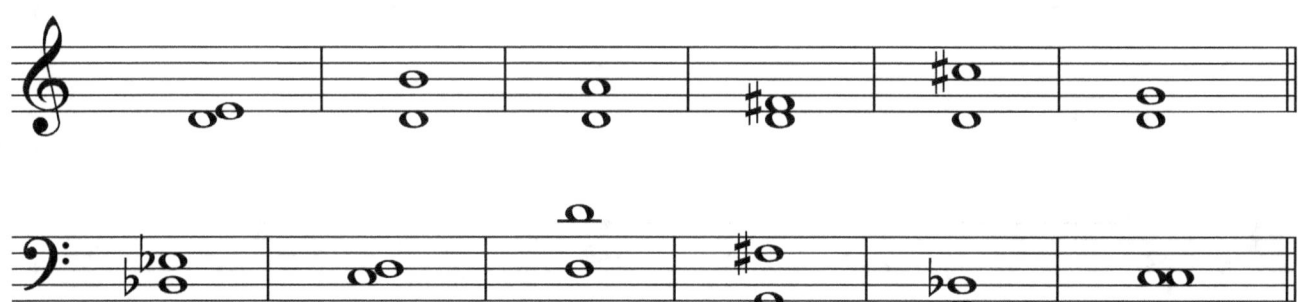

Page 62, No. 3

Page 63, No. 4

I   V   I   i

i   V   V   V

Page 63, No. 5

marcato	marked, stressed
cantabile	in a singing style
maestoso	majestically
grazioso	gracefully
dolce	sweetly
ottava	the interval of an octave
dal segno	from the sign

Page 64, No. 6

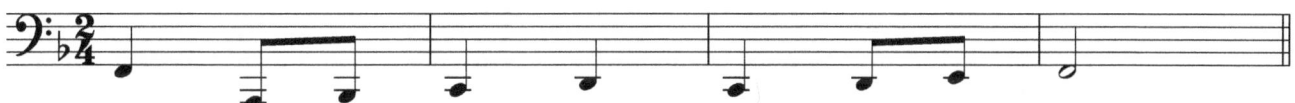

Page 64, No. 7

a) Johann Sebastian Bach
b) Bach's second wife
c) Carl Phillip Emmanuel Bach, Johann Christian Bach
d) Dances, Arias, Chorales
e) Harpsichord
f) Keyboard

Page 68, No. 1 (other options are possible)

Page 68, No. 2 (other options are possible)

Page 68, No. 3 (other options are possible)

Page 69, No. 4 (other options are possible)

Page 69, No. 5 (other options are possible)

Page 71-72, No. 1

Page 73

Allegro

Alexander Reinagle
(1756 - 1809)

a. Add the correct time signature directly on the music.

b. Name the key of this piece. **C major**

c. Name the composer of this piece. **Alexander Reinagle**

d. Draw a phrase mark over each phrase.

e. Label the phrases according to the form (a, a¹, b)

f. These two phrases form a: ☑ contrasting period ☐ parallel period

g. Does the second phrase end on a stable or unstable degree? **stable**

h. Define *Allegro*. **fast**

i. How are measure 1 and 2 similar to 5 and 6? **The rhythm is the same.**

i. Locate and circle a half step in this piece.

© San Marco Publications 2022   Level 3

Page 74

Carefree

Daniel Gottlob Turk
((1756 - 1813))

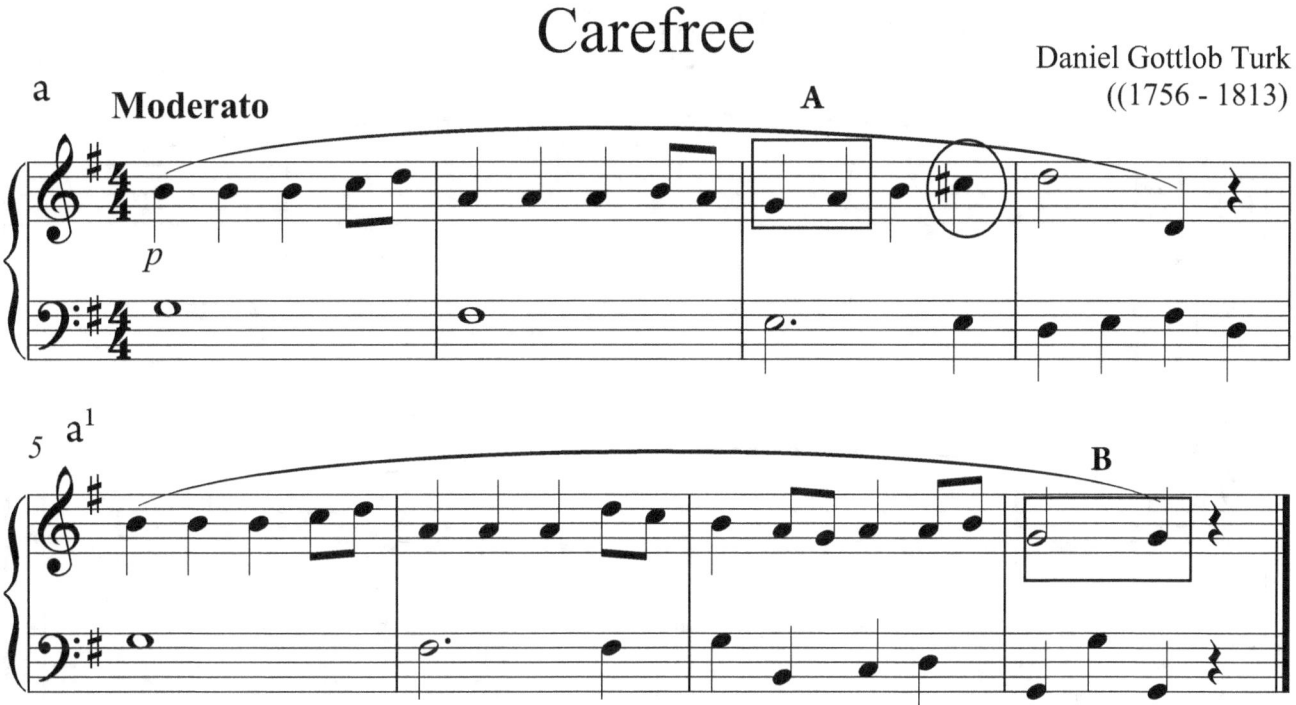

a. Add the correct time signature directly on the music.

b. Name the key of this piece. **G major**

c. Name the composer of this piece. **Daniel Gottlob Turk**

d. Draw a phrase mark over each phrase.

e. Label the phrases according to the form (a, a¹, b)

f. These two phrases form a: ☐ contrasting period   ☑ parallel period

g. Does the second phrase end on a stable or unstable degree? **stable**

h. Define *Moderato*. **at a moderate speed**

i. Find and circle one accidental in this piece.

j. Name the interval at letter A. **maj 2**

k. Name the interval at letter B. **per 1**

Level 3

Page 75

Bagatelle

Anton Diabelli

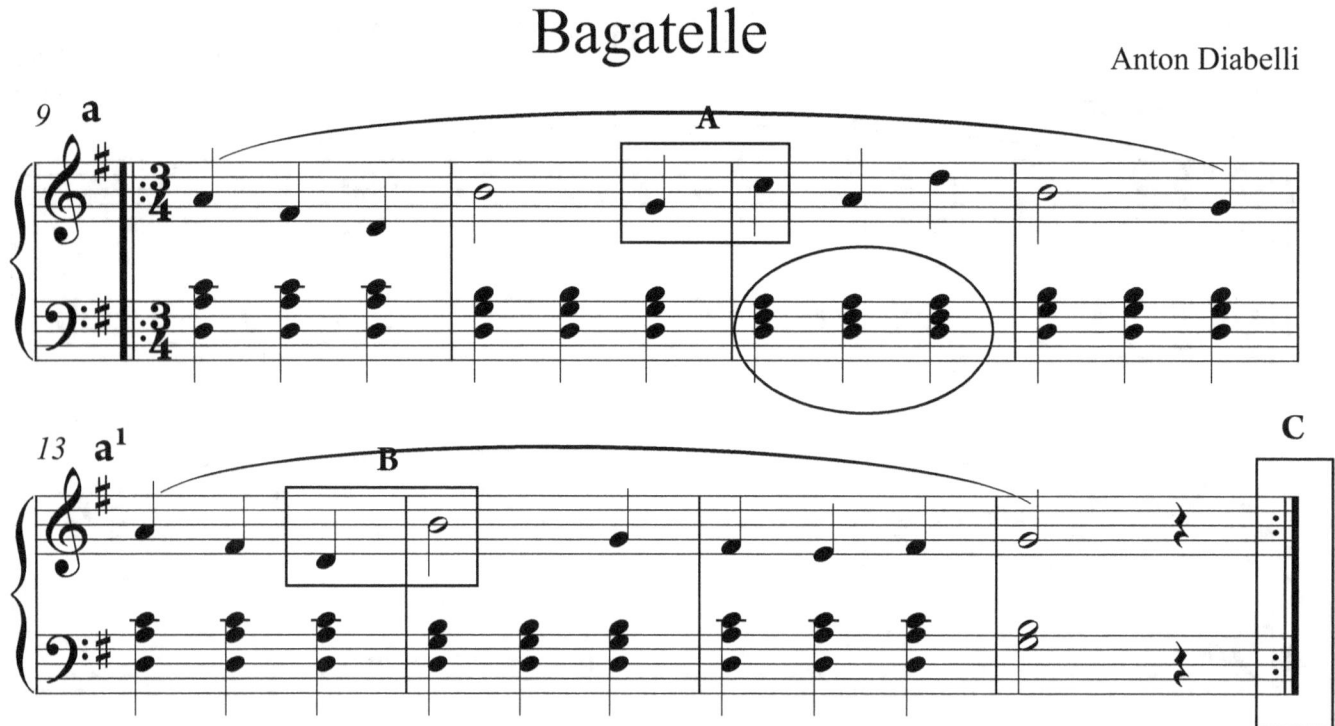

a. Add the correct time signature directly on the music.

b. Name the key of this piece. **G major**

c. Name the composer of this piece. **Anton Diabelli**

d. Draw a phrase mark over each phrase.

e. Label the phrases according to the form (a, a¹, b)

f. Does the second phrase end on a stable or unstable degree? **stable**

g. Find and circle one dominant triad in this piece.

h. Name the interval at letter A. **per 4**

i. Name the interval at letter B. **maj 6**

j. Explain the sign at letter C. **Repeat sign. Repeat the music between the repeat signs.**

k. On what measure does this piece begin? **9**

© San Marco Publications 2022

Level 3

Page 79, No. 1   Review 3

per 5   maj 2   maj 7   maj 6   min 3   per 1

maj 3   per 4   per 8   maj 7   maj 6   maj 2

Page 79, No. 2

Page 80, No. 3

Page 81, No. 4

Page 81, No. 5

Page 81, No. 6

marcato	marked or stressed
grazioso	graceful
dolce	sweet
maestoso	majestic
cantabile	in a singing style
ottava	the interval of an octave
dal segno	from the sign

Page 82, No. 7

a) Baroque
b) 1600 -1750
c) Germany
d) A book of Baroque keyboard pieces
e) Carl Phillip Emmanuel Bach, Johann Christian Bach
f) Dances, Arias, Chorales, Minuet, Gavotte, Gigue
g) Harpsichord
h) Keyboard
i) France
j) 3/4
k) France
l) Yes
m) Allegro, Presto
n) three
o) At the end

Level 4

Page 4, No. 1

Page 4, No. 2

Page 4, No. 3

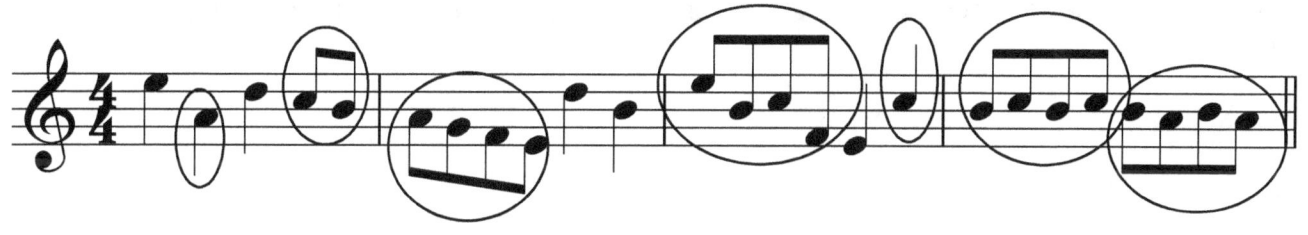

Page 6, No. 1

Mikhail Glinka
Souvenir of a Night in Madrid

Page 6, No. 2

Wolfgang Amadeus Mozart
Piano Concerto K270

Page 8, No. 1

Page 8, No. 2

3/4	3/4
2/4	2/4
4/4	4/4
3/4	4/4
2/4	3/4

Page 10, No. 1

Page 10, No. 2

3/4
2/4
4/4
3/4

Page 12, No. 1

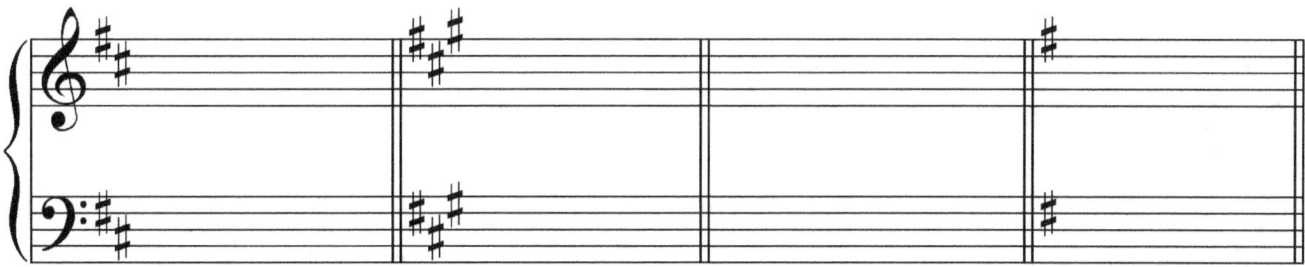

Page 12, No. 2

Page 14, No. 1

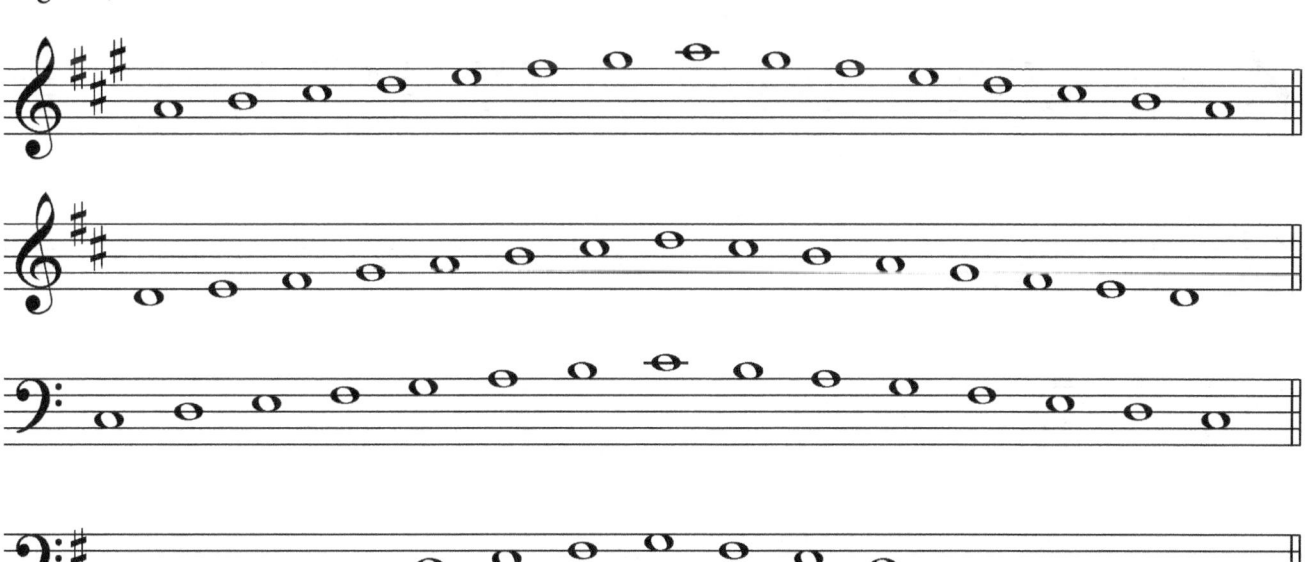

Page 15, No. 1

Page 16, No. 2 (other options for this question are possible)

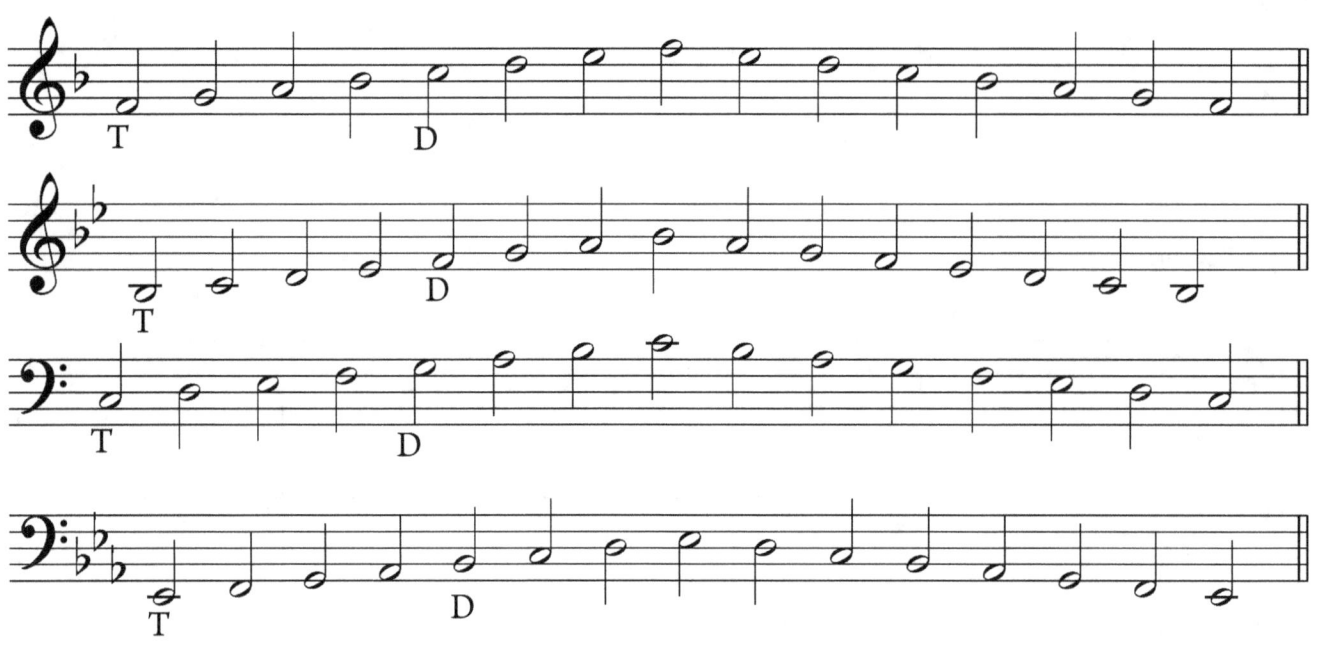

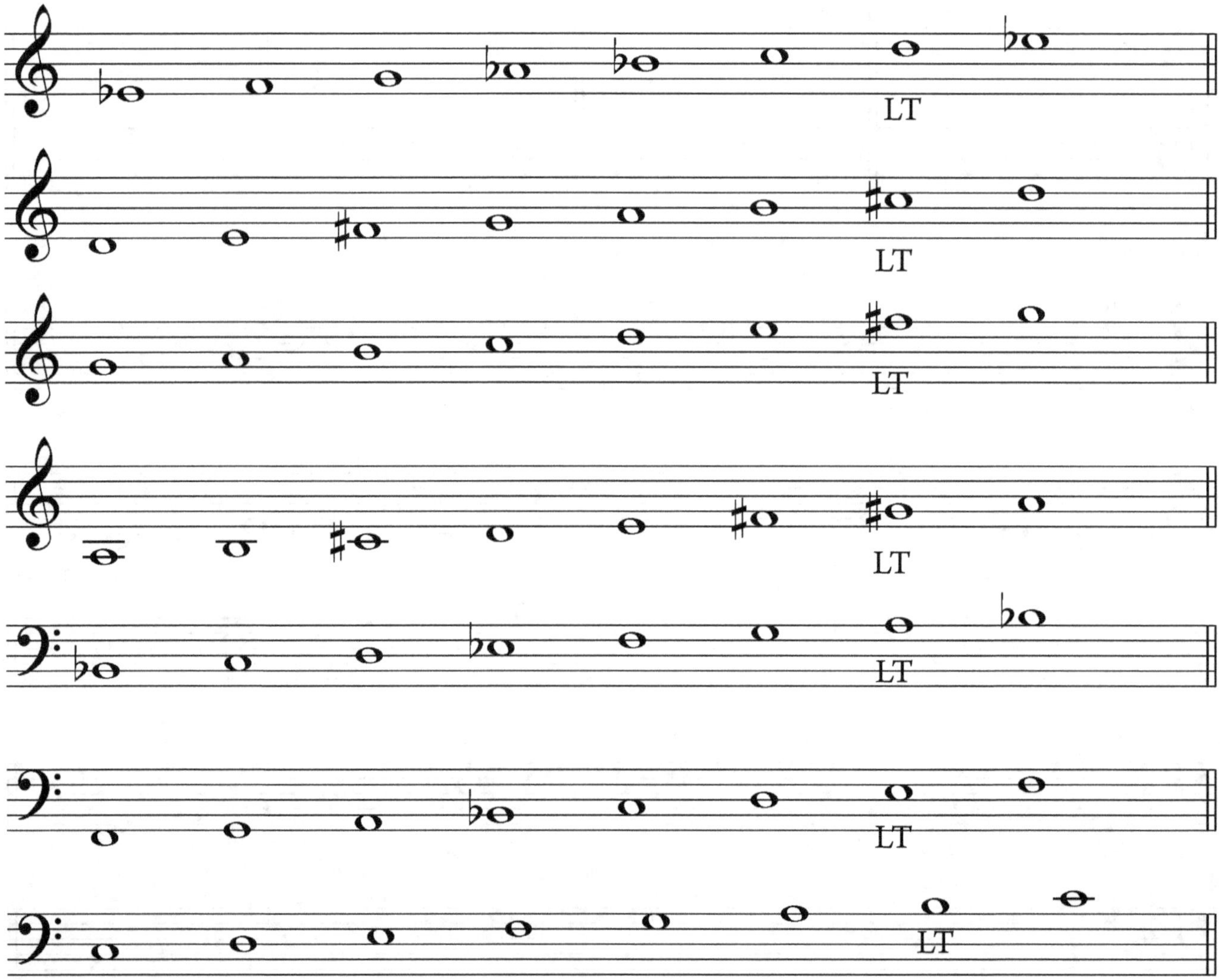

© San Marco Publications 2022   85   Level 4

Page 17, No. 3

Page 21, No. 1 Review 1

Page 21, No. 2

Claude Debussy
Prelude "Voiles"

Page 21, No. 3

Page 22, No. 4

Page 22, No. 5

4/4	4/4
2/4 3/4	
3/4	2/4
2/4	4/4

Page 23, No. 6

Page 23, No. 7

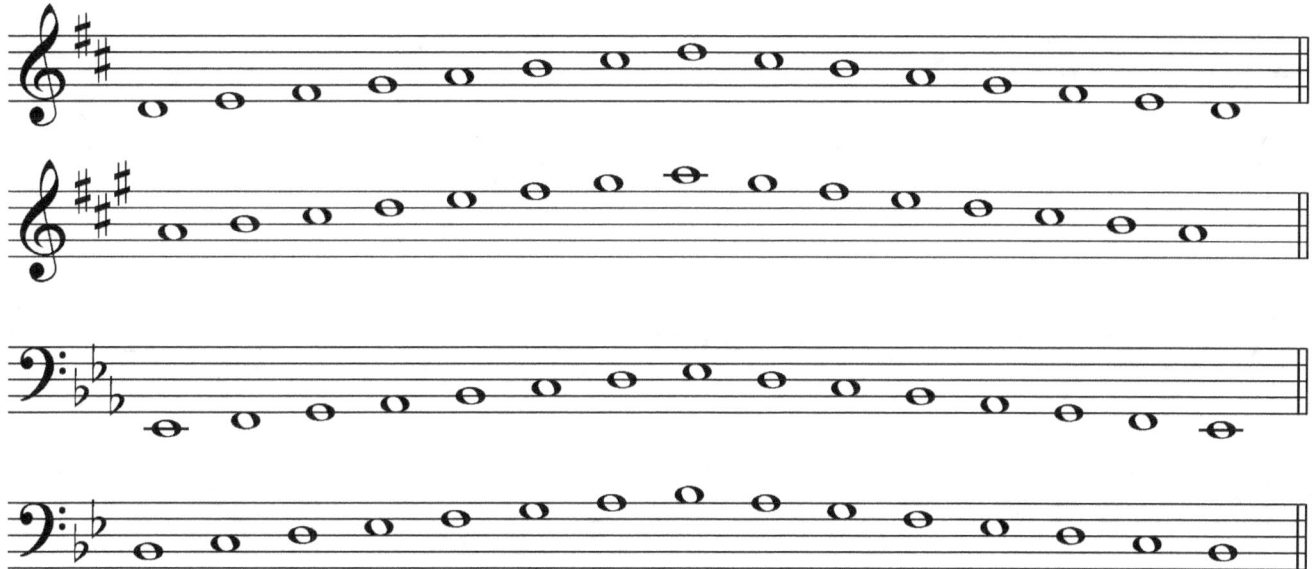

Page 24, No. 8

1. **Strings** (violin, viola, cello, double bass, harp)

2. **Woodwinds** (flute, clarinet, oboe, bassoon, piccolo, saxophone, double bassoon)

3. **Brass** (horn, trumpet, trombone, tuba)

4. **Percussion** (Bass drum, Chimes, Gong, Triangle, Cymbals, Snare drum, Tambourine, Drum, Timpani, Xylophone, Marimba)

Page 24, No. 9

cantabile	in a singing style
dolce	sweetly
grazioso	gracefully
maestoso	majestically
marcato	marked or stressed

Page 27, No. 1

D minor	F major	B♭ major	G minor
E minor	G major	C major	A minor
B minor	D major	D major	B minor
C minor	E♭ major	E♭ major	C minor
F# minor	A major	A major	F# minor

Page 29, No. 1

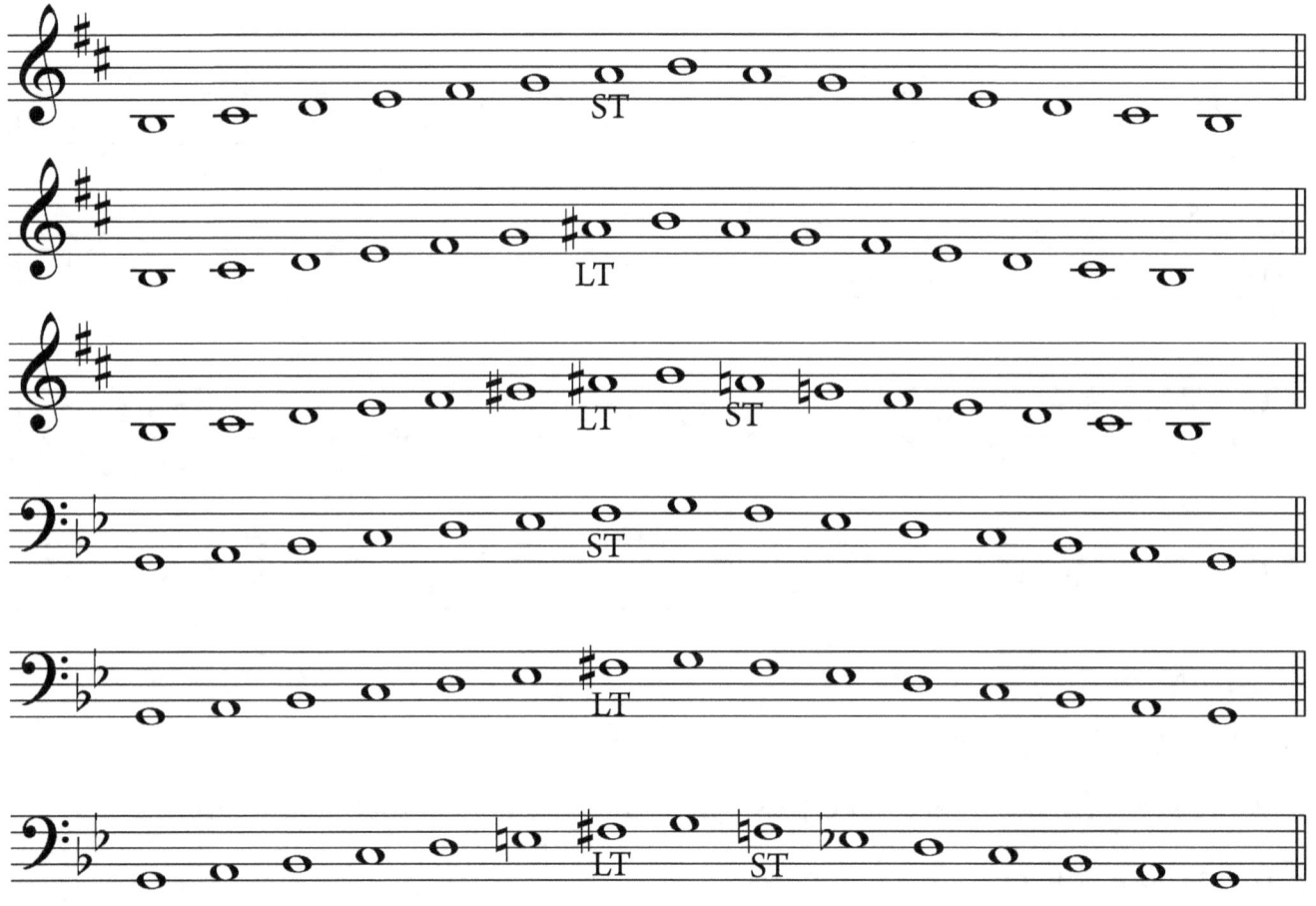

Page 30, No. 2

E natural minor
C harmonic minor
F# melodic minor
D harmonic minor
A harmonic minor
B harmonic minor
G melodic minor

Page 31, No. 3

Page 33, No. 1

per 5, maj 3, maj 6, maj 2, per 8, maj 7, maj 6

per 1, per 4, maj 6, maj 3, per 5, per 8, maj 2

Page 34, No. 1

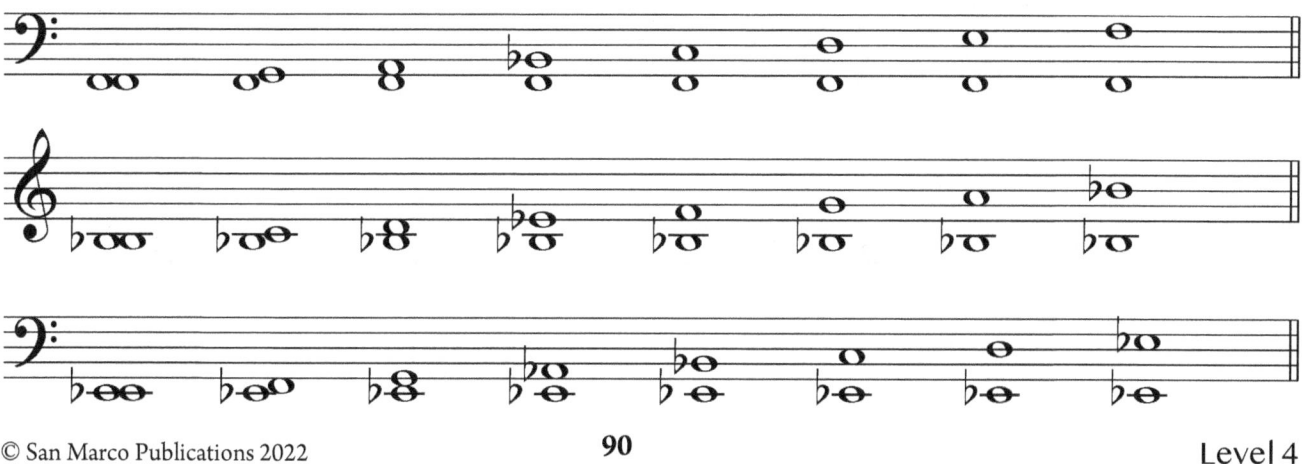

Page 35, No. 1

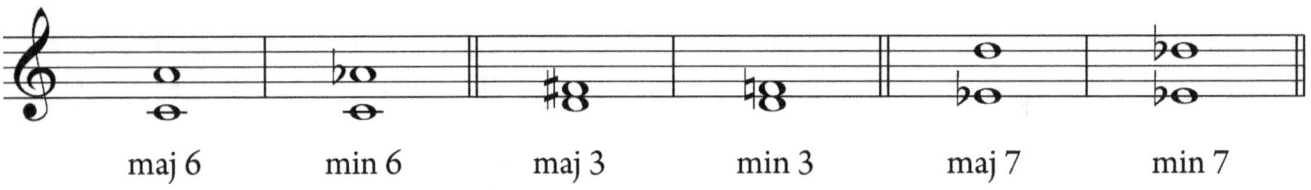

     maj 6   min 6   maj 3   min 3   maj 7   min 7

     maj 7   min 7   maj 2   min 2   maj 7   min 7

Page 36, No. 2

maj 6, per 4, maj 3, min 7, min 7, min 6, per 5

maj 2, per 4, min 6, min 7, maj 3, maj 3, per 4

Page 37, No. 3

Page 37, No. 4

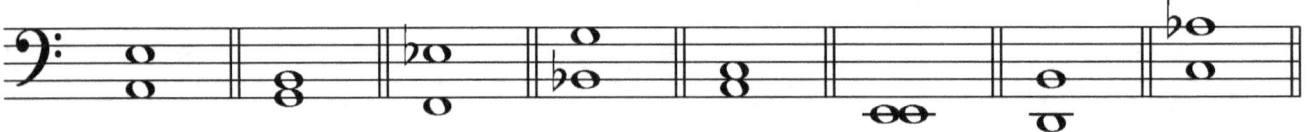

Level 4

Page 38, No. 5

Page 39, No. 6

min 7, maj 6

maj 2, maj 2, per 1

maj 3, maj 2, min 3, min 3

per 5, maj 2, min 2, maj 2, min 2, maj 2

Page 40, No. 1

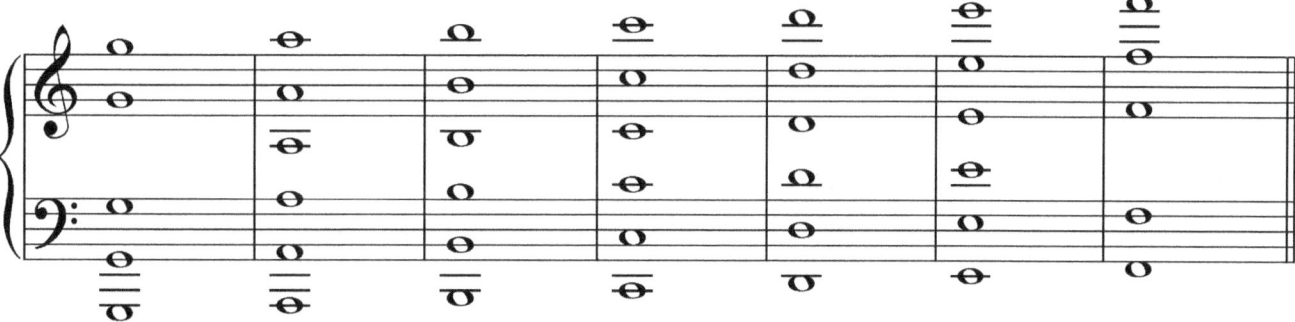

Page 40, No. 2

Page 42, No. 1

Page 43, No. 2

Page 43, No. 3

Ludwig van Beethoven
Leonore, No. 2

Enrique Granados
Spanish Dance, No. 6

Page 44, No. 4

Johannes Brahms
Seranade in D, V

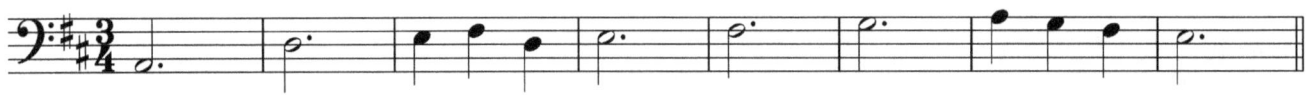

Frederic Chopin
Nocturne Op. 72, No. 1

Page 47, No. 1

4/8 or 2/4
2/8
3/8
4/8 or 2/4
2/8
3/8

Page 48, No. 2

Page 49, No. 3

Page 50, No. 4

Page 58, No. 1 Review 2

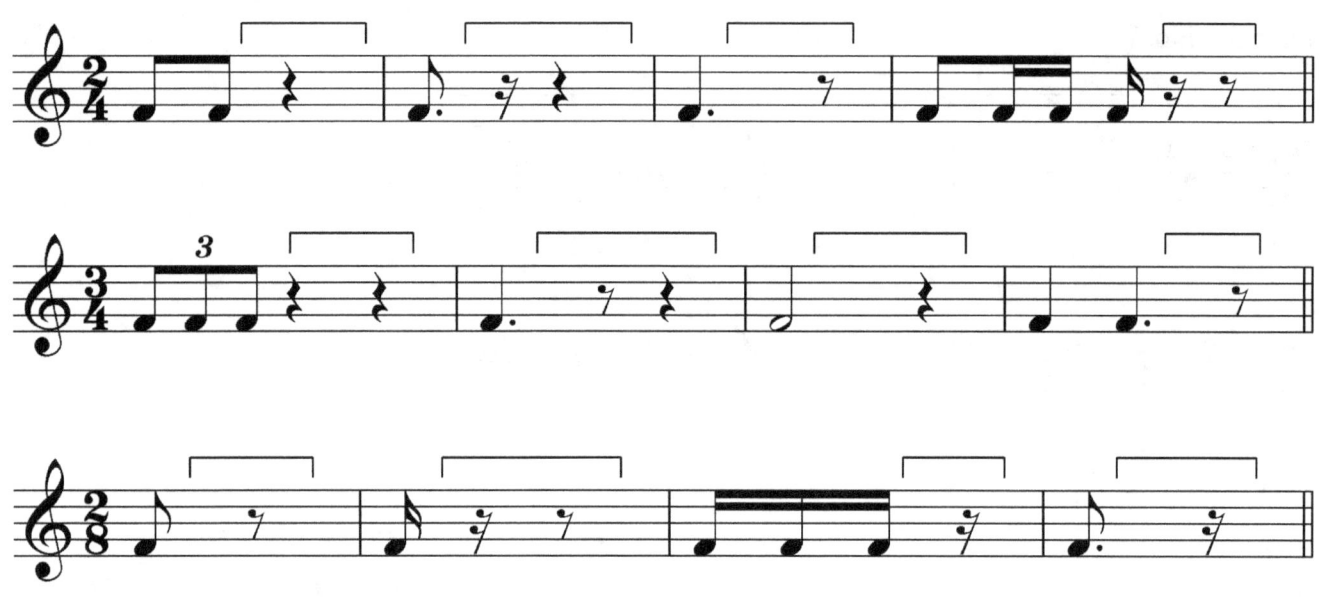

Page 59, No. 2

Page 59, No. 3

Page 59, No. 4

per 4, maj 7, min 3, per 8, maj 7, maj 2, min 6, per 8

Page 59, No. 5

Page 60, No. 6

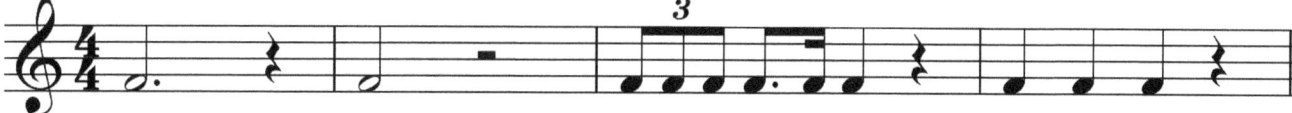

Page 60, No. 7

William Byrd
Pavan

Page 60, No. 8

Felix Mendelssohn
Faith from Song Without Words

Page 61, No. 9

accelerando	becoming quicker
adagio	slow
mano destra	right hand
mano sinistra	left hand
prestissimo	as fast as possible
Tempo primo	return to the original tempo or speed
vivace	lively, quick

Page 61, No. 10

a. Who composed Young Persons Guide to the Orchestra? **Benjamin Britten**

b. In what country was he born? **England or Great Britain**

c. In what era did he live? **Modern**

d. Who composed the theme on which this work is based? **Henry Purcell**

e. What era did this composer live? **Baroque**

f. How many variations are in Young Persons Guide to the Orchestra? **13**

g. What are the four instrument families featured in this composition?

    1. **Strings**
    2. **Woodwinds**
    3. **Brass**
    4. **Percussion**

h. What type of piece is the final movement of this composition? **Fugue**

Page 64, No. 1

Page 65, No. 2

Page 65, No. 3

Key:	G major	B♭ major	A major	E♭ major
Triad:	tonic	dominant	subdominant	tonic

Key:	D major	F major	A major	E♭ major
Triad:	subdominant	dominant	tonic	dominant

Page 67, No. 1

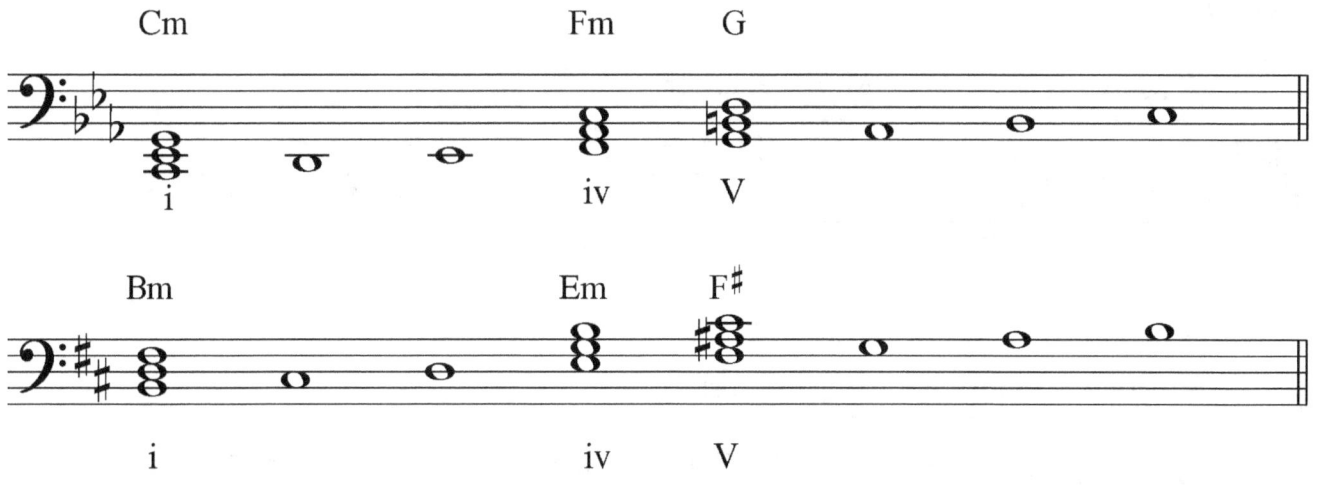

Page 68, No. 2

Page 68, No. 3

Key:	E minor	G minor	F# minor	C minor
Triad:	tonic	dominant	subdominant	tonic
	i	V	iv	i

Key:	B minor	D minor	F# minor	C minor
Triad:	dominant	subdominant	tonic	dominant
	V	iv	i	V

© San Marco Publications 2022   Level 4

Page 69, No. 1

Page 70, No. 2

Page 73, No. 1 (other options are possible)

Page 73, No. 2 (other options are possible)

Page 73, No. 3 (other options are possible)

Page 74, No. 4 (other options are possible)

Page 74, No. 5 (other options are possible)

Page 74, No. 6 (other options are possible)

Page 81, No. 1

Franz Schubert
Slumber Song

a. Add the time signature directly on the music.

b. Name the key of this piece. **G major**

c. Mark the phrases with slurs.

d. Label the phrases with *a*, *a¹*, and *b*.

e. Name the chord formed by the notes at A: **G major**   B: **D major**

Piano Sonata, Mvt. I

Franz Joseph Haydn
(1732-1809)

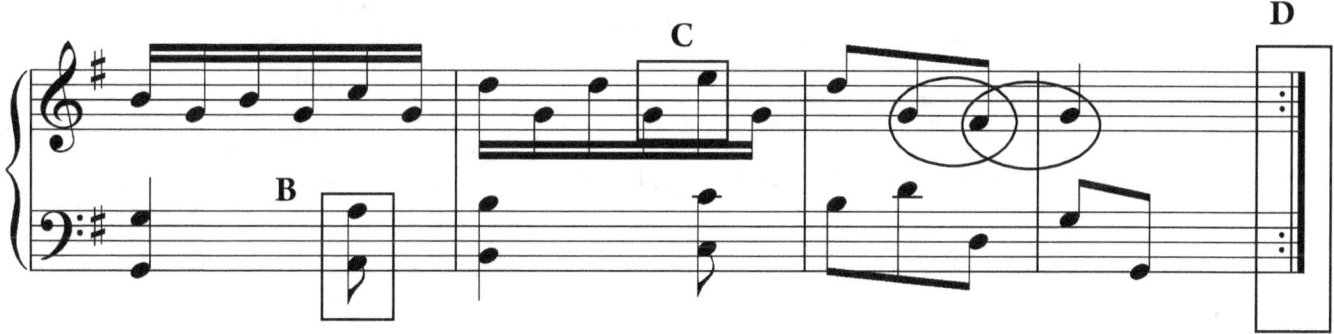

a. Add the correct time signature directly on the music.

b. Name the key of this piece. **G major**

c. Name the composer of this piece. **Franz Joseph Haydn**

d. On which beat does this piece begin? **3**

e. Name the intervals at : A **maj 3** B **per 8** C **maj 6**

f. Does this piece end on a stable or unstable degree? **stable**

g. Explain the sign at D. **Repeat sign, repeat from the beginning**

h. Define *Presto* **Very fast**

i. Find one half step and circle it.

Menuetto

Wolfgang Amadeus Mozart
(1756-1791)

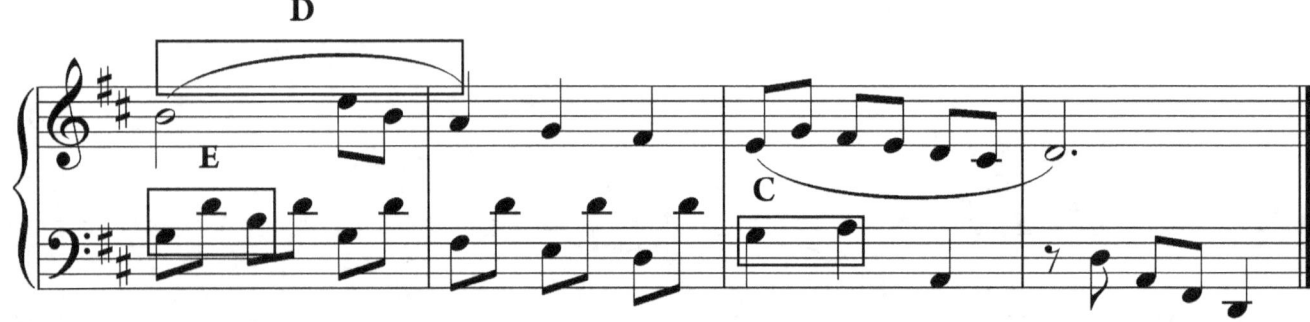

a. Add the correct time signature directly on the music.

b. Name the key of this piece. **D major**

c. Name the composer of this piece. **Wolfgang Amadeus Mozart**

d. When did this composer live? **1756-1791**

e. Name the intervals at : A **per 4** B **per 5** C **maj 2**

f. Explain the sign at D. **slur, play the notes smoothly connected**

h. Define *andante*. **moderate walking pace**

i. Does this piece end on a stable or unstable scale degree? **stable**

j. Name the triad formed by the notes at E: **G major**

k. In this key, this triad is the: ❏ tonic triad   ☑ subdominant triad   ❏ dominant triad

Page 84, No. 1 Review 3

Page 84, No. 2

Key:	E♭ major	G major	A major	B♭ major
Triad:	tonic	dominant	subdominant	tonic
	I	V	IV	I

Page 85, No. 3

	D	F♯m	Gm	F♯
Key:	G minor	F♯ minor	D minor	B minor
Triad:	dominant	tonic	subdominant	dominant

Page 85, No. 4 (other options are possible)

Page 85, No. 5 (other options are possible)

Page 86, No. 6

a. Who composed *The Nutcracker*? **Piotr Ilyich Tchaikovsky**
b. In what country was he born? **Russia**
c. In what era did he live? **Romantic**
d. How many symphonies did he write? **Six**
e. What type of work is *The Nutcracker*? **Ballet**
f. Name a dance from *The Nutcracker*. **Waltz of the flowers, Dance of the Sugar Plum Fairy**
g. Who choreographed *The Nutcracker*?
        1. **Marius Petipa**
        2. **Lev Ivanov**
h. What is a choreographer? **A choreographer designs the dances for a ballet.**
i. What unique instrument is featured in *The Nutcracker*? **Celesta**

Page 87, No. 7

n) cantabile	a) becoming quicker
m) vivace	b) a slow tempo between andante and largo
i) rallentando	c) fairly fast, a little slower than allegro
o) dolce	d) fast
r) marcato	e) slow
l) Tempo primo	f) at a moderate tempo
e) adagio	g) very fast
j) ritardando	h) as fast as possible
c) allegretto	i) slowing down
h) prestissimo	j) slowing down gradually
p) grazioso	k) speed at which music is performed
f) moderato	l) return to the original tempo
g) presto	m) lively, brisk
a) accelerando	n) in a singing style
q) maestoso	o) sweetly
k) tempo	p) gracefully
d) allegro	q) majestically
b) lento	r) marked or stressed

Level 5

Page 2, No. 1

Page 2, No. 2

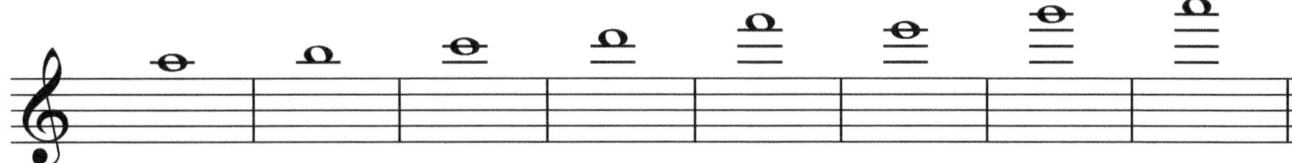

Page 2, No. 3

Page 2, No. 4

Page 3, No. 5

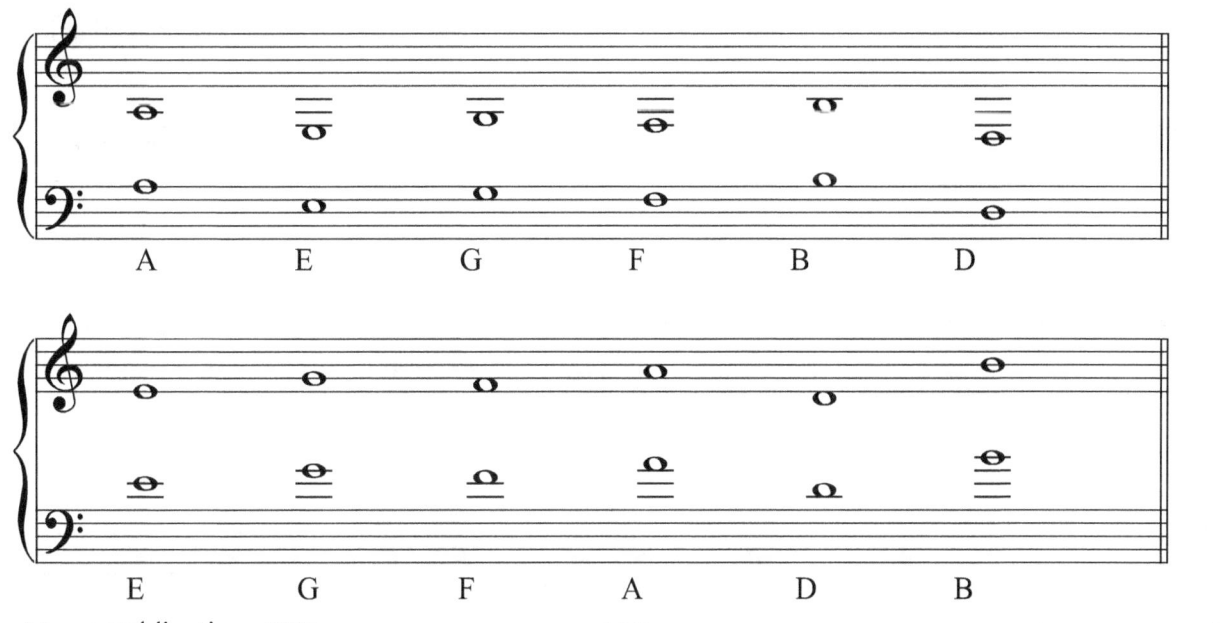

Page 3, No. 6

Jean Sibelius
Symphony No. 3, III

Page 4, No. 1

G♭	B♭	E#
A#	C♭	F#
D♭	A♭	C#
E♭	B#	G#
F	A#	D#

Page 5, No. 1

3/4	3/4
2/4	2/4
4/4	4/4
3/4	4/4
2/4	3/4

Page 7, No. 1

2/4   2/2   2/4   2/8   2/2   2/8   2/4

Page 9, No. 1

George Frideric Handel
Water Music, X

Joseph Haydn
Symphony No. 92

George Frideric Handel
Concerto Grosso
Op. 6, No. 3

Domenico Scarlatti
The Good Humored Ladies Ballet Suite

J.S. Bach
English Suite No. 2

Ludwig van Beethoven
Symphony No. 9, IV

Page 11, No. 1

4/2   4/4   4/2   4/4

Page 12, No. 2

Page 12, No. 3

4/4   4/2   3/2

© San Marco Publications 2022   112   Level 5

Page 13, No. 1

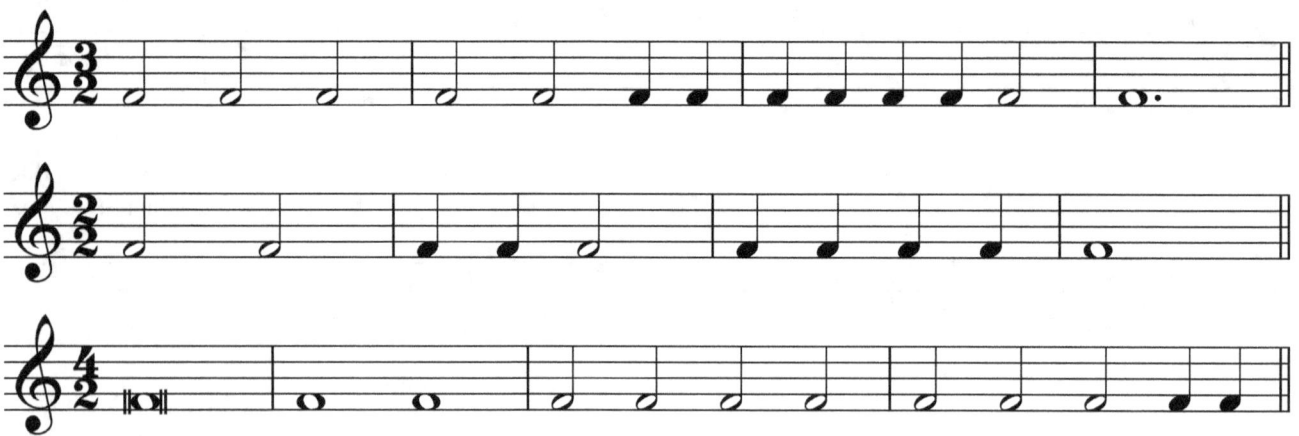

Page 13, No. 2

Page 14, No. 1

2/4   3/8
4/4   3/2
3/4   2/8

Page 15-16, No. 1

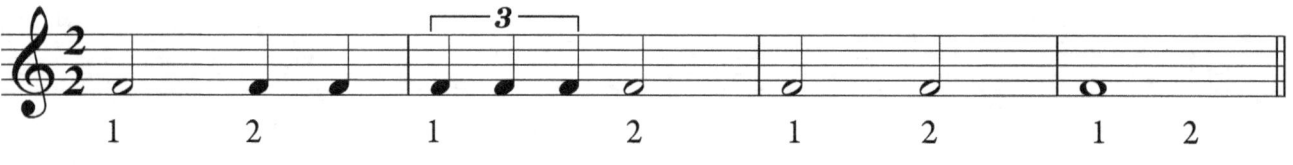

© San Marco Publications 2022 — Level 5

Page 17, No. 1

Page 18, No. 2

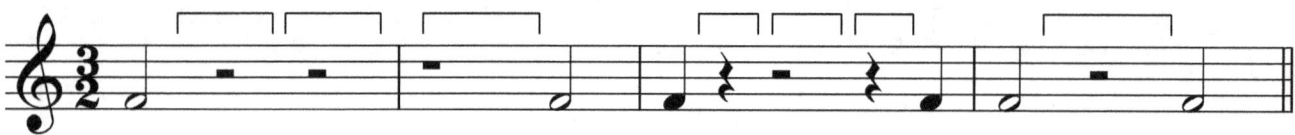

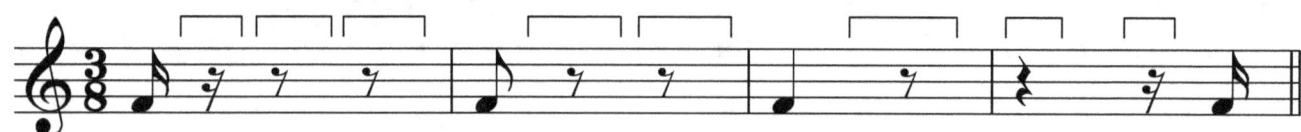

Page 19, No. 3

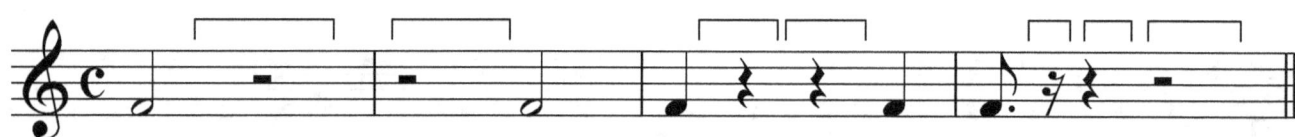

Page 20, No. 4

Page 22, No. 1

Page 23, No. 2

Edvard Grieg
Norwegian Melody

Robert Schumann
Symphony No. 3

Gustav Mahler
Resurrection Symphony No. 1

Page 25, No. 1

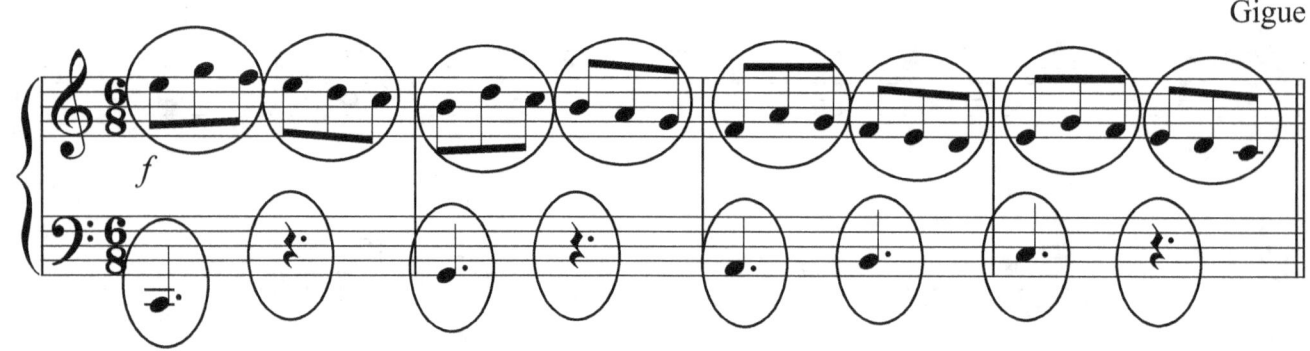

Page 26, No. 2

3/4
6/8
6/8
3/4

Page 26, No. 3

Page 27, No. 1

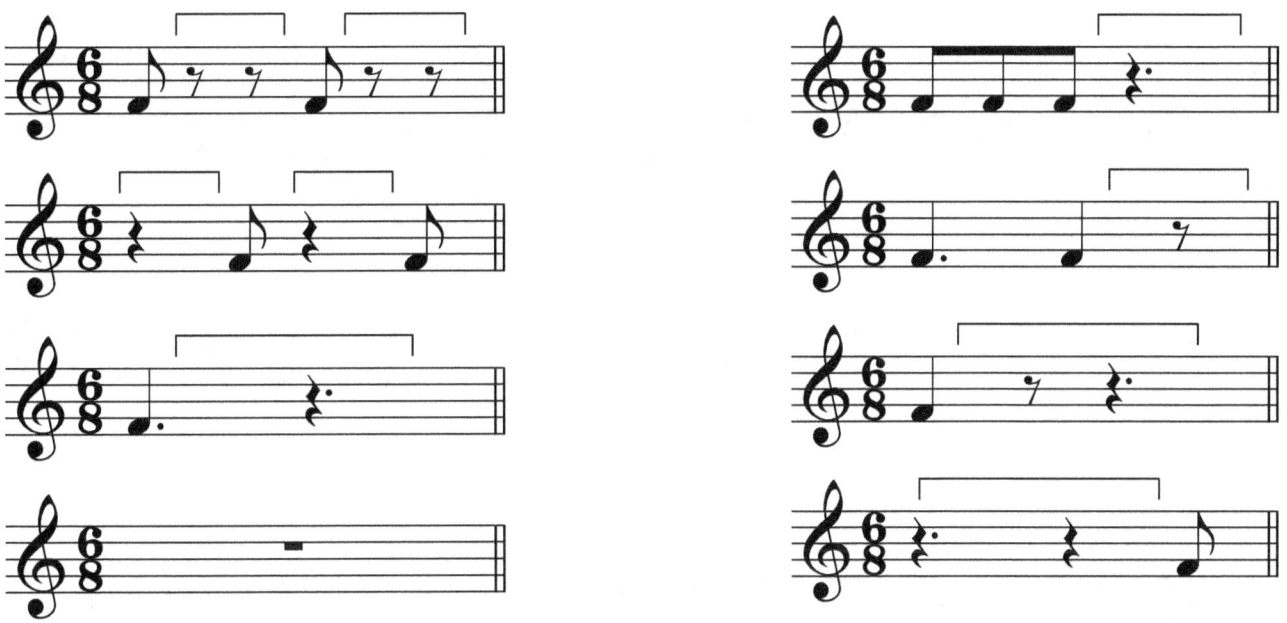

Page 28, No. 2

Page 33, No. 1

Page 34, No. 2

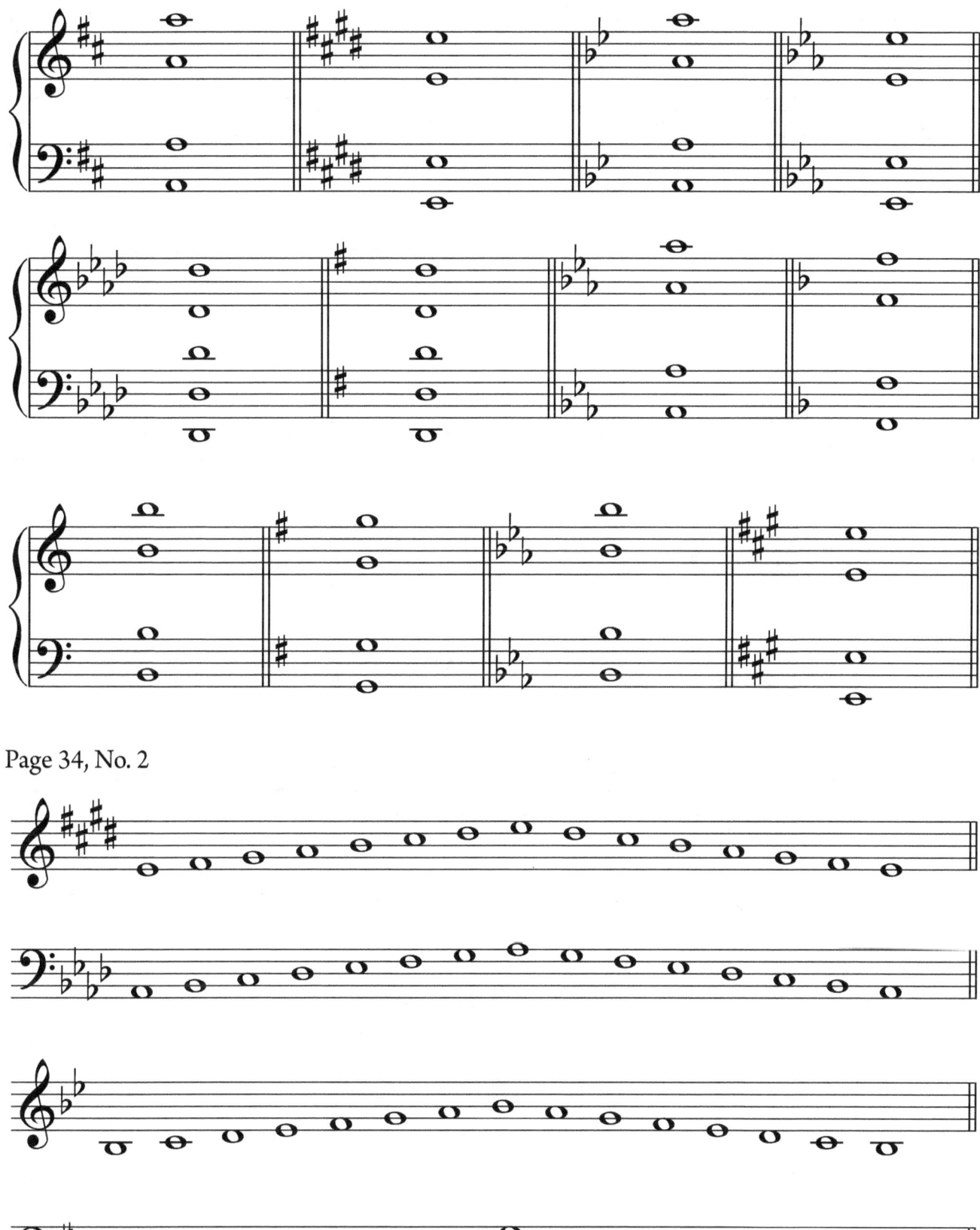

Page 35, No. 3

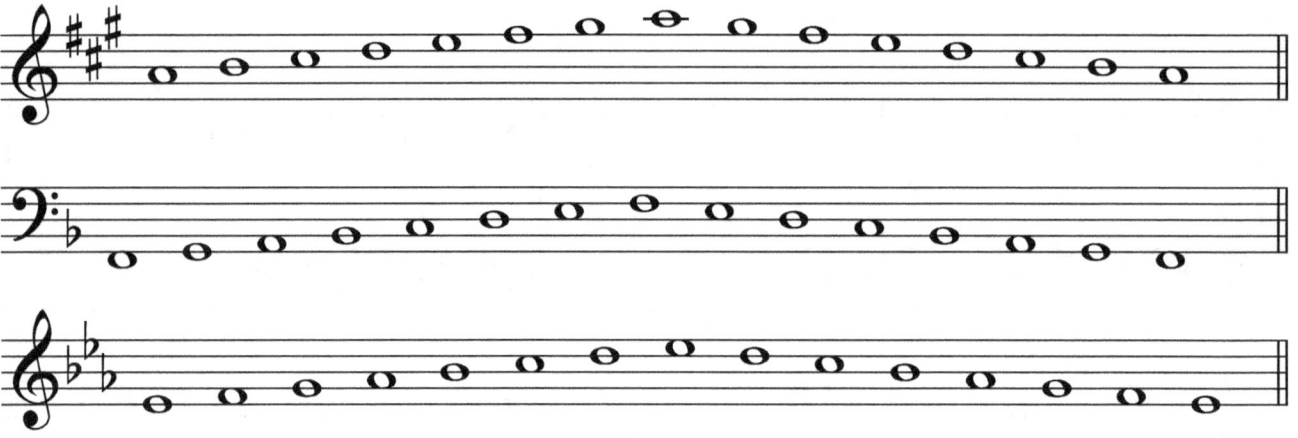

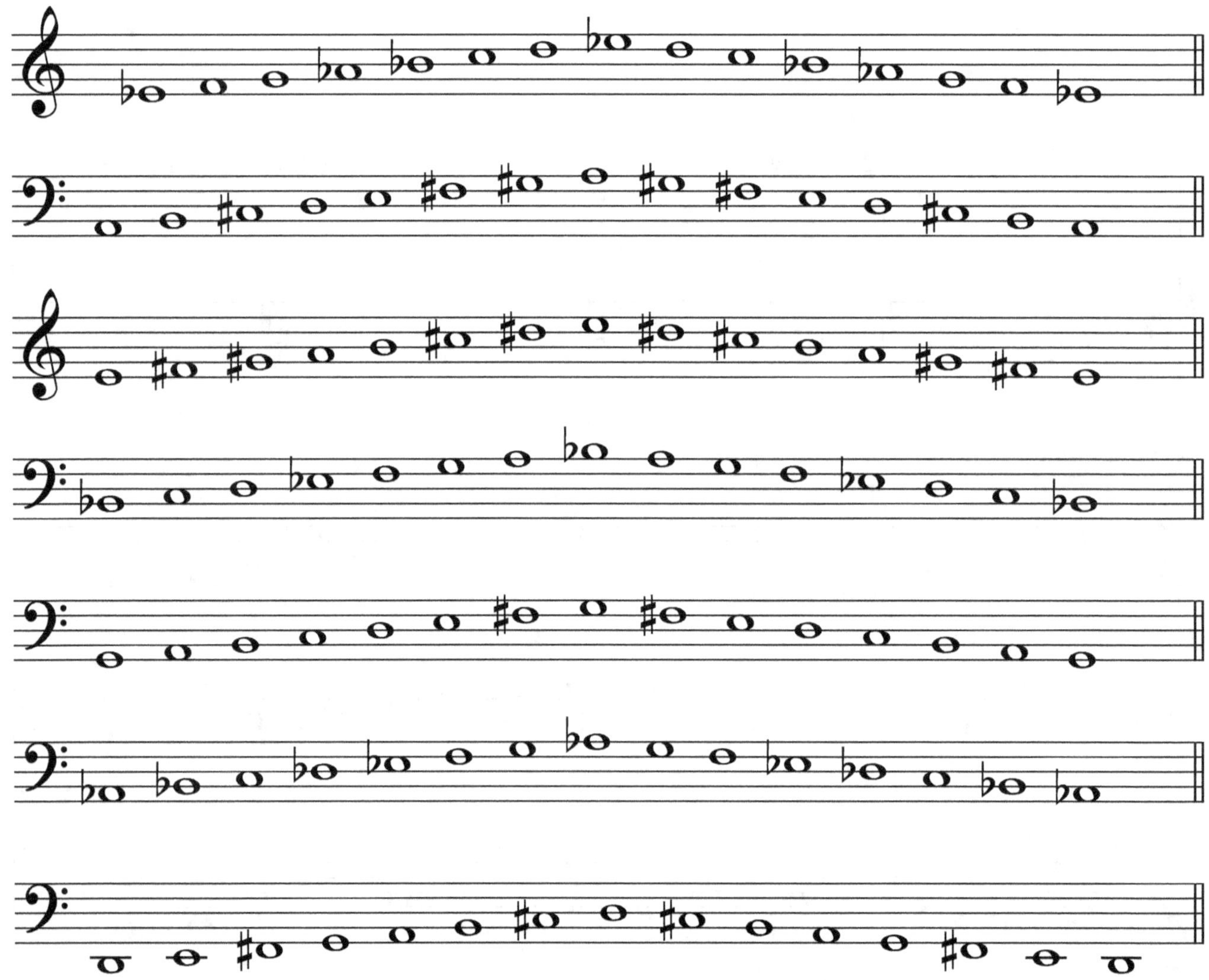

Page 36, No. 4

Page 40, No. 1 Review 1

Wolfgang Amadeus Mozart
Piano Concerto K270

Mikhail Glinka
Souvenir of a Night in Madrid

Page 40, No. 2

C#	Db		G#	Ab		F	E#
Ab	G#		B	Cb		Gb	F#
F#	Gb		A#	Bb		Eb	D#
D#	Eb		C	B#		Bb	A#

Page 41, No. 3

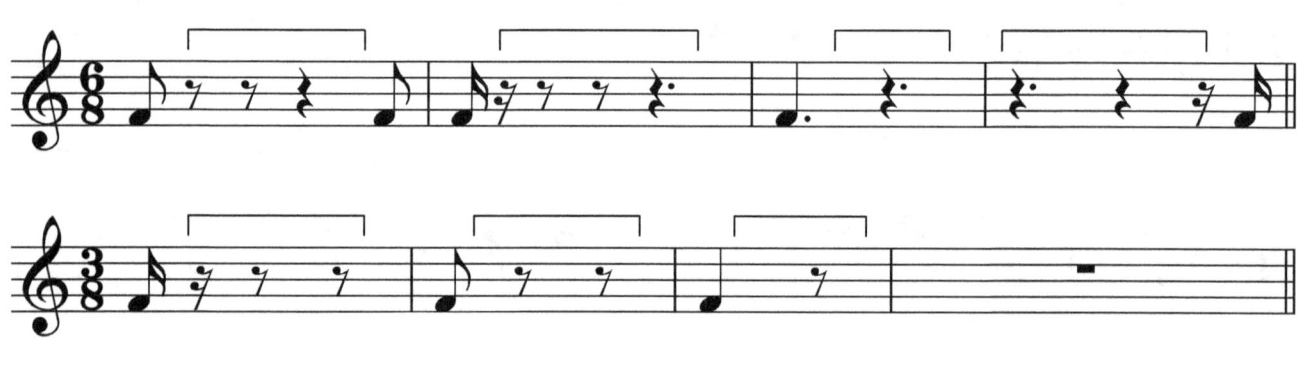

Page 41, No. 4

Page 42, No. 5

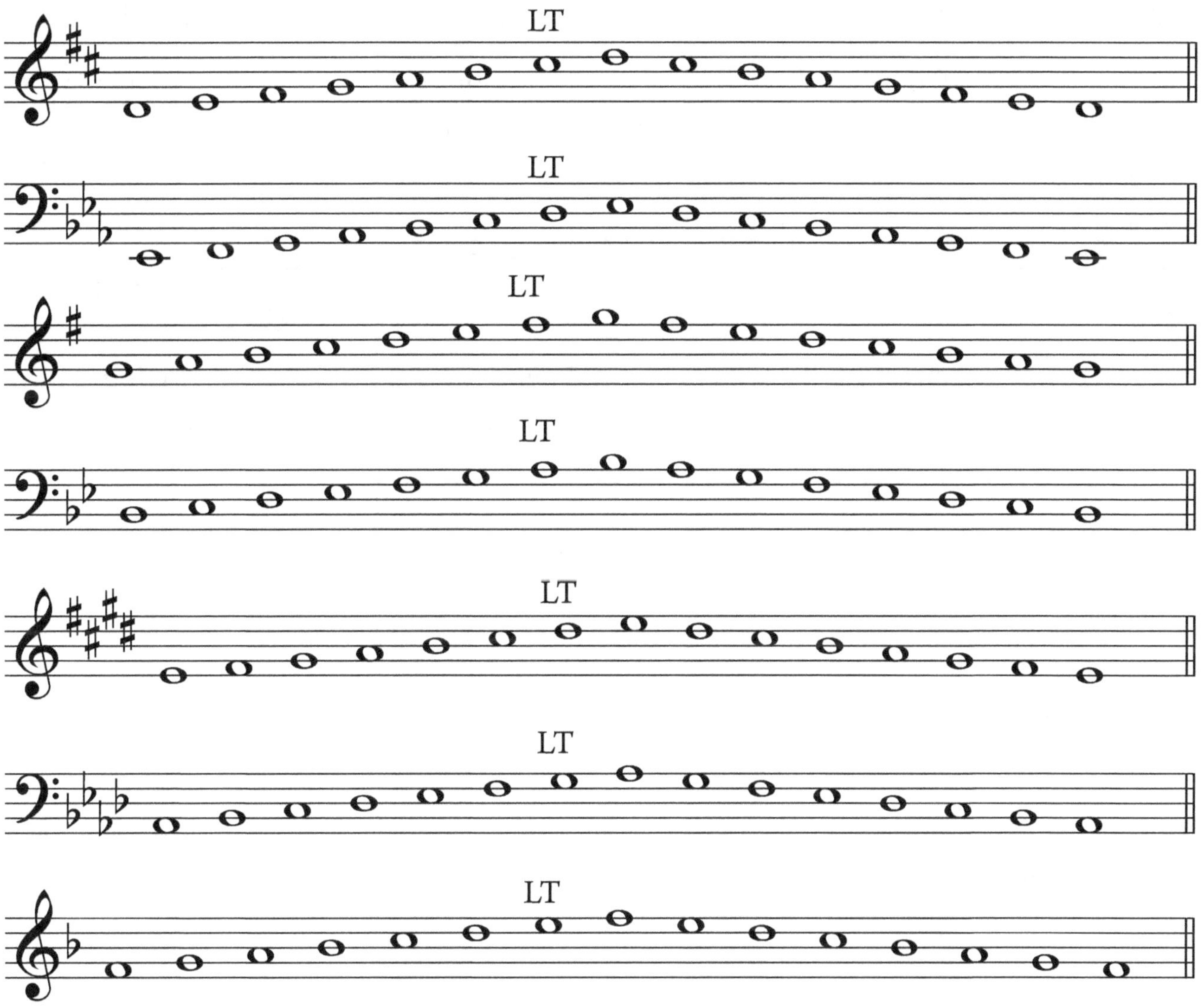

Page 43, No. 6

a) Germany
b) Baroque
c) England
d) A large composition for orchestra, choir and soloists based on a religious theme.
e) 1741
f) Soprano   Alto   Tenor   Bass
g) Technique of writing music that mirrors the meaning of a piece.
h) The text "Forever and ever" is repeated over and over.

Page 44, No. 1

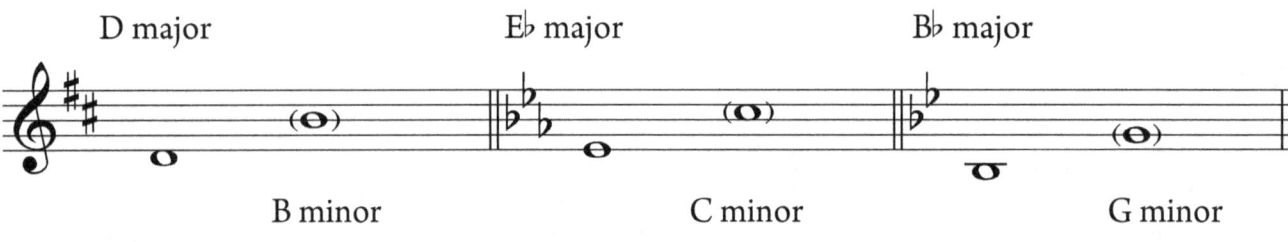

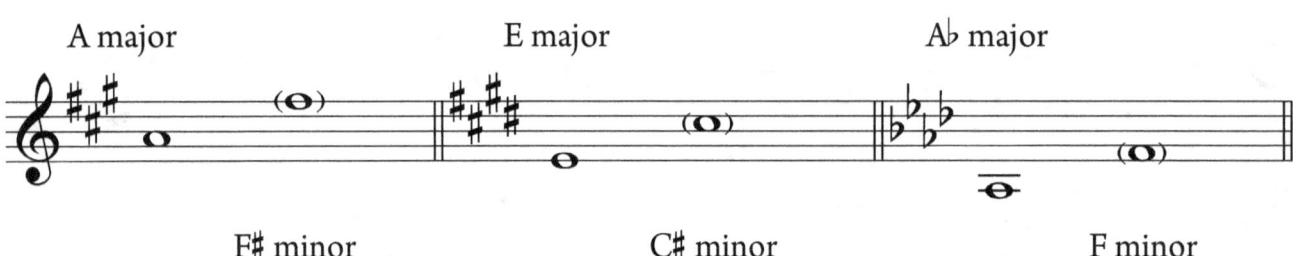

Page 47, No. 1

E natural minor

B harmonic minor

C♯ harmonic minor

C melodic minor

F harmonic minor

A melodic minor

G natural minor

Page 48, No. 2

Page 49, No. 3

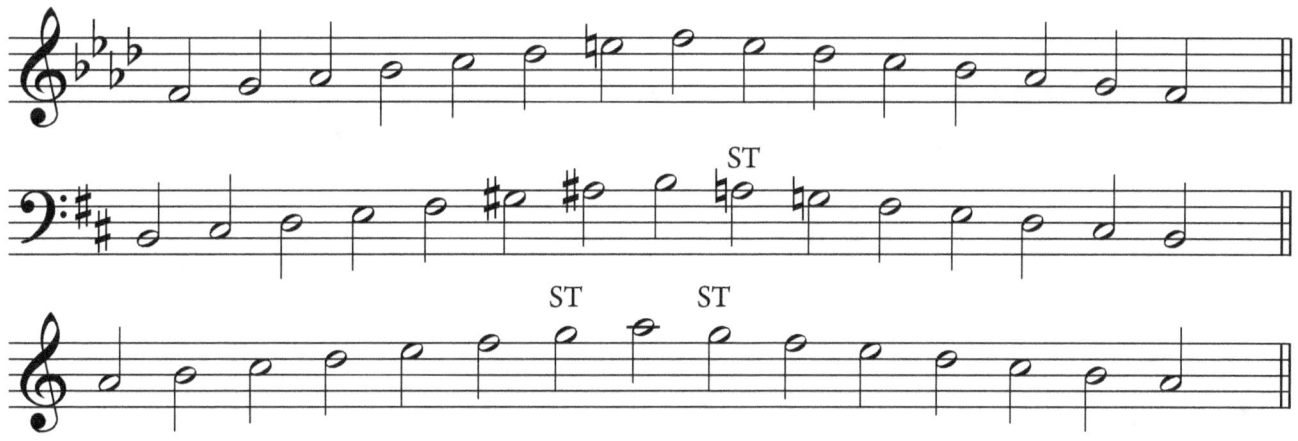

Page 50-51, No. 1

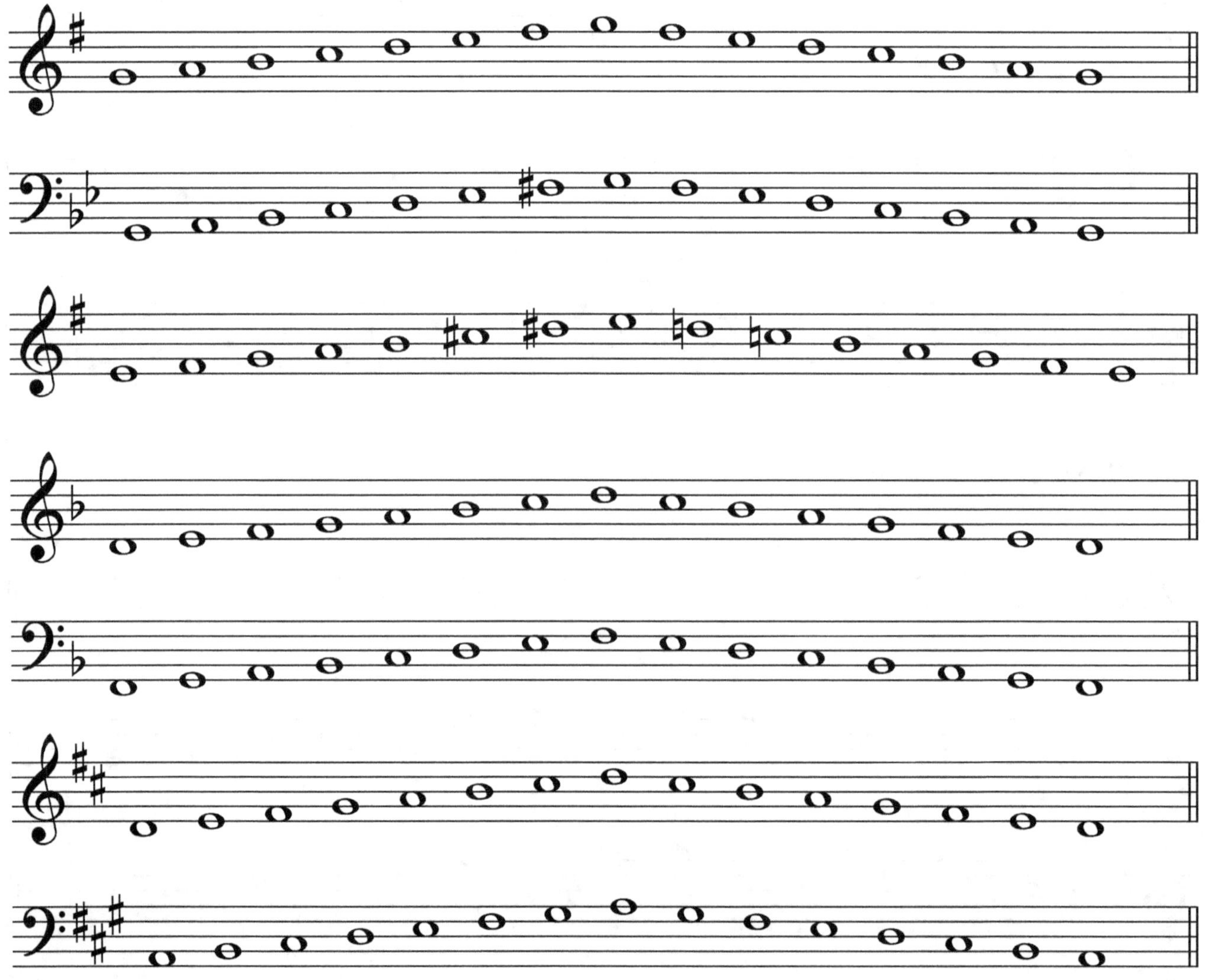

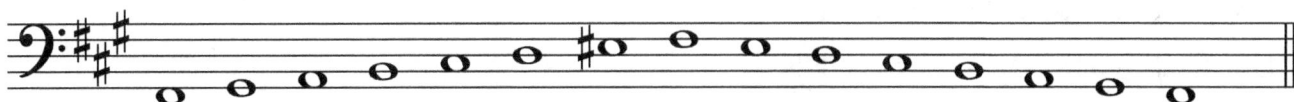

Page 53, No. 1

E♭ major
B♭ major
D minor
G minor
E minor
A♭ major
C minor

Page 55, No. 1

Page 55, No. 2

Page 56, No. 1

Page 56, No. 2

Page 56, No. 3

CHS DHS DHS CHS CHS DHS
DHS CHS DHS CHS CHS DHS
CHS DHS DHS CHS DHS DHS
DHS CHS CHS DHS CHS DHS

Page 57, No. 1

Page 57, No. 2

Page 58, No. 1

per 1   maj 2   maj 3   per 4   per 5   maj 6   maj 7   per 8

Page 58, No. 2

per 1   maj 2   maj 3   per 4   per 5   maj 6   maj 7   per 8

Page 59, No. 3

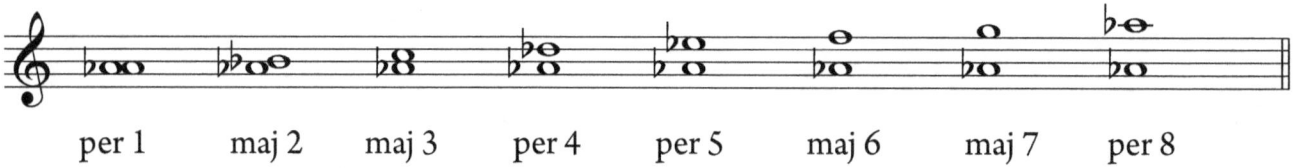

Page 59, No. 4

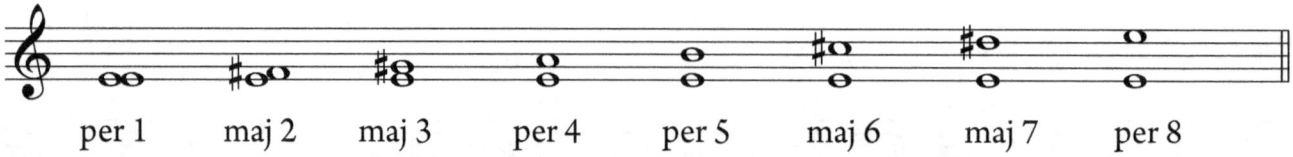

Page 60, No. 1

Page 60, No. 2

per 8   per 4   min 3   maj 2
per 5   per 4   maj 6   maj 3   min 2

Page 61, No. 3

per 5   min 3   per 4   maj 2   per 8   min 7   maj 7   per 5
per 5   min 6   per 5   min 6   min 7   maj 3   min 7   per 4

Page 61, No. 4

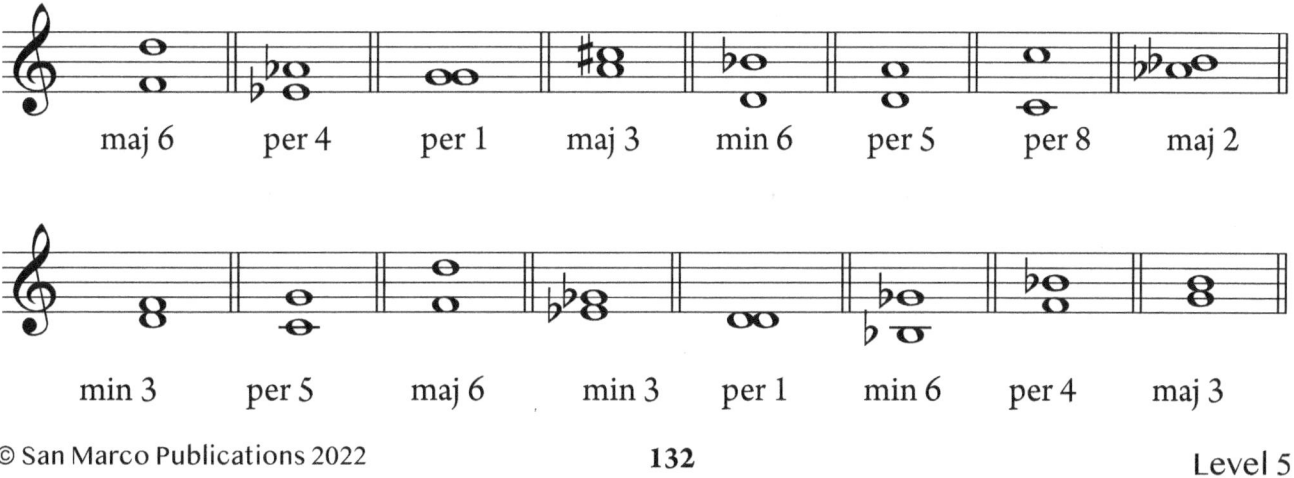

Page 67, No. 1 Review 2

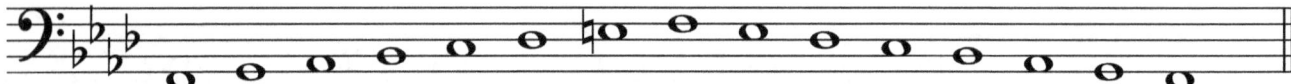

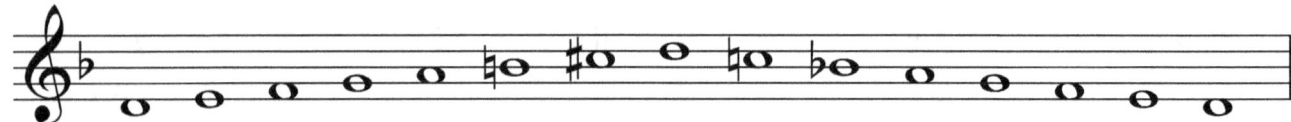

Page 67, No. 2

CHS DHS WS DHS DHS CHS

WS WS WS CHS CHS CHS

Page 68, No. 3

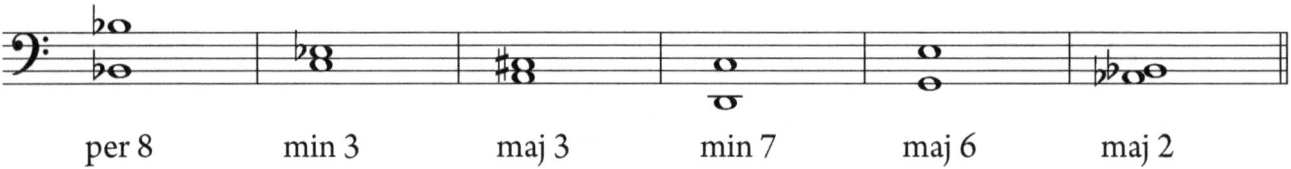

Page 68,

4. An opera is a play with music.
5. Classical era
6. 1791
7. Singspiel
8. German
9. A song in an opera that can be taken out and sung in a musical performance.
10. Coloratura

Page 68, No. 11

b) ***andantino***   a) expressive
a) ***espressivo, espress.***   b) a little faster than andante
d) ***larghetto***   c) very slow
c) ***largo***   d) fairly slow, not as slow as largo

Page 72, No. 1

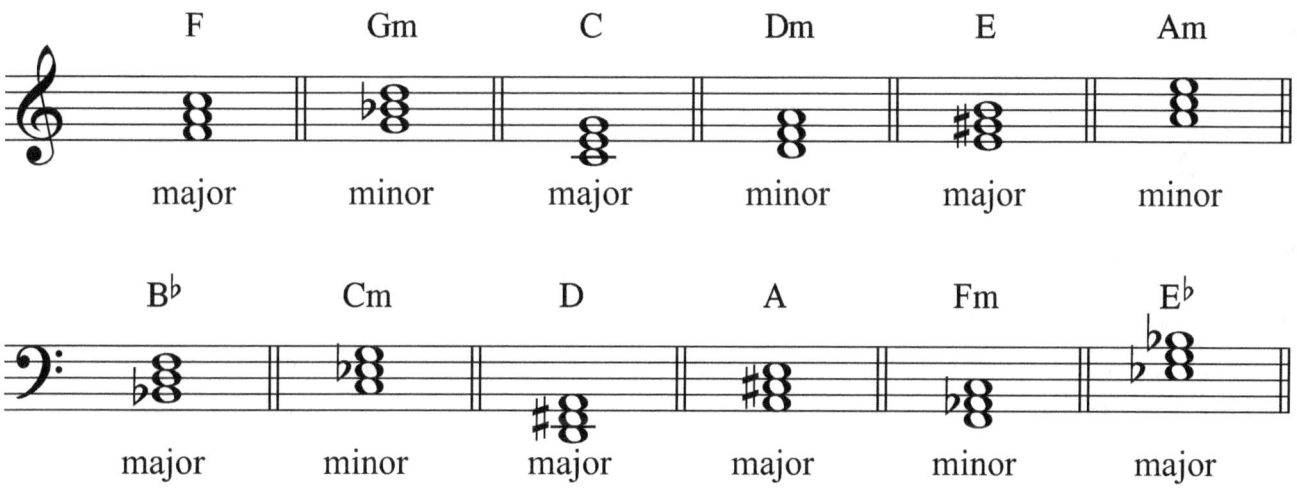

Page 72, No. 2

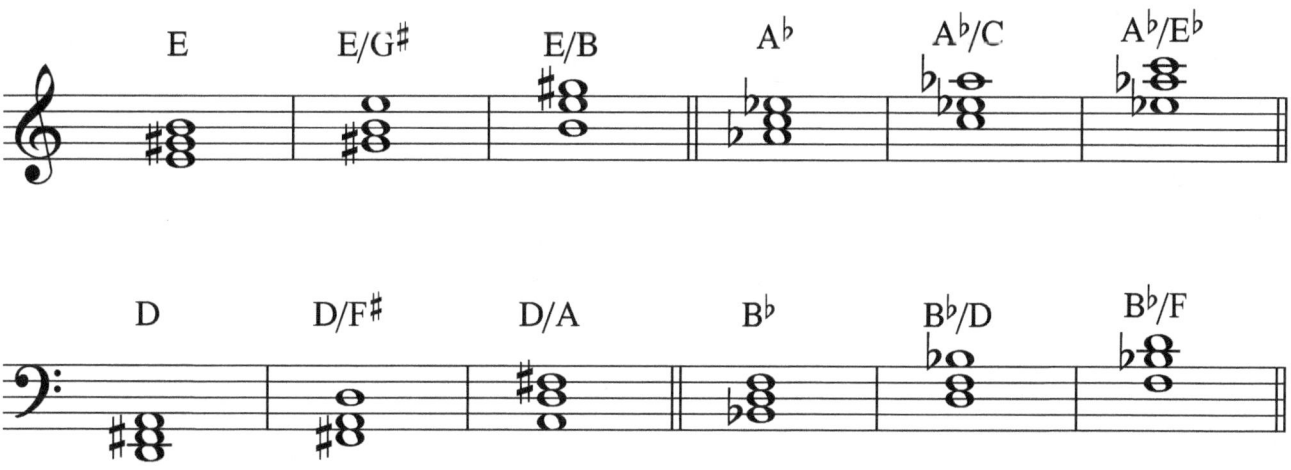

Page 73, No. 3

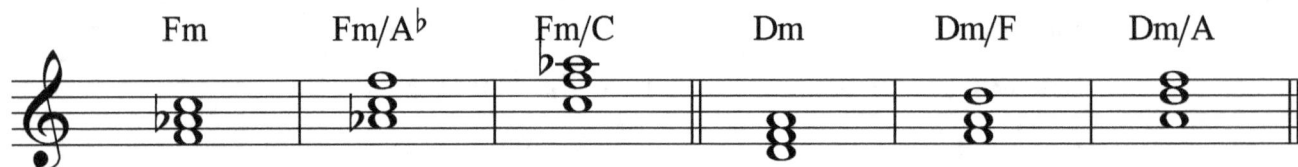

Page 74, No. 1

B♭ C E G D D
F   E♭ D E C A

Page 74, No. 2

E	F	G	D	A	A
minor	minor	major	minor	major	minor
2nd inv	1st inv.	root pos.	1st inv.	root pos.	1st inv.

B♭	A♭	B	G	E	F
major	major	minor	minor	minor	major
1st inv.	root pos.	2nd inv.	root pos.	2nd inv.	root pos.

Page 76, No. 1

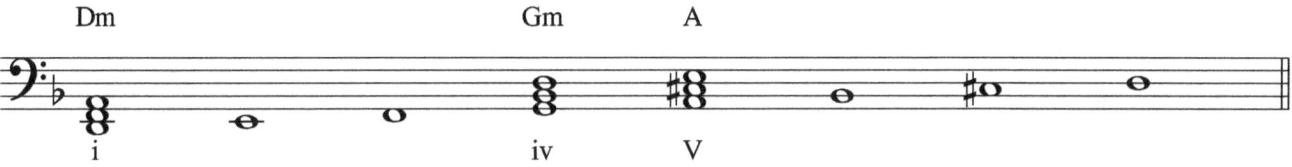

Page 76, No. 2

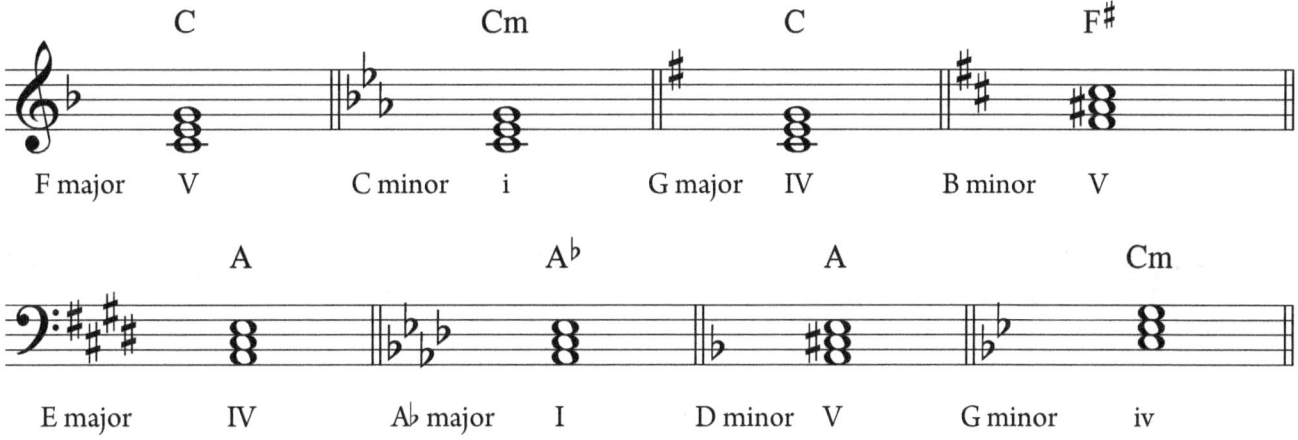

Page 77, No. 3

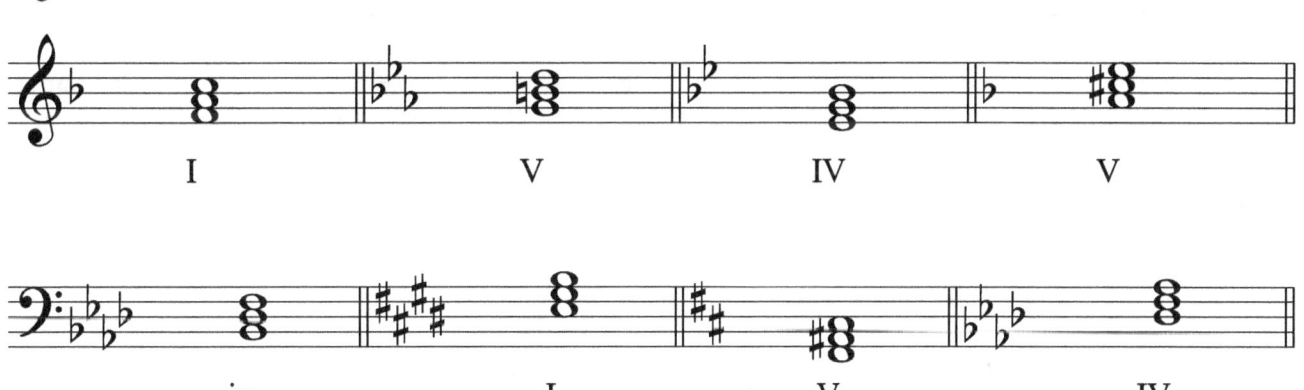

Page 77, No. 4

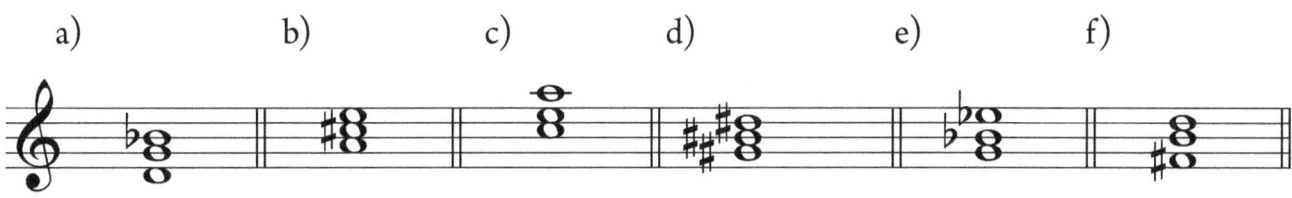

Page 79, No. 1

D major   G major   C major   F major   B♭ major   E♭ major

Page 79, No. 2

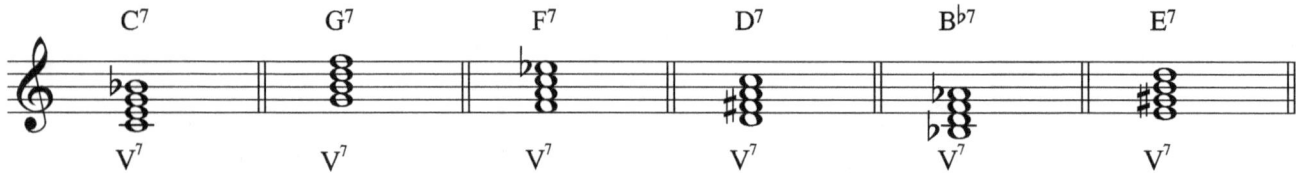

Page 79, No. 3

Page 79, No. 4

Page 81, No. 1

Page 82, No. 2

William Byrd
Pavan

J. S. Bach
Toccata and Fugue in G minor

Page 83, No. 3

Dimitri Shostakovich
Symphony No.7, Op. 60

J.S. Bach
Fugue 24 From WTC Book 2

Page 83, No. 4

Frederic Chopin
Sonata in G minor

Claude Debussy
Petite Suite

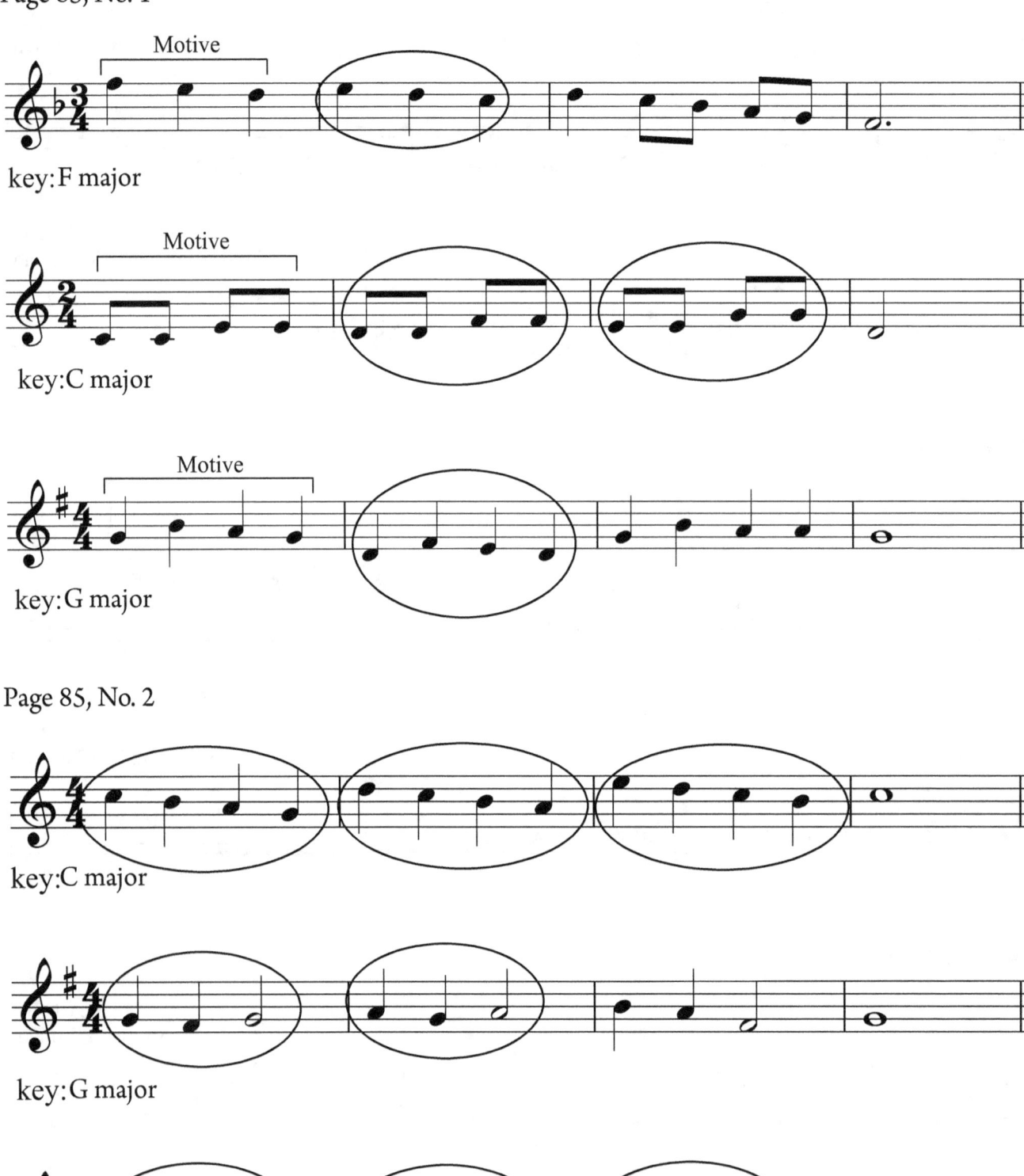

Page 86, No. 1

Page 88, No. 1

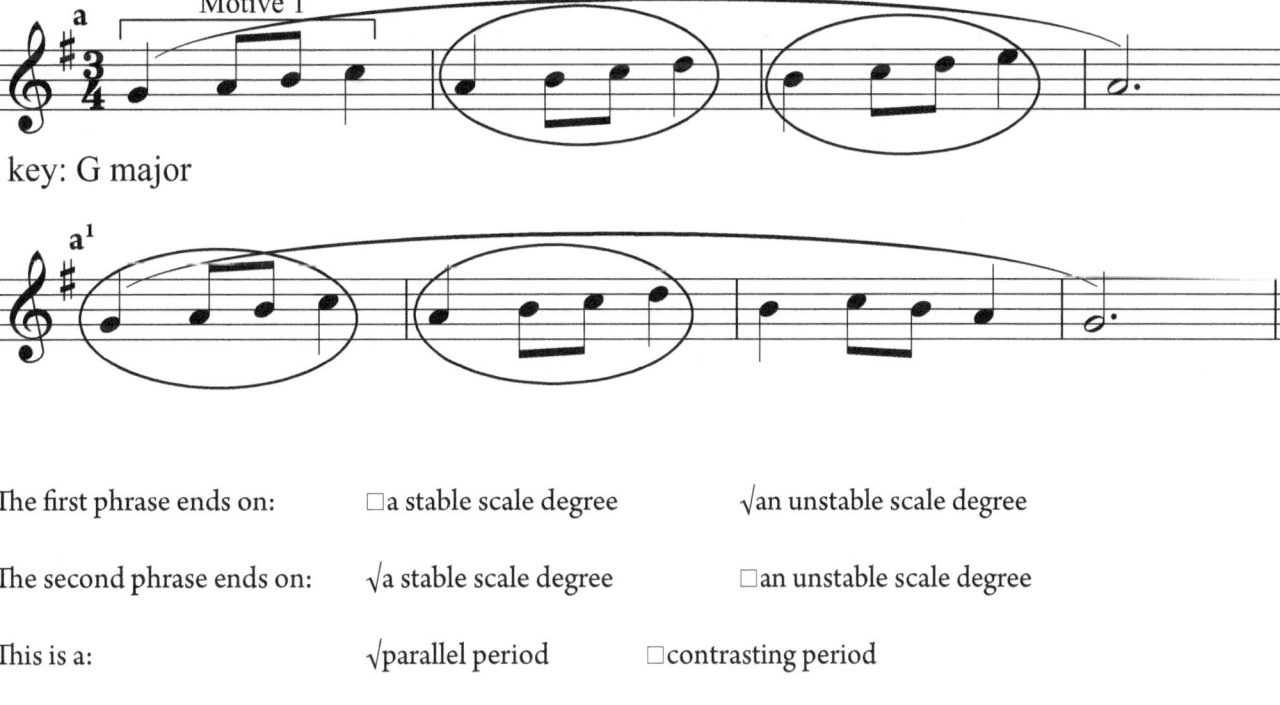

The first phrase ends on: □ a stable scale degree   √ an unstable scale degree

The second phrase ends on: √ a stable scale degree   □ an unstable scale degree

This is a: √ parallel period   □ contrasting period

© San Marco Publications 2022   140   Level 5

Page 89, No. 2

key: F major

The first phrase ends on: ☐ a stable scale degree ☑ an unstable scale degree
The second phrase ends on: ☑ a stable scale degree ☐ an unstable scale degree
This is a: ☐ parallel period ☑ contrasting period

Page 90 - 91, No. 1 (other options are possible)

Page 92

1. Who composed the music shown above? **George Frideric Handel**

2. What is the name of the composition? **Messiah - Hallelujah Chorus**

3. What key is it in? **D major**

4. What four voices are used to sing this piece? **soprano alto tenor bass**

5. Name the triad formed by the notes at A **D major triad**

6. Name the interval at B. **per 4**

7. Name the interval at C. **maj 3**

8. Name the interval at D. **per 5**

Page 93

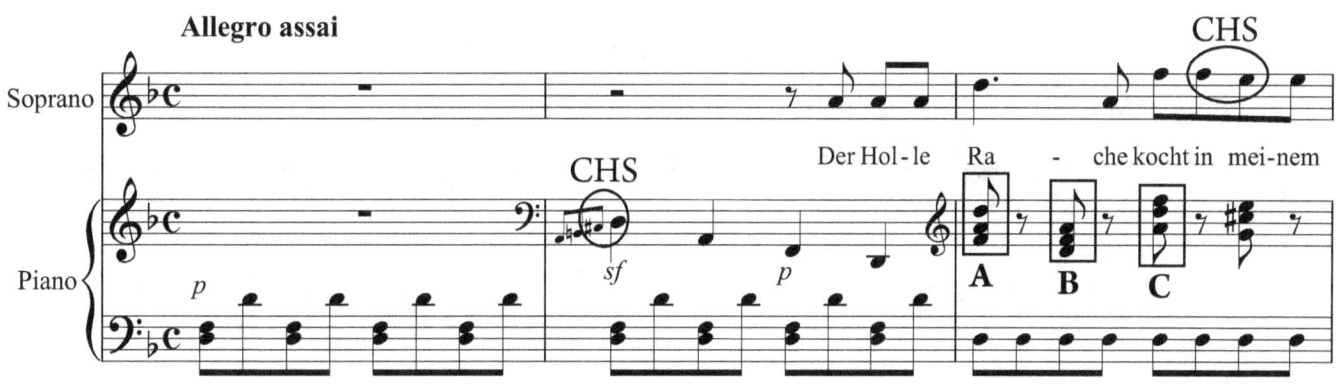

1. Who wrote the above musical example? **Wofgang Amadeus Mozart**

2. What musical era was it written? **Classical**

3. What character is singing in this passage? **The Queen of the Night**

4. In what language is she singing? **German**

5. What is the key of this piece? **D minor**

6. Name the triad and inversion at A: **D minor 1st inversion**
   B: **D minor Root position**
   C: **D minor 2nd inversion**

7. Circle one chromatic half step on the score. Label it CHS.

8. Define Allegro assai: **Very fast**

9. How many measures are in this example? **6**

Sonatina

Cornelius Gurlitt
1820 -1901

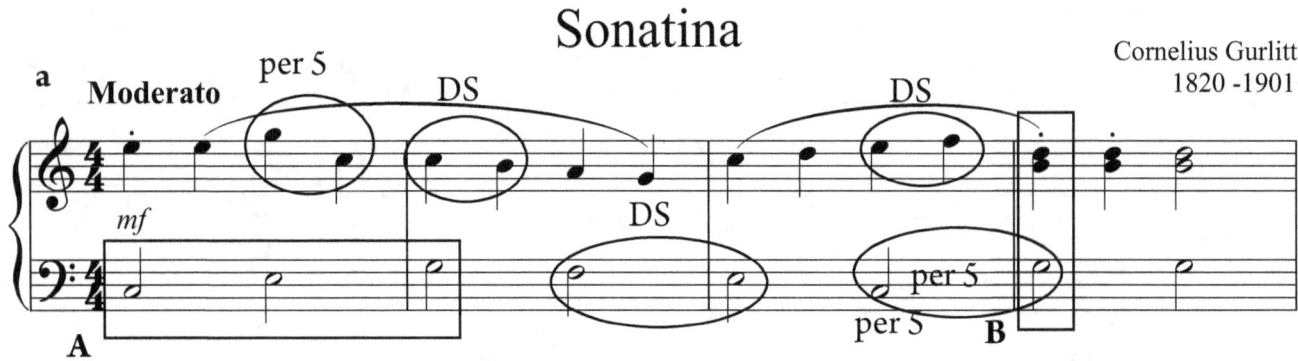

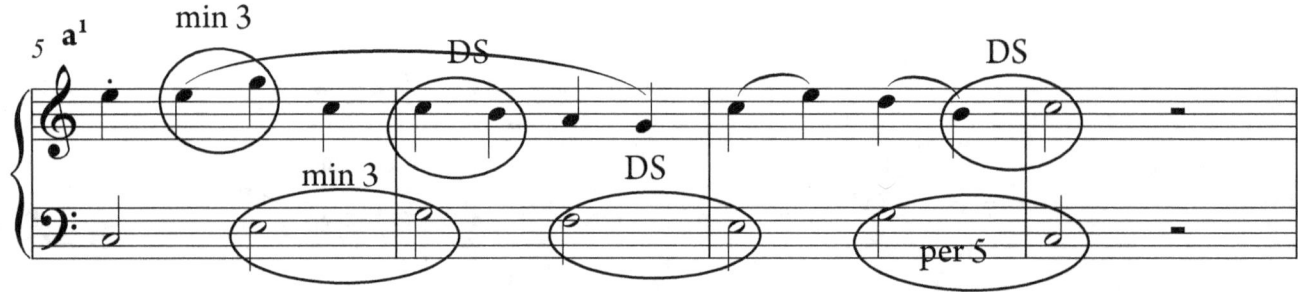

1. Name the composer of this piece? **Cornelius Gurlitt**

2. Name the key of this piece. **C major**

3. Write the time signature on the score.

4. Define "moderato" **at a moderate tempo or speed**

5. How many phrases are in this example? **2**

6. Does the first phrase end on a stable or unstable degree? **unstable**

7. Does the second phrase end on a stable or unstable degree? **stable**

8. Label the phrases either: (a - a¹) or (a - b) depending on the form.

9. What triad is formed by the notes in the box at letter A: **C major triad**

10. What triad is formed by the notes in the box at letter B: **G major triad**

11. Find the interval of a harmonic minor 3rd, circle it, and label it maj 3.

12. Find the interval of a melodic perfect 5th, circle it, and label it per 5.

13. Find two different diatonic semitones, circle them, and label them DS.

14. How many slurs occur in this piece? **5**

Page 95

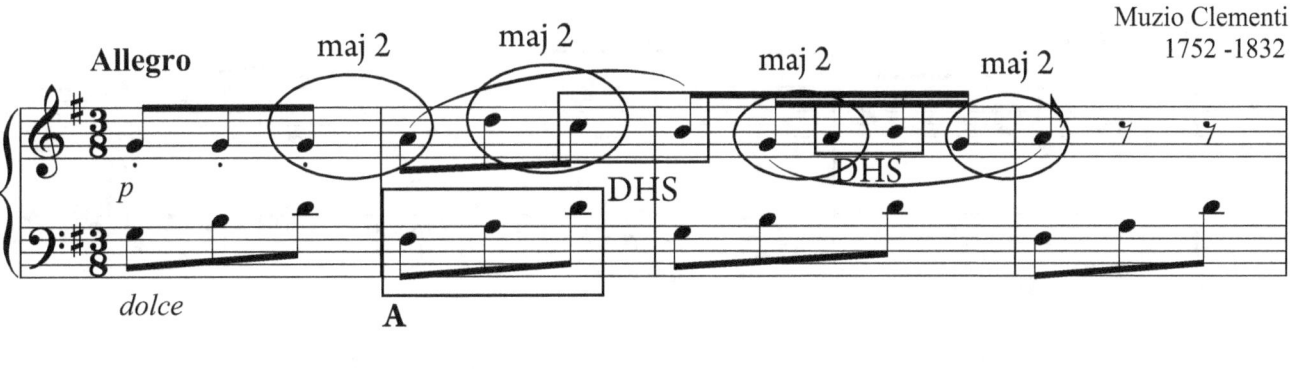

1. Name the composer of this piece? **Muzio Clementi**

2. When did he live? **1752-1832**

3. Write the time signature on the score.

4. Name the key of this piece. **G major**

5. Define "allegro." **fast**

6. Define "dolce." **sweetly**

7. For the triad at letter A, name the: Root **D** Quality **major** Position **1st**

8. For the triad at letter B, name the: Root **G** Quality **major** Position **root**

9. How many times does the broken tonic triad occur in the bass clef. **4**

10. Find a melodic major 2nd, circle it and label it maj 2.

11. Find a melodic major 3rd, circle it and label it maj 3.

12. Find a diatonic half step, put a box around it and label is DHS.

Page 96

1. Name the key of this piece? **F major**

2. Write the time signature on the score.

3. Check the terms that apply to this time signature. ☑compound ☐triple ☐simple ☑duple

4. Mark the phrases with a slur.

5. Label each phrase using the letters *a*, *a¹* or *b*.

6. Define "andantino." **a little faster than andante**

7. Name the triad at letter A.   root: **F**   quality: **major**

Page 99, No. 1   Review 3

F	G	E♭	D	C	E
major	major	major	minor	major	minor
root	1st	root	2nd	1st	root

A	B♭	A	F	G	C
minor	major	major	minor	major	minor
1st	2nd	root	2nd	root	root

Page 99, No. 2

Page 99, No. 3

c)
d)
a)
b)

Page 100, No. 4

Franz Schubert
Waltz, Op. 50

Page 100, No. 5

Page 100, No. 6

The composer of the Wizard of Oz:
☑Harold Arlen ☐George Gershwin ☐Irving Berlin

Harold Arlen was:
☐French ☐Russian ☑American

"Over the Rainbow" was written for:
☐Bette Davis ☑Judy Garland ☐Beyonce

The song form of "Over the Rainbow" is:
☑AABA ☐ABBA ☐ABAB

Page 105, No. 1 **Exam**

B A G♯ D A

Page 105, No. 2

DHS WS CHS DHS DHS

Page 105, No. 3

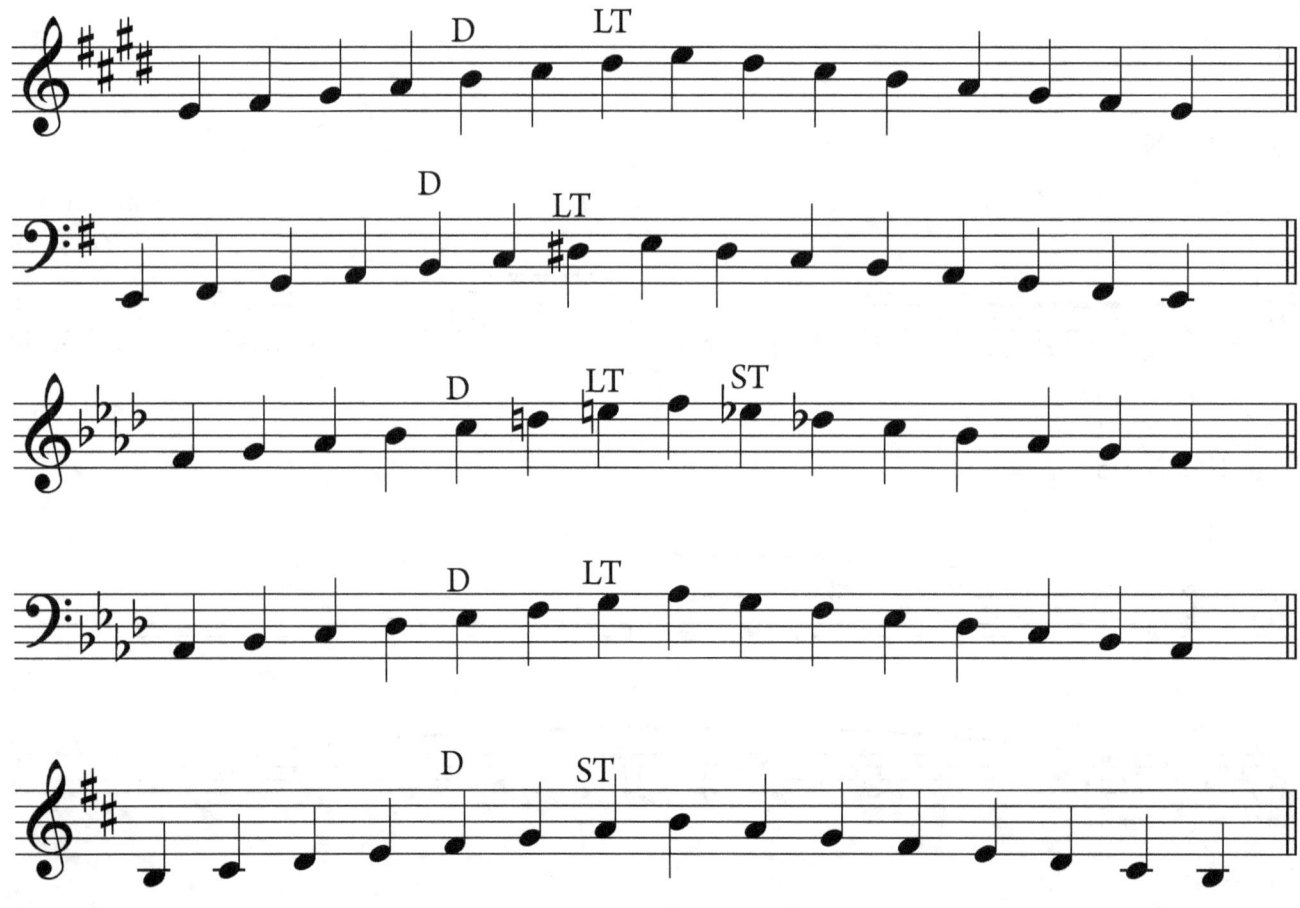

Page 106, No. 4

maj 3   maj 7   per 5   min 6   maj 2

Page 106, No. 5

Page 106, No. 6

Page 106, No. 7

W.A. Mozart
Concerto K218

D major

Page 107, No. 8

F major

Page 107, No. 9

i.   ii.   iii.   iv.   v.

© San Marco Publications 2022   Level 5

Page 107, No. 10

i)
h)
e)
f)
j)
a)
g)
d)
b)
c)

Page 108, No. 11

andantino - a little faster than andante

larghetto - fairly slow, not as slow as largo

rubato - flexible tempo with slight variations of speed to enhance musical expression

largo - very slow

mano destra - right hand

poco - little

lento - slow

pedale - pedal

spiritoso - spirited

marcato - well marked or stressed

prestissimo - as fast as possible

tranquillo - tranquil

dolce - sweetly

leggiero - light

molto - much, very

espressivo - expressive

vivace - lively

fine - the end

marcato - well marked

adagio - slow

Page 109, No. 12

Muzio Clementi
1752-1832

1. What is the key of this piece? **G major**

2. Write the time signature on the score.

3. Define *dolce*   **sweetly**

4. Define *Un poco adagio*   **a little slow**

5. Label the two phrases as: a - a¹ or a - b.

6. For the triad at A, name the: Root: **G**   Quality: **major**   Position: **root**

7. For the triad at B, name the: Root: **D**   Quality: **major**   Position: **1st inversion**

8. Find a chromatic half step in the score. Circle it and label it: CHS.

9. Find and circle a G major scale on the score. Label it: G major.

10. Name the highest note in this piece.   **B**

© San Marco Publications 2022   152   Level 5

Level 6

Page 2, No. 1

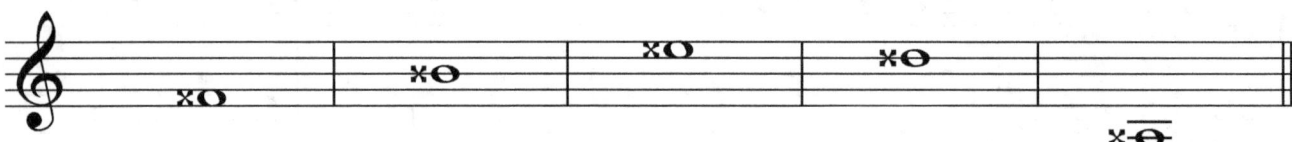

Page 2, No. 2

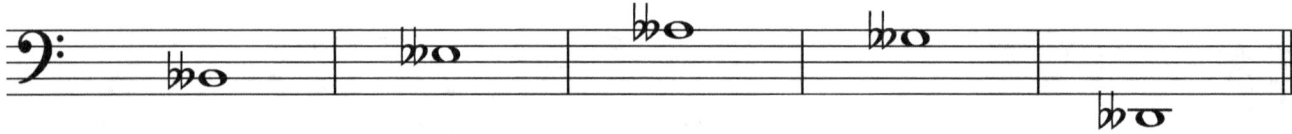

Page 3, No. 1

Page 4, No. 2

Jean Sibelius
Symphony No. 3, III

Wolfgang Amadeus Mozart
Piano Concerto K270

Page 6, No. 1

a. Sixteenth note.

b. Eighth note.

c. Half note.

d. Dotted quarter note.

e. Whole note.

f. Quarter note.

Page 6, No. 2

2/4
3/8
2/4
4/4
3/4

Page 7, No. 1

Page 8, No. 1

Page 10, No. 1

Page 11, No. 2

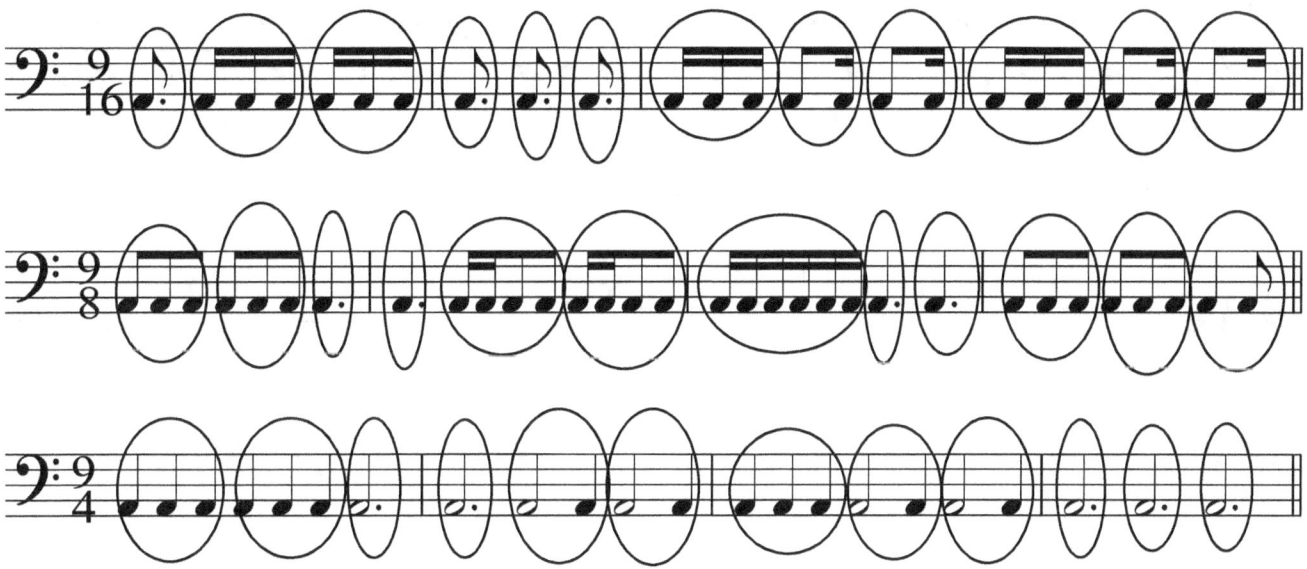

Page 12, No. 3

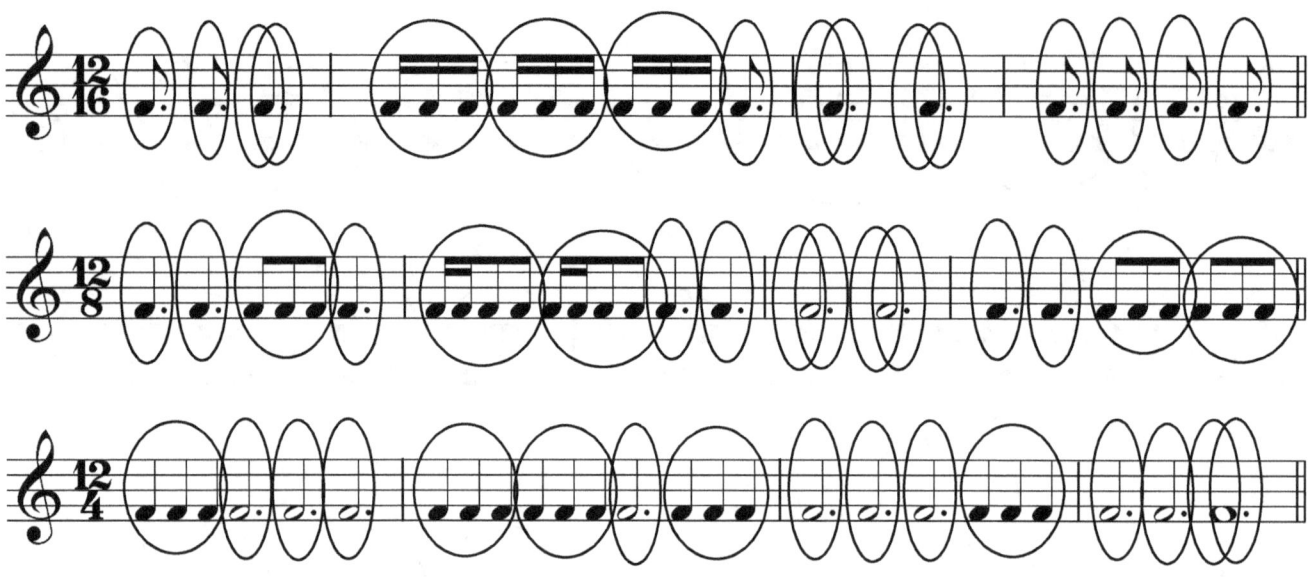

Page 13, No. 4

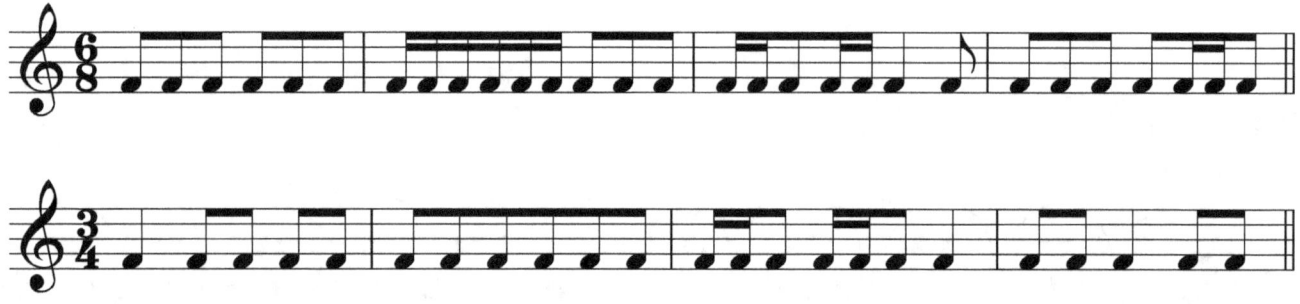

Page 15, No. 5

Page 16, No. 5

Page 16 - 17, No. 6

12/8
6/8
3/2
9/8
4/2
4/4
6/8
2/4
9/8
12/8

Page 21, No. 1

C#	D	F#	
FCGDAEB	FC	FCGDAE	

G	A	B	E
F	FCG	FCGDA	FCGD

G♭	A♭	C♭	
BEADGC	BEAD	BEADGCF	

B♭	F	E♭	D♭
BE	B	BEA	BEADG

© San Marco Publications 2022   158   Level 6

Page 22, No. 1

Page 23, No. 2

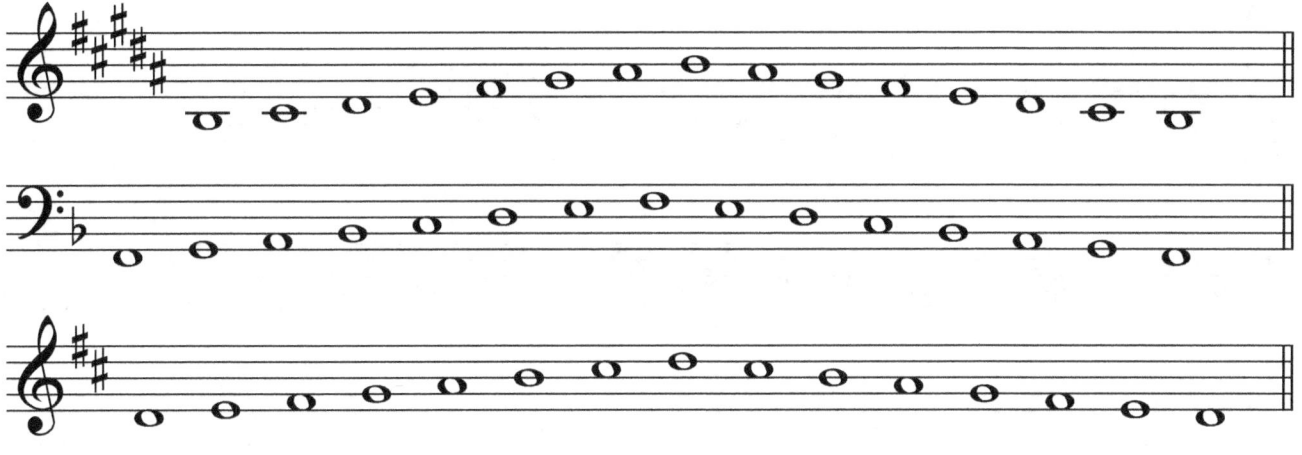

Page 24, No. 3 (accidentals are not required descending)

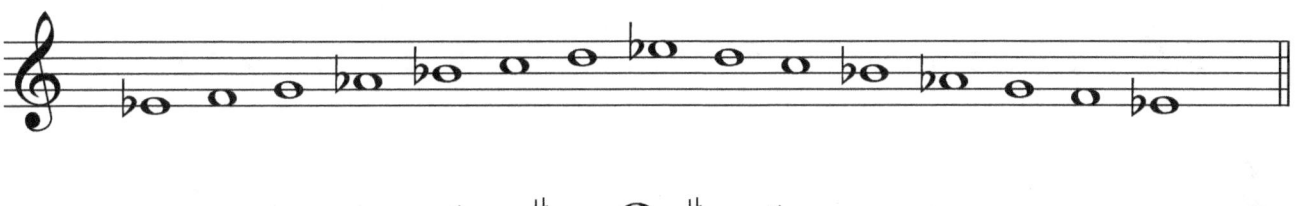

Page 25, No. 4

Page 30, No. 1 **Review 1**

D = E♭♭, C𝑥

F = E♯, G♭♭

F♯ = G♭, E𝑥

C = B♯, D♭♭

B♭ = A♯, C♭♭

Page 30, No. 2

Page 31, No. 3

Page 31, No. 4
j)
i)
h)
e)
d)
f)
g)
c)
b)
a)

Page 32, No. 5

a. The Baroque period occurred approximately:	☐	1600-1700	☐	1650-1725
	☐	2010-2015	☑	1600-1750
b. The following are famous Baroque composers:	☑	J.S. Bach	☑	Vivaldi
	☐	Mozart	☑	Handel
c. These elements can be used to describe Baroque music:	☑	counterpoint	☑	doctrine of affections
	☐	romantic	☑	highly ornamented
d. These are Bach's 3 main periods.	☑	Leipzig	☑	Weimar
	☐	Berlin	☑	Cöthen
e. Bach composed for the following mediums.	☑	keyboard	☑	orchestra
	☑	choir	☑	chamber music
f. How many 2 part inventions did J.S. Bach write?	☐	21	☑	15
	☐	12	☐	6
g. The 3-part inventions are also known as:	☐	sonatas	☑	sinfonias
	☐	dances	☐	fugues
h. The 2-part inventions are written for this many voices:	☑	2	☐	3
	☐	6	☐	32
i. 3 elements found in the 2-part inventions are:	☑	motives	☑	sequence
	☑	imitation	☐	monophony
j. This is the numbering system used to identify Bach's works:	☐	NRA	☑	BWV
	☐	BVW	☐	BMW

© San Marco Publications 2022   163   Level 6

Page 33, No. 1

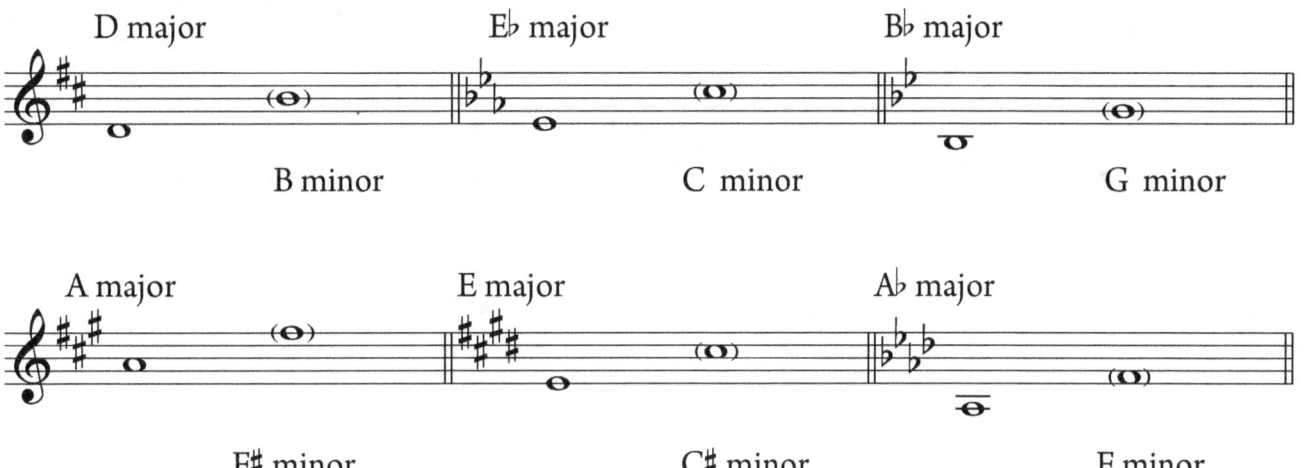

Page 36, No. 1

E natural minor
B♭ harmonic minor
G♯ harmonic minor
C melodic minor
D♯ harmonic minor
A melodic minor
G natural minor

Page 37, No. 2

Page 38, No. 1

a. The enharmonic tonic major of C# major is Db major.
b. The enharmonic tonic minor of Bb major is A# minor.
c. The enharmonic tonic major of Cb major is B major.
d. The parallel minor of D major is D minor.
e. The tonic major of G minor is G major.
f. The enharmonic tonic minor of Eb major is D# minor.

Page 39, No. 2

Page 41, No.1

| per 5 | min 3 | per 4 | maj 2 | per 8 | min 7 | maj 7 | per 5 |
| per 5 | min 6 | per 5 | min 6 | min 7 | maj 3 | min 7 | per 4 |

Page 41, No. 2

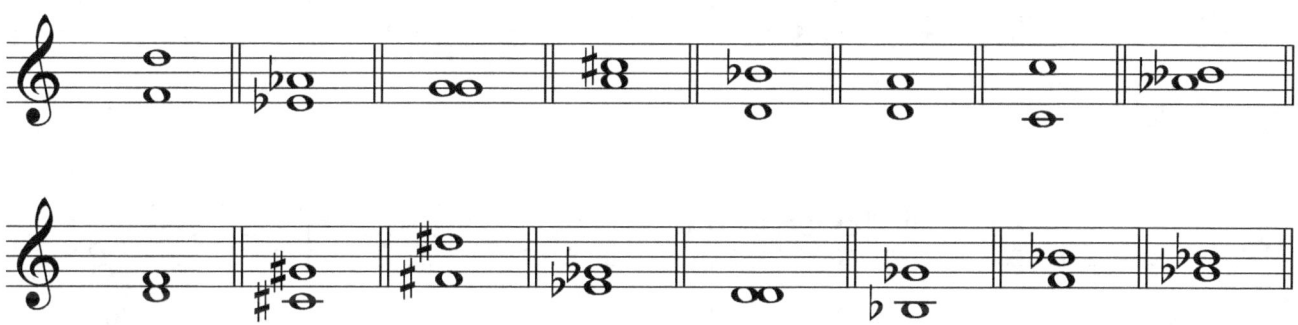

Page 42, No. 1

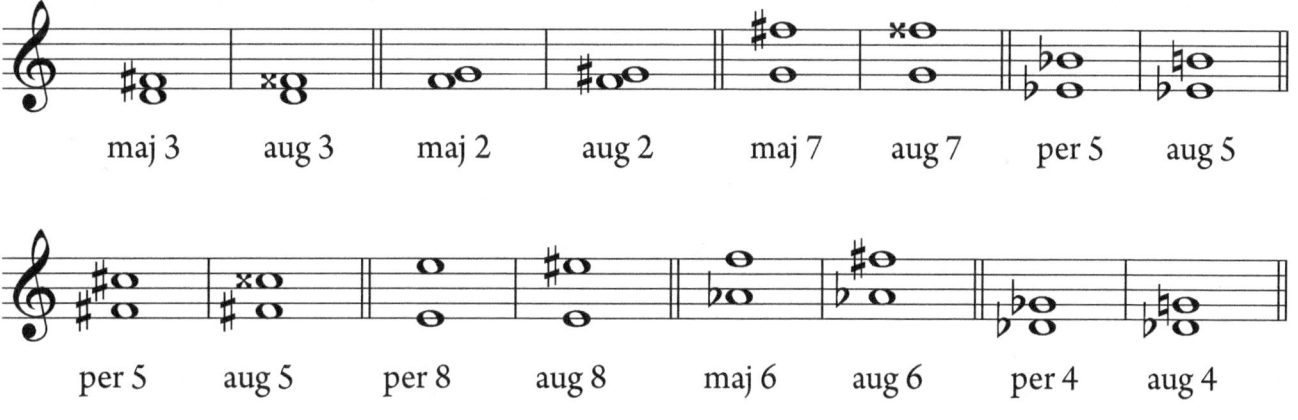

| maj 3 | aug 3 | maj 2 | aug 2 | maj 7 | aug 7 | per 5 | aug 5 |
| per 5 | aug 5 | per 8 | aug 8 | maj 6 | aug 6 | per 4 | aug 4 |

Page 43, No. 2

per 4 aug 4 maj 3 aug 3 maj 2 aug 2 per 8 aug 8

maj 7 aug 7 maj 6 aug 6 per 5 aug 5 maj 3 aug 3

Page 43, No. 3

Page 46, No. 1

per 5 dim 5 maj 6 dim 6 maj 3 dim 3 per 4 dim 4

maj 7 dim 7 per 8 dim 8 per 4 dim 4 per 5 dim 5

Page 46, No. 2

maj 6 dim 7 maj 7 dim 7 maj 3 dim 3 per 5 dim 5

per 4 dim 4 maj 6 dim 6 per 5 dim 5 maj 7 dim 7

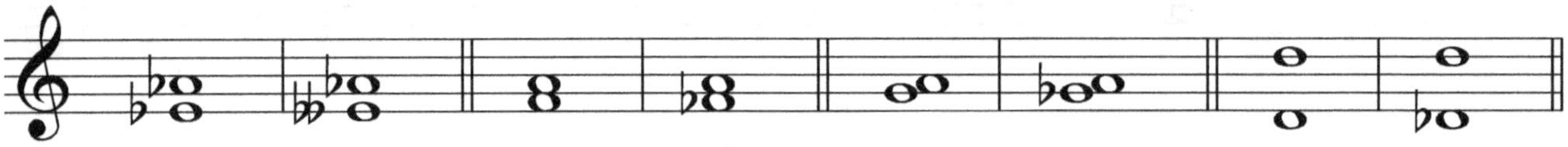

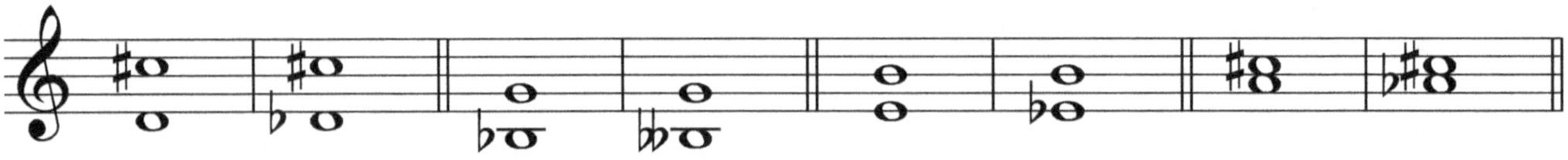

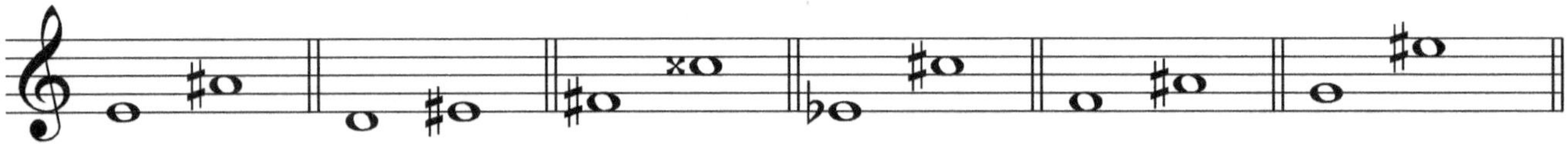

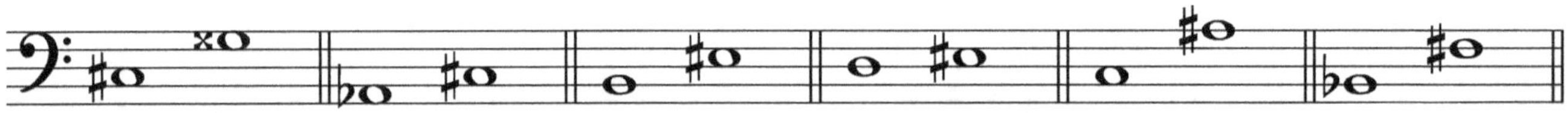

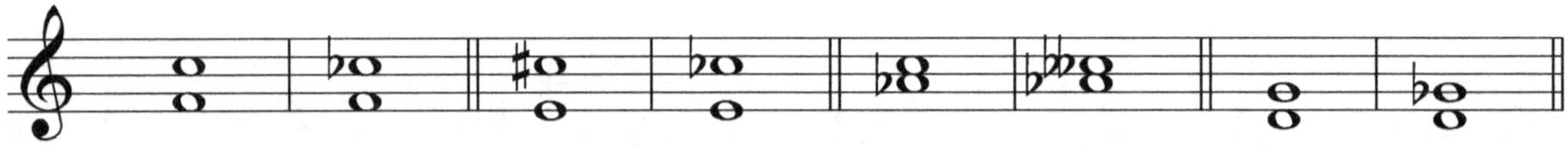

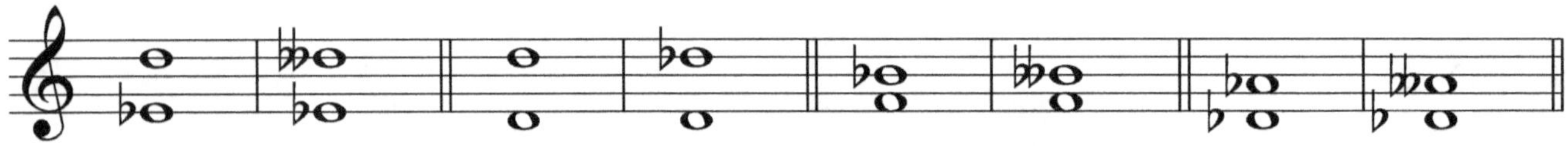

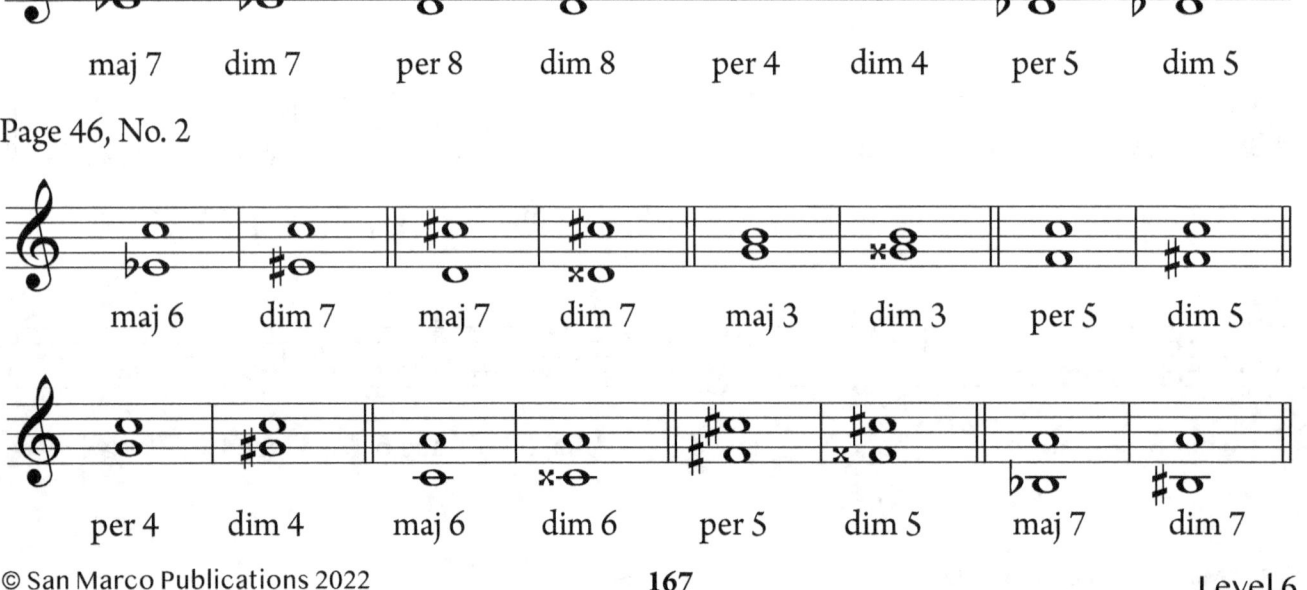

Page 46, No. 3

Page 47, No. 4

aug 5   min 6   per 5   maj 2   aug 3   aug 4
maj 3   per 8   dim 6   dim 5   dim 2   per 1

Page 47, No. 5

maj 2   dim 4   per 5   per 8   maj 3   min 2   min 3   maj 2

Page 47, No. 6

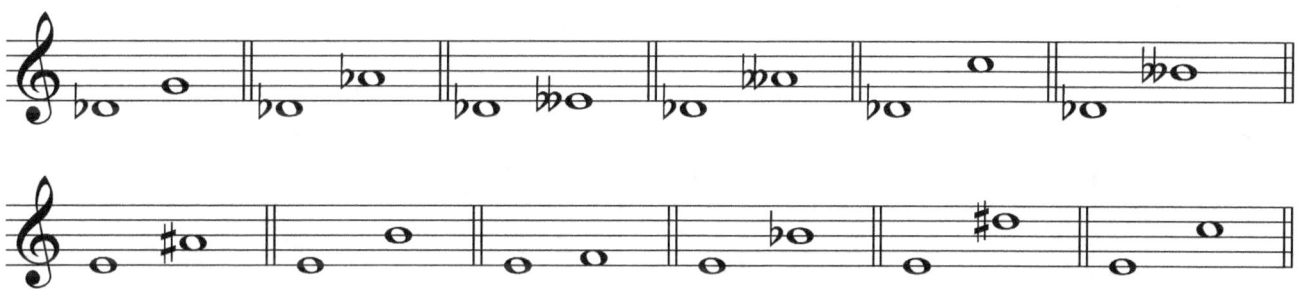

Page 49, No. 1

per 5   dim 3   maj 6   min 7   aug 2   dim 5

Page 49, No. 2

per 4   aug 5   aug 2   dim 7   dim 7   min 7

Page 49, No. 3

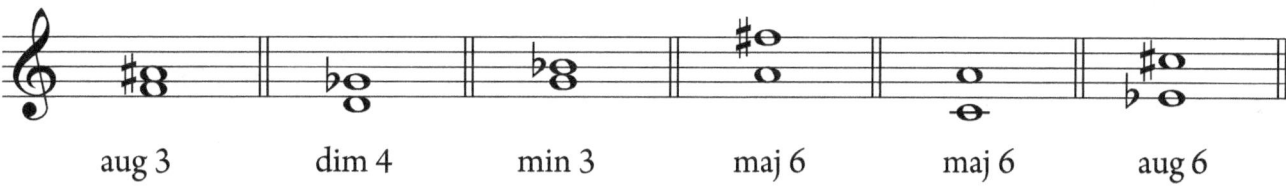

Page 49, No. 4

min 6   min 2   per 4   maj 3
per 4   per 4   min 3   min 3   per 4
per 4   per 4   min 2   maj 2   min 3
maj 2   dim 5   min 2   min 3   per 4

Page 50, No. 1

major   minor   minor   major   minor   major
major   minor   minor   minor   major   major

Page 53, No. 1

B♭   C   E   G   D   D
F   G♭   D   E   C   C♯

Page 53, No. 2

E	F	G	D	A	A
minor	minor	major	minor	major	minor
2nd inv	1st inv	root pos	1st inv	root pos	1st inv

B♭	A♭	B	G	E	F♯
major	major	minor	minor	minor	minor
1st inv	root pos	2nd inv	root pos	2nd inv	root pos

Page 54, No. 1

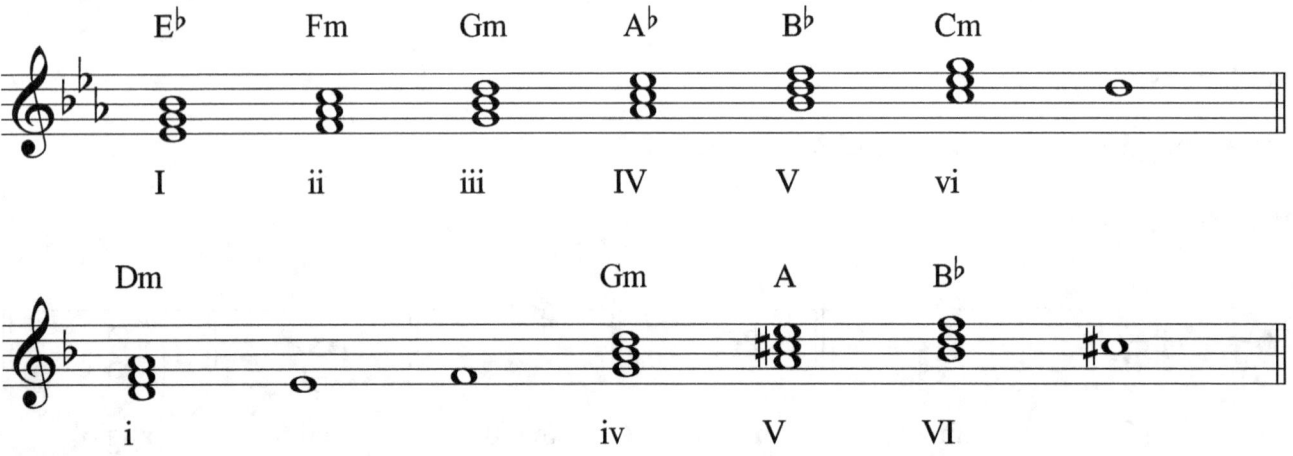

Page 55, No. 2

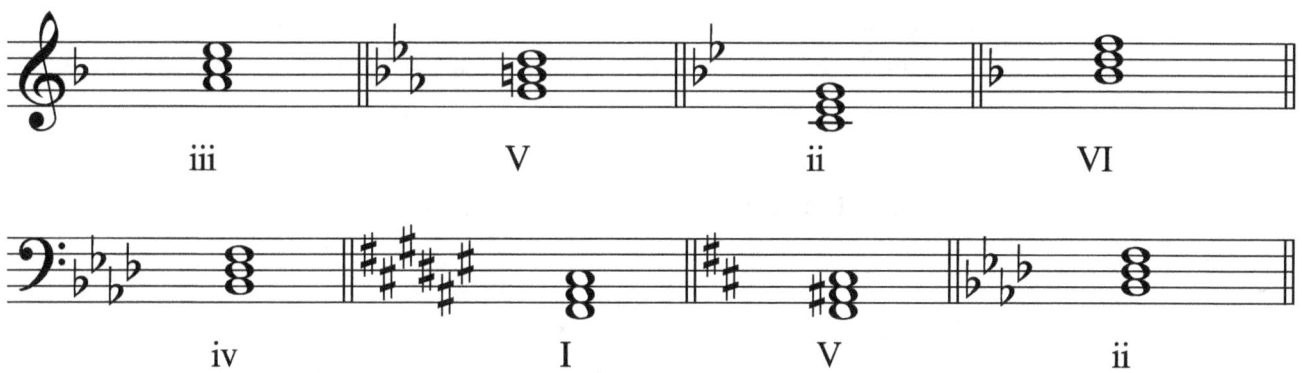

Page 55, No. 3

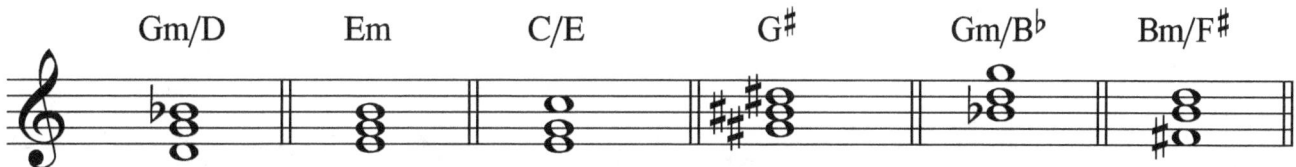

Page 56, No. 1

C	B♭	E	G	A	E♭
minor	major	major	major	minor	major
root pos	1st inv	root pos	root pos	1st inv	2nd inv

C♯	F	B	G♭	E	F♯
major	minor	major	major	minor	minor
root pos	root pos	2nd inv	2nd inv	2nd inv	2nd inv

Page 58, No. 1

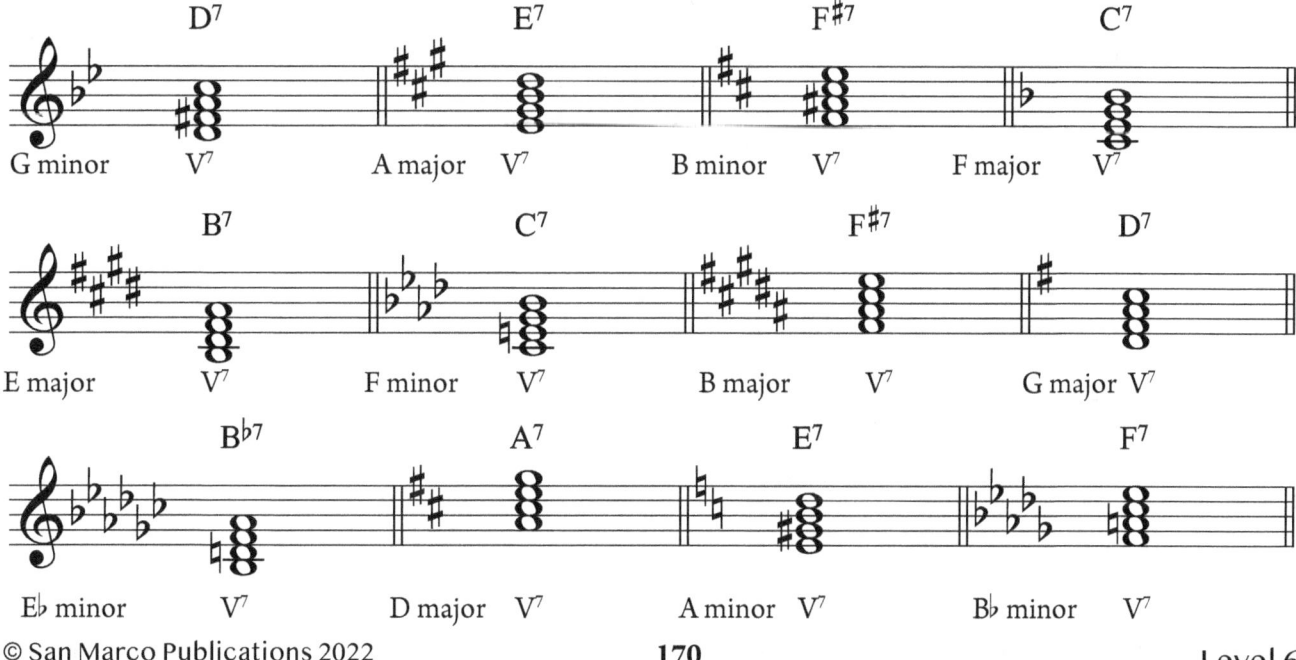

Page 58, No. 2

| F major | D major | E♭ major | G major | B major | A major |
| F minor | D minor | E♭ minor | G minor | B minor | A minor |

Page 59, No. 1

D major   G major   C major   F major   B♭ major   E♭ major

Page 59, No. 2

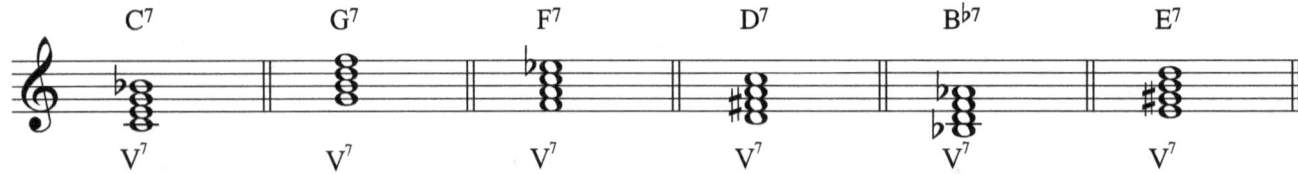

Page 59, No. 3

Page 59, No. 4

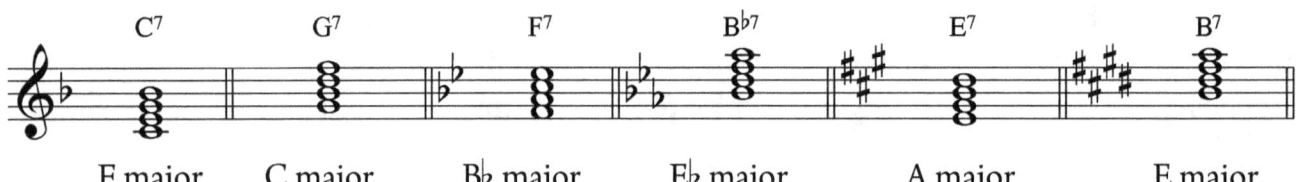

Page 62-63, No. 1

A major:	A major root pos $\hat{1}$	D major root pos $\hat{4}$	A major root pos $\hat{1}$	
C major:	C major root pos $\hat{1}$	G major 1st inv $\hat{5}$	A minor root pos $\hat{6}$	D minor 1st inv $\hat{2}$
A minor:	A minor root pos $\hat{1}$	E major root pos $\hat{5}$		
G major:	G major root pos $\hat{1}$	D major 1st inv $\hat{5}$		
E minor:	E minor root pos $\hat{1}$	B major root pos $\hat{5}$		

Page 67, No. 1   **Review 2**

Page 68, No. 2

dim 5   dim 5   maj 2

maj 6   min 2   min 7

per 4   per 4   min 3   min 3   maj 3

dim 4   min 2   per 4   min 3

Page 68, No. 3

C	E	B♭	F	A	G
minor	major	dom 7	minor	dom 7	minor
root pos	1st inv	root pos	root pos	root pos	root pos

Page 69, No. 4

k m g i l h c f d j a e b

Page 69, No. 5

a. Who composed Brandenburg Concerto No. 5? **Johann Sebastian Bach**

b. What genre is this work? **concerto grosso**

c. What 3 instruments are featured in this work? **violin, flute, harpsichord**

d. What is this group of instruments called? **concertino**

e. The full string orchestra in a concerto grosso is called a

☑ripieno ☐concertino ☐oratorio ☐sequence

f. The form of the first movement of Brandenburg Concerto No. 5 is

☐rondo ☑ritornello ☐sonata ☐binary

Page 72 - 73, No. 1

	E A			F B♭
	V I			V I
A major:	perfect authentic		B♭ major:	imperfect authentic
	G C			G Cm
	V I			V i
C major:	perfect authentic		C minor:	imperfect authentic
	B E			A Dm
	V I			V i
E major:	perfect authentic		D minor:	perfect authentic
	F B♭m			B Em
	V i			V i
B♭ minor:	imperfect authentic		E minor:	perfect authentic

Page 75, No. 1

Page 81, No. 1

F major

Page 85, No. 1

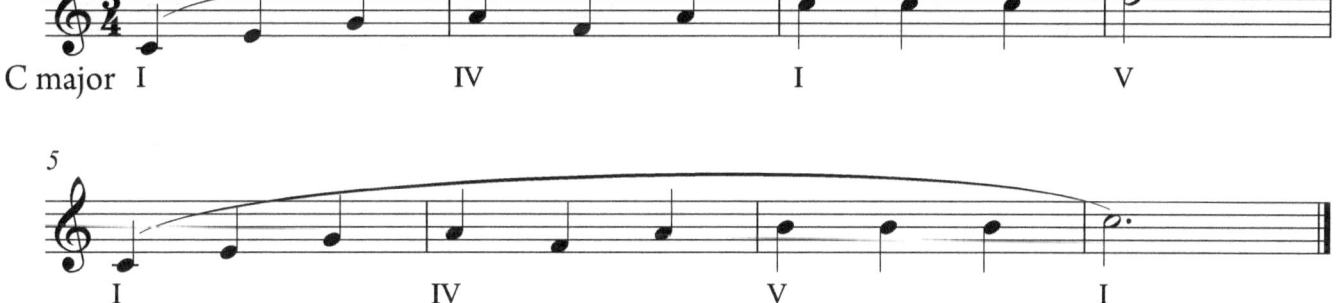

C major

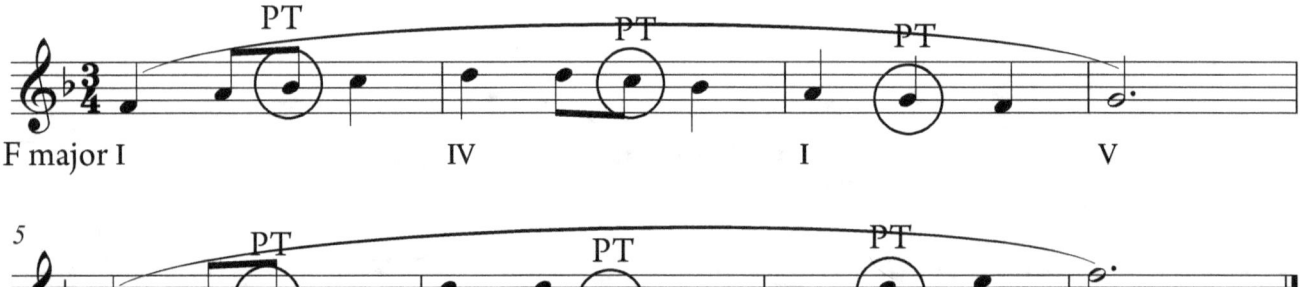

Page 88, No. 1

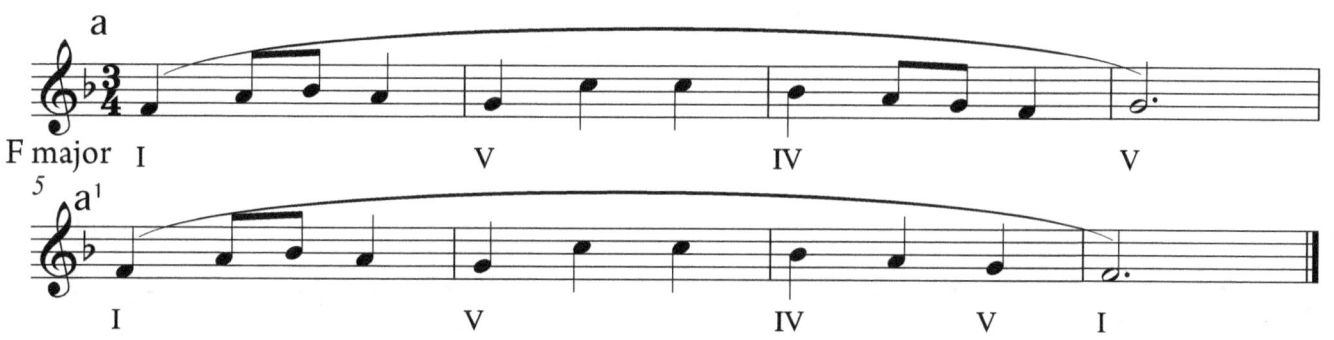

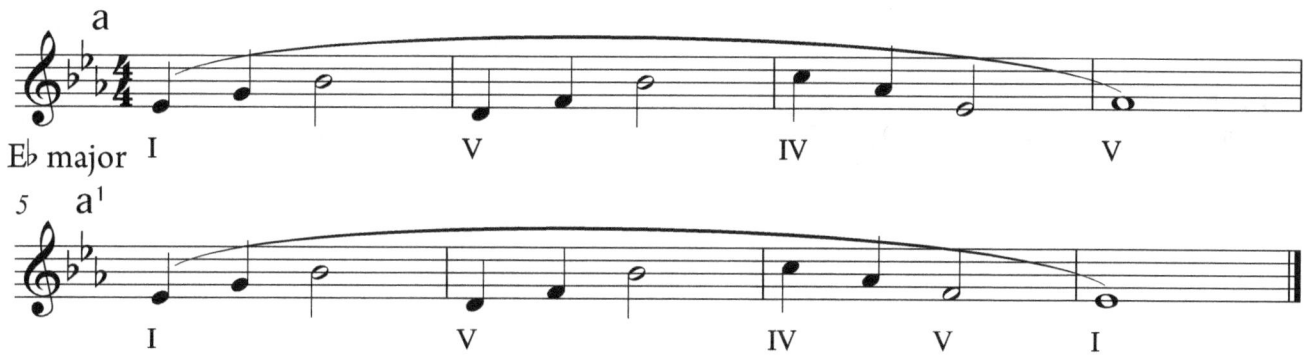

Page 93, No. 1 **Review 3**

F major		F	C	
		I	V	
		half		
		C	F	
		V	I	
		perfect authentic		

D major		G	A	
		IV	V	
		half		
		A	D	
		V	I	
		perfect authentic		

Page 94, No. 2

G major

Bb major

maj 2

Page 94, No. 3

Eb major

Page 95, No. 4

9
7
6
8
5
3
2
4
1

Page 95, No. 5

a. T
b. F
c. T
d. F
e. T
f. F
g. T
h. T
i. F
j. T

Page 100

1. Name the key of this piece. **C major**

2. Write the time signature directly on the score.

3. The form of this piece is: ☐ binary ☑ ternary

4. Label the score by using A, A¹, and B to define the form.

5. Define *Allegretto*. **fairly fast, a little slower than allegro**

6. Check all statements below that apply to the chord at A:

    ☑ tonic triad ☐ subdominant triad ☑ C major triad ☑ root position ☐ broken chord

7. Check all statements below that apply to the chord at B:

    ☐ tonic triad ☑ dominant triad ☑ G major triad ☐ 1st inversion ☑ solid or blocked chord

8. Name the cadence at C:

    ☑ perfect authentic cadence   ☐ half cadence   ☐ imperfect authentic cadence

9. Symbolize the chords of this cadence on the score using functional chord symbols.

Page 101

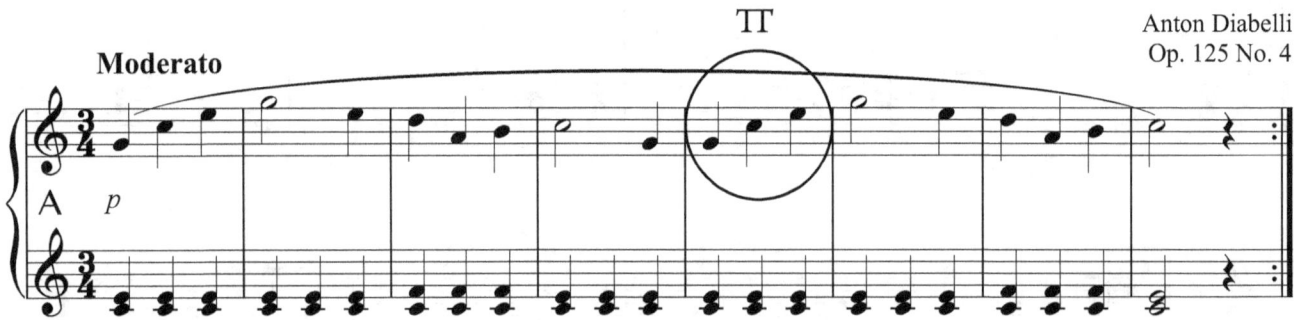

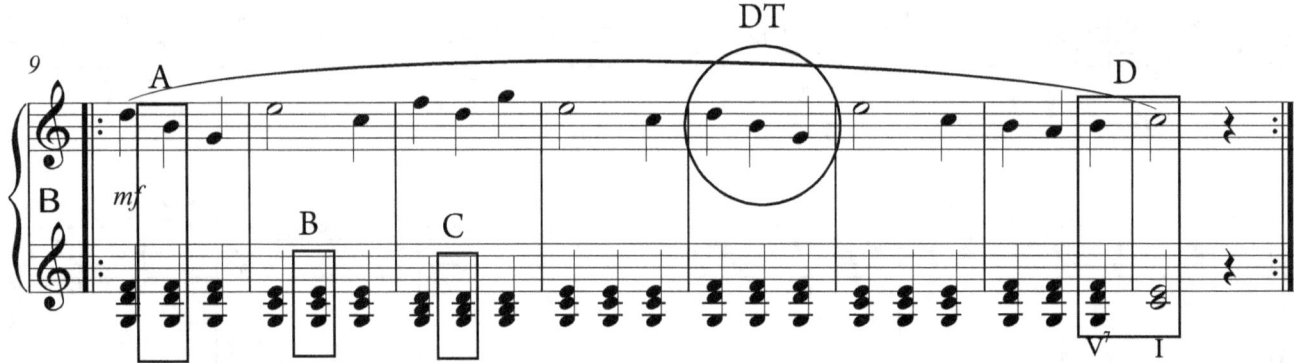

1. Name the key of this piece. **C major**

2. Write the time signature directly on the score.

3. Check the words below that apply to this time signature.

   ☑triple   ☐compound   ☐duple   ☑simple   ☐quadruple

4. Mark the phrases using a slur.

5. The form of this piece is: ☑binary   ☐ternary

6. Label the score by using A, A¹, and B to define the form.

7. Define *Moderato*. **at a moderate speed or tempo**

8. Name the chord at letter A: **G⁷, the dominant 7th**

9. For the chord at letter B name the: root **C**   quality **major**   position **2nd inv.**

10. For the chord at letter C name the: root **G**   quality **major**   position **root pos.**

11. The cadence at D is: ☐half   ☑perfect authentic   ☐imperfect authentic

12. Write the functional chord symbols for this cadence directly on the score.

13. Find and circle a broken dominant triad on the score. Label it DT.

14. Find and circle a broken tonic triad on the score. Label it TT.

Page 102

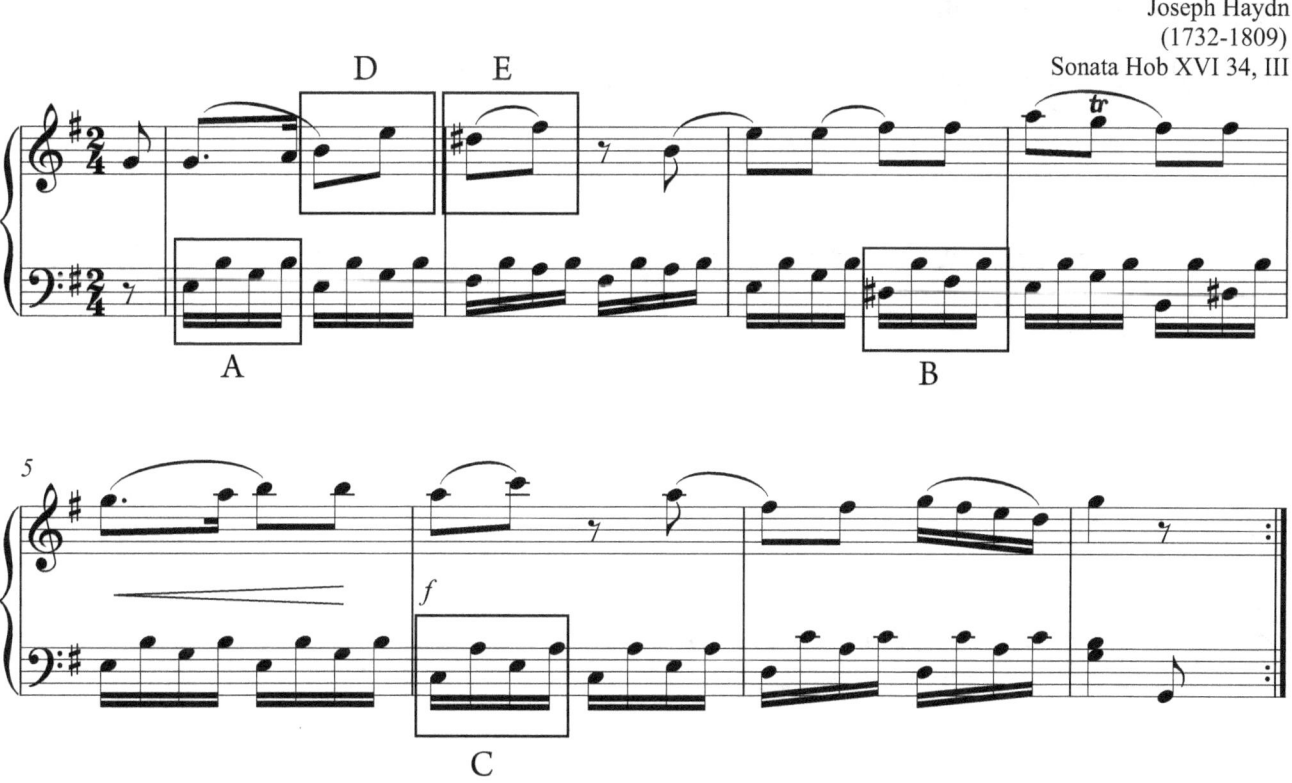

Joseph Haydn
(1732-1809)
Sonata Hob XVI 34, III

1. Name the key of this piece. **E minor**
2. Write the time signature directly on the score.
3. This excerpt is written for a right hand melody with left hand accompaniment. This is and example of:

    ❏ polyphonic music ☑ homophonic music ❏ contrapuntal music ❏ absolute music

4. What musical era was this piece composed? **Classical**
5. Name the chord at A: root **E**   quality **minor**   position **root pos**
6. Name the chord at B: root **B**   quality **major**   position **1st inv**
7. Name the chord at C: root **A**   quality **minor**   position **1st inv.**
8. In this piece, chord A is the: ☑ tonic triad   ❏ subdominant triad   ❏ dominant triad
9. In this piece, chord B is the: ❏ tonic triad   ❏ subdominant triad   ☑ dominant triad
10. In this piece, chord C is the: ❏ tonic triad   ☑ subdominant triad   ❏ dominant triad
11. Define *Molto vivace*: **Very lively**
12. This excerpt is an example of a: ❏ parallel period   ☑ contrasting period
13. Name the interval at D: **min 3**
14. Name the interval at E: **per 4**

Page 109, No. 1 Final Exam

dim 5   dim 3   min 6   dim 8   maj 2

Page 109, No. 2

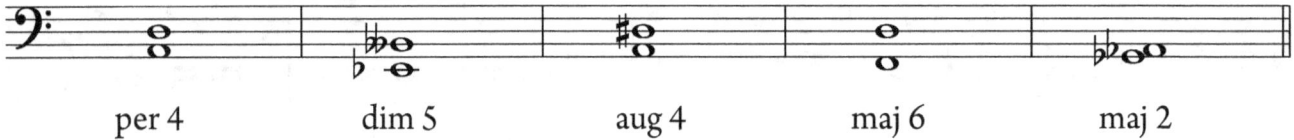

per 4   dim 5   aug 4   maj 6   maj 2

Page 109, No. 3

G major I   IV   V   I

Page 109, No. 4

F major

Page 110, No. 5

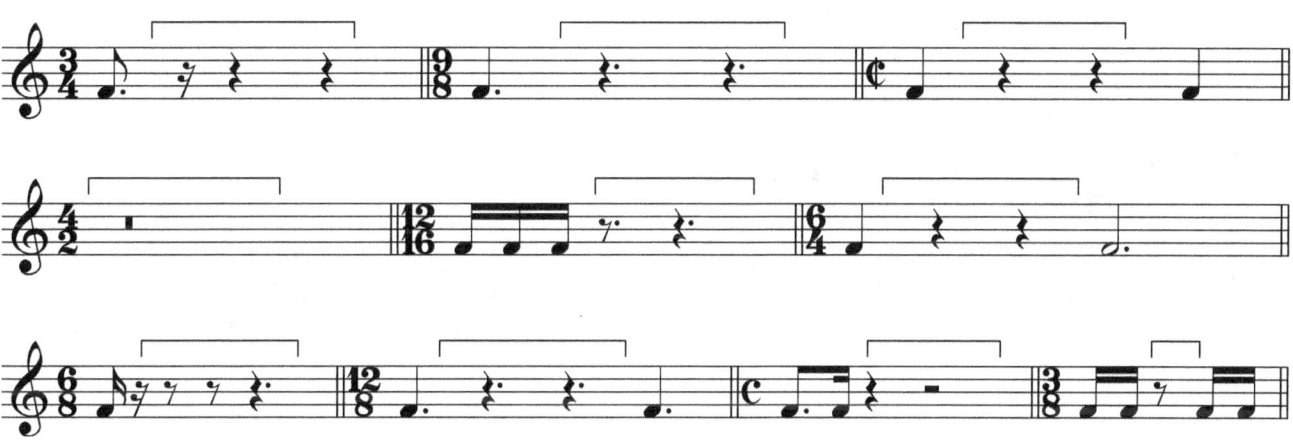

Page 110, No. 6

Eb major

A major

maj 3

Page 111, No. 7

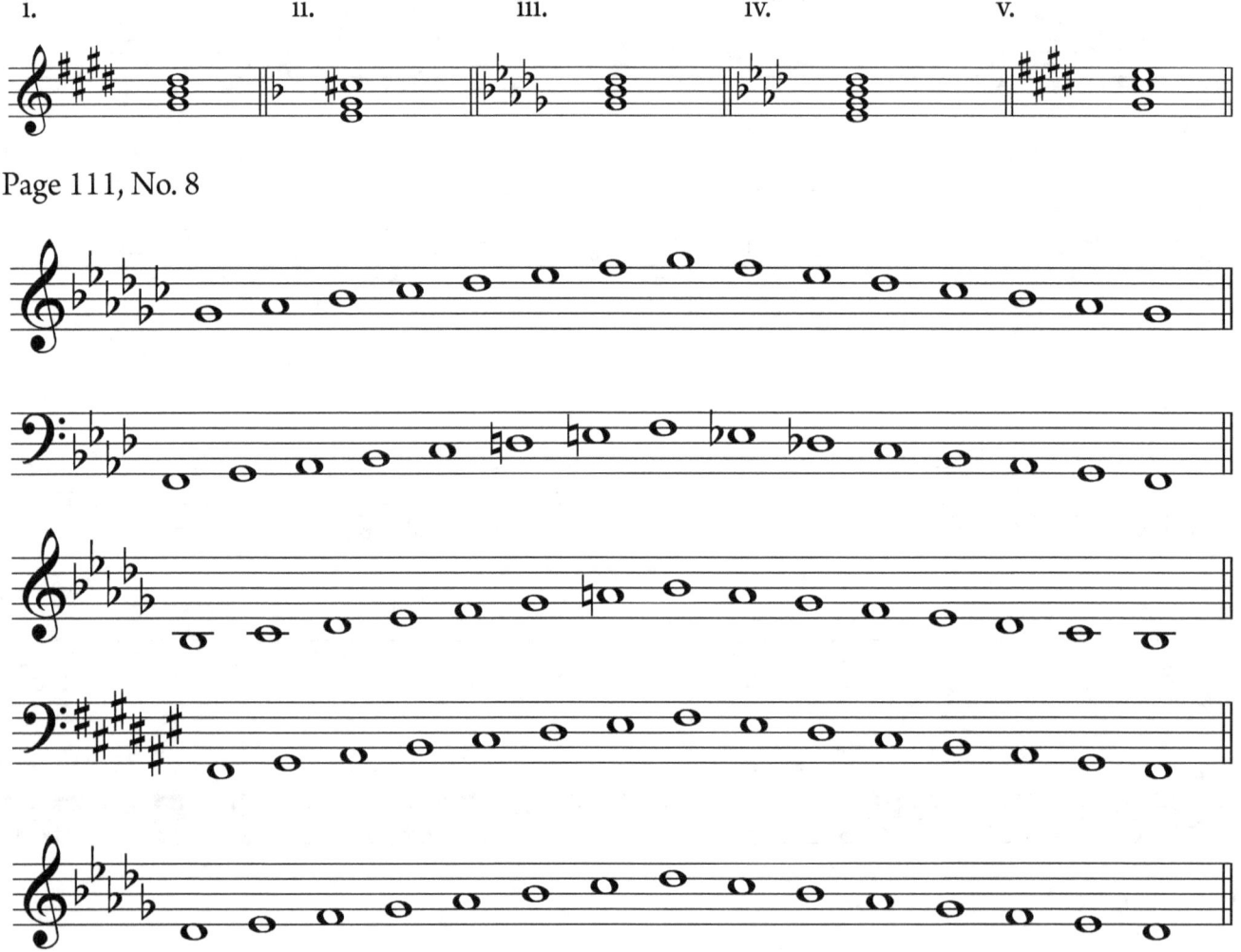

Page 111, No. 8

Page 112, No. 9

Bb major

Bb   F
I   V
half

F   Bb
V   I
perfect authentic

Page 112, No. 10

h g d i f c e b a

Page 112, No. 11

a. animato   lively, animated
b. con fuoco   with fire
c. piu mosso   more motion, movement
d. senza   without
e. subito   suddenly

Page 113

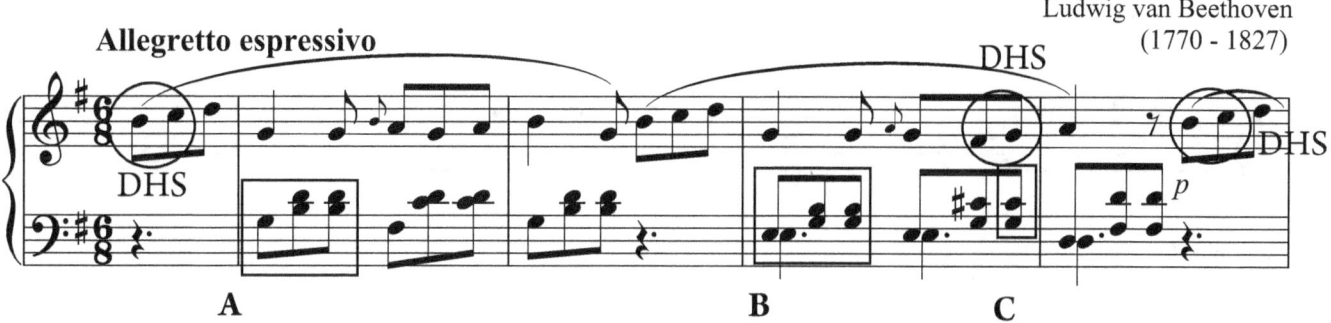

1. What is the key of this piece? **G major**
2. Write the time signature on the score.
3. In what era was this composed? **classical**
4. Define *Allegretto espressivo* **fairly fast and expressive**
5. For the triad at A, name the: Root: **G**   Quality: **major**   Inversion: **root pos**
6. For the triad at B, name the: Root: **E**   Quality: **minor**   Inversion: **root pos**
7. Find a diatonic half step in the score. Circle it and label it: DHS.
8. Find a broken C major triad on the score. Circle it and label it: C major.
9. Name the interval at C. **aug 4**

Level 7

Page 2, No. 1

Page 4, No. 1

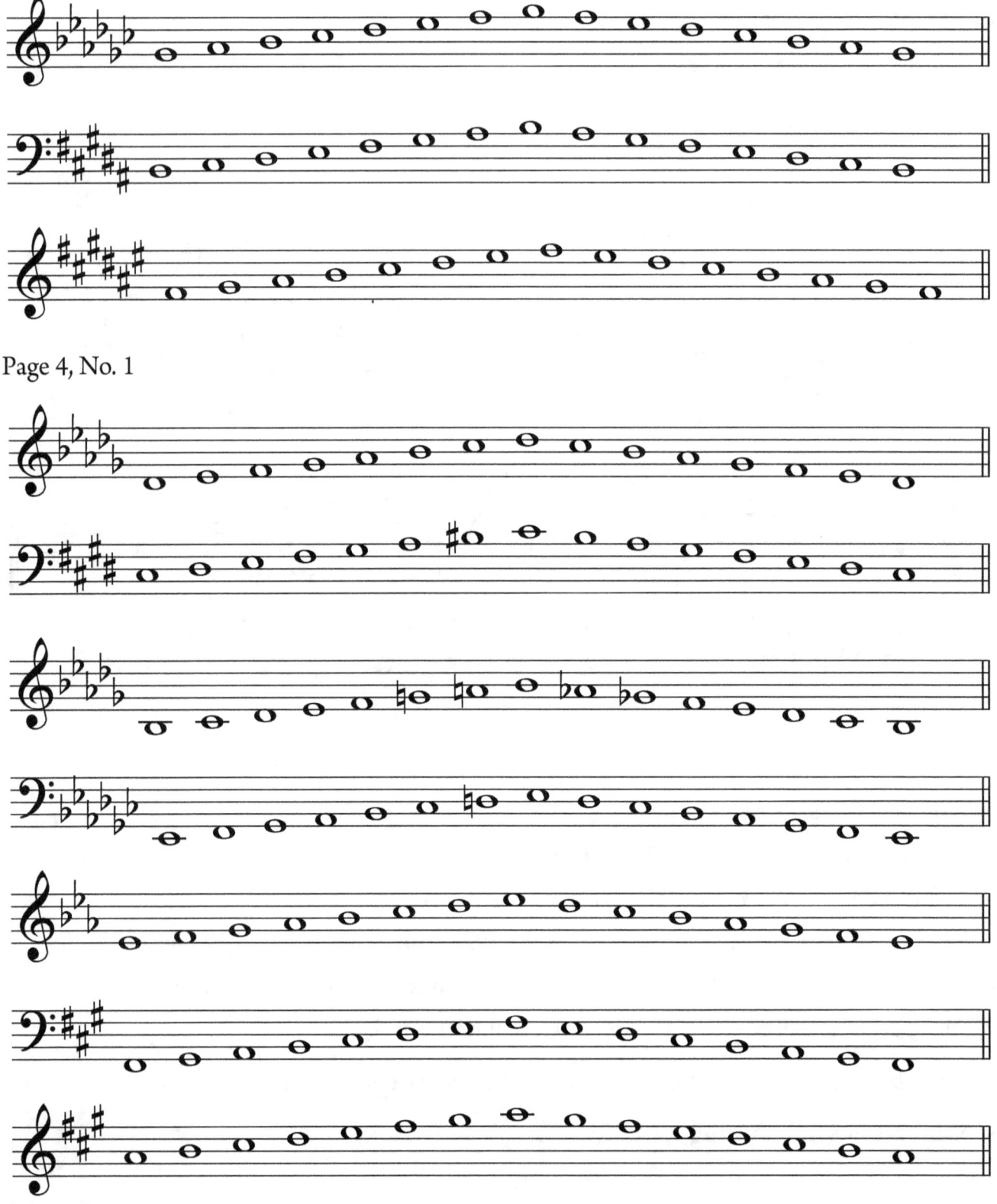

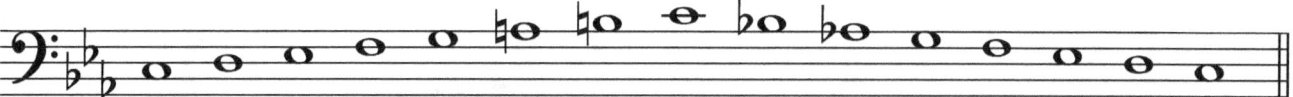

Page 7, No. 1

G major
B minor
C minor
E major
F minor
B♭ major
G♯ minor
A minor

Page 8, No. 2

C major
F major
D minor
G♯ minor

Page 10 - 11, No. 1

Joseph Haydn
Quartet, Op. 76

G minor

Joseph Haydn
Symphony No. 99

E♭ major

Johann Sebastian Bach
English Suite 6, Courante

D minor

Frederic Chopin
Nocturne Op. 72. No. 1

E minor

Frederic Chopin
Sonata for Cello and Piano

D minor

Page 13 - 14, No. 1

Page 16, No. 1

Page 17, No. 2

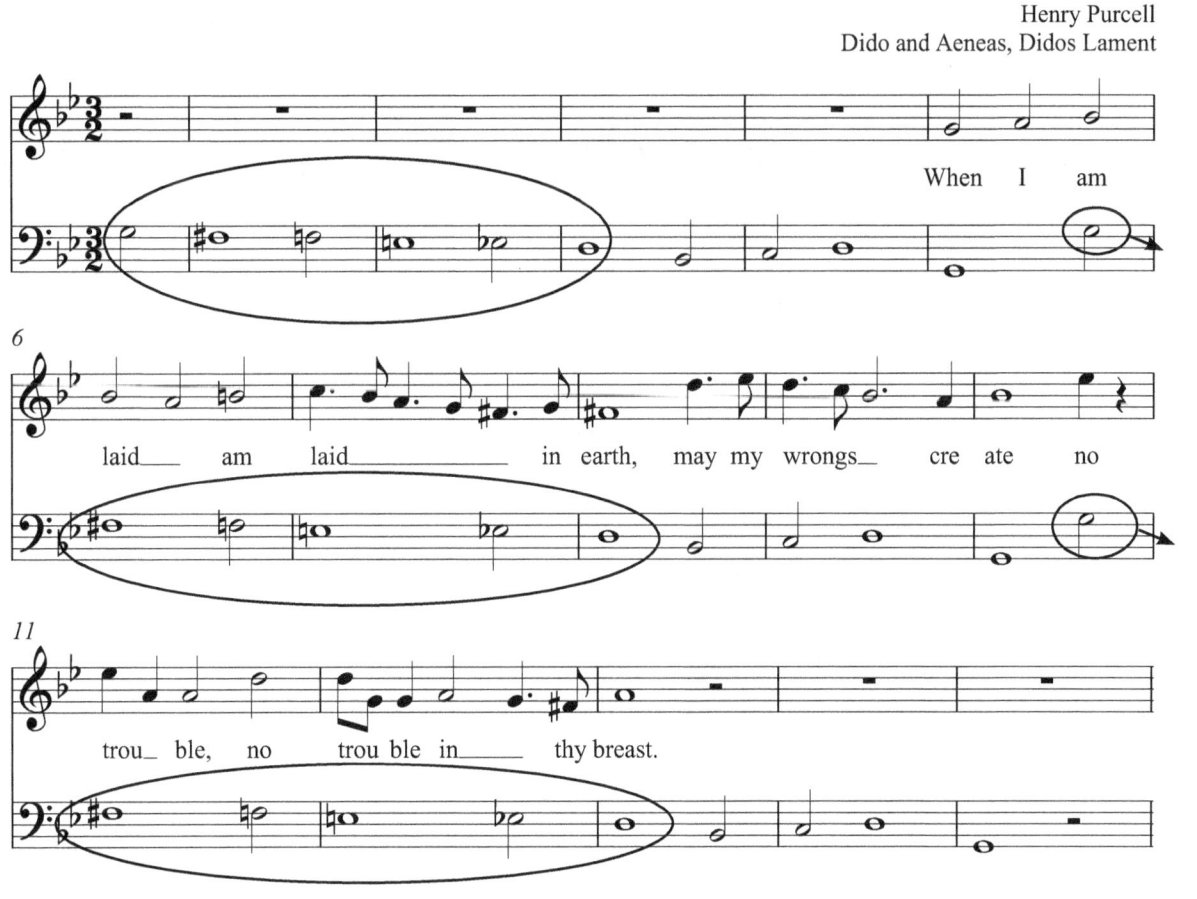

Henry Purcell
Dido and Aeneas, Didos Lament

© San Marco Publications 2022　　　190　　　Level 7

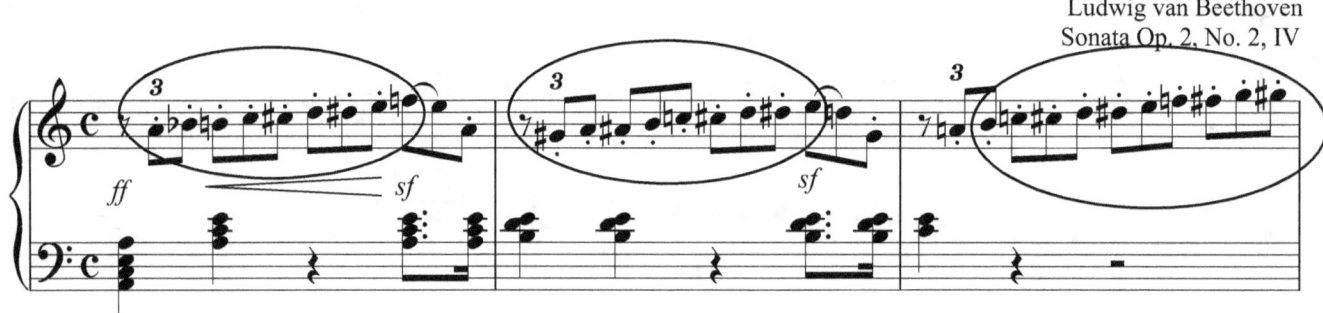

Ludwig van Beethoven
Sonata Op. 2, No. 2, IV

Page 19, No. 1

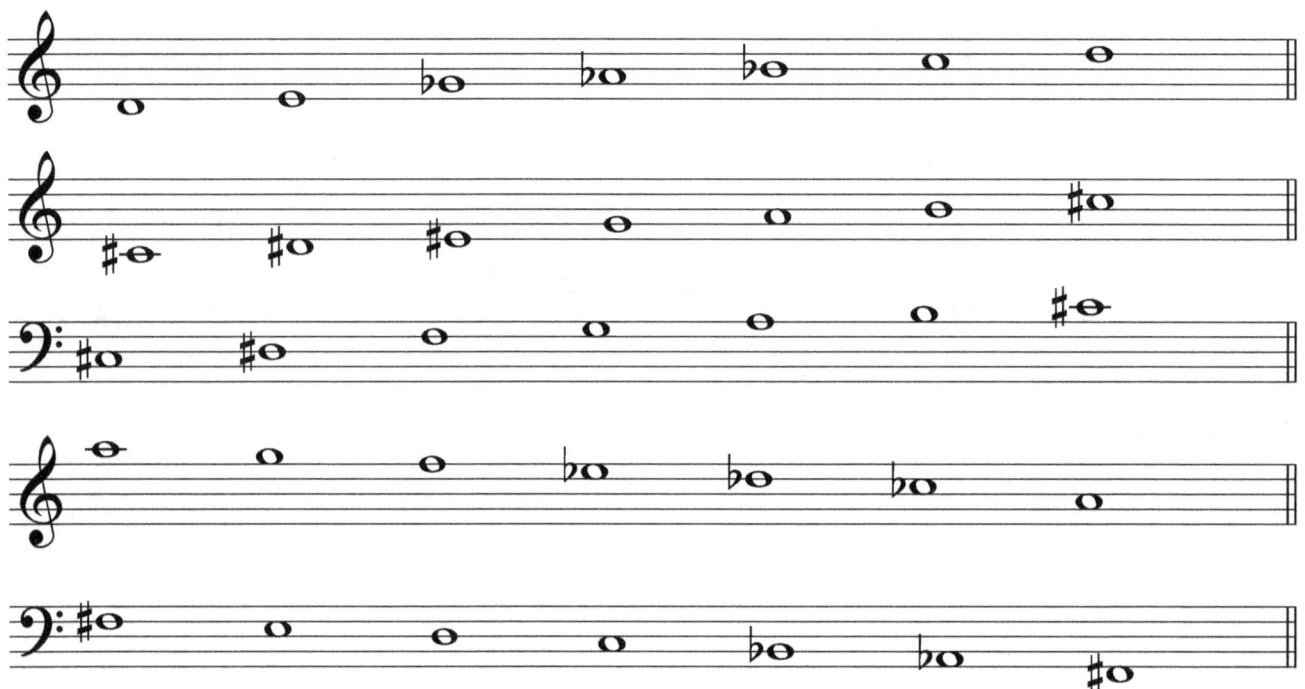

Page 19, No. 2 (other answers are possible)

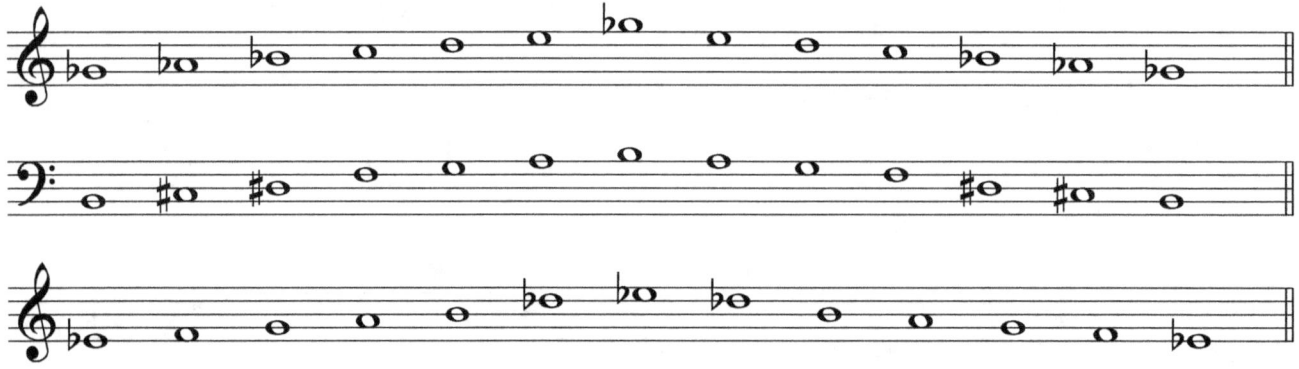

Page 21, No. 1 (other answers are possible)

Page 21, No. 2 (other answers are possible)

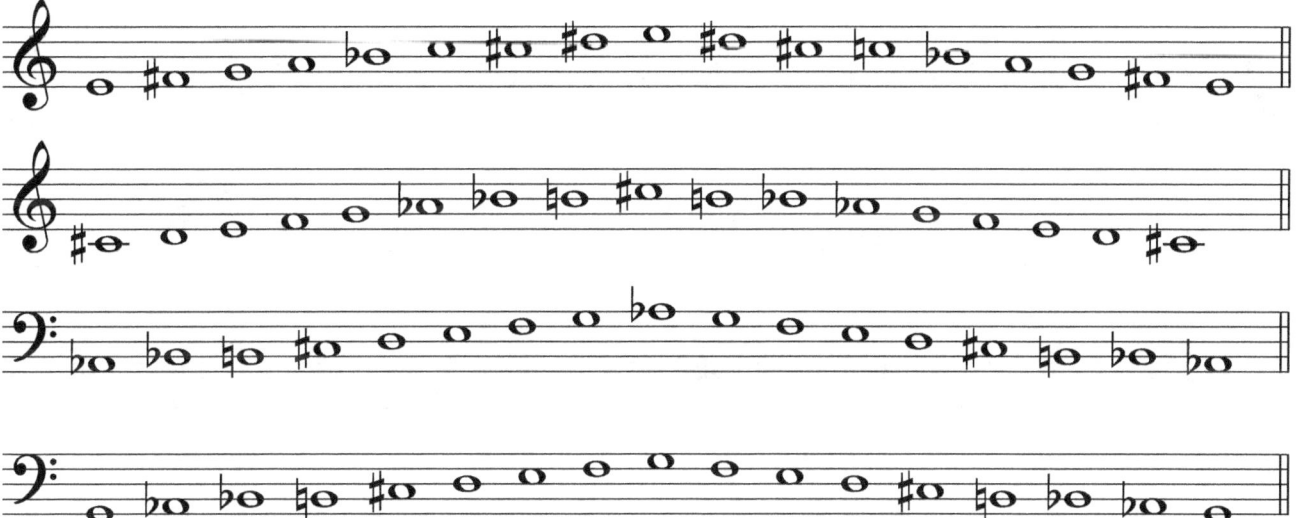

Page 22, No. 1

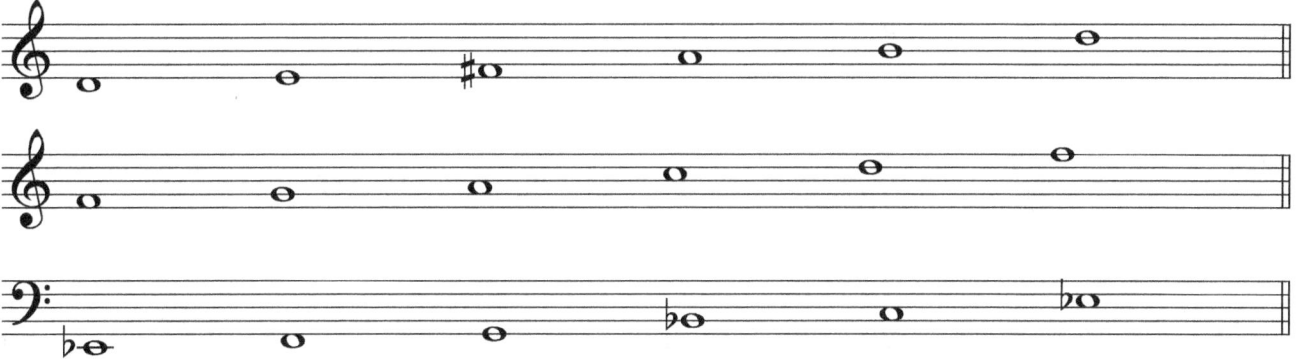

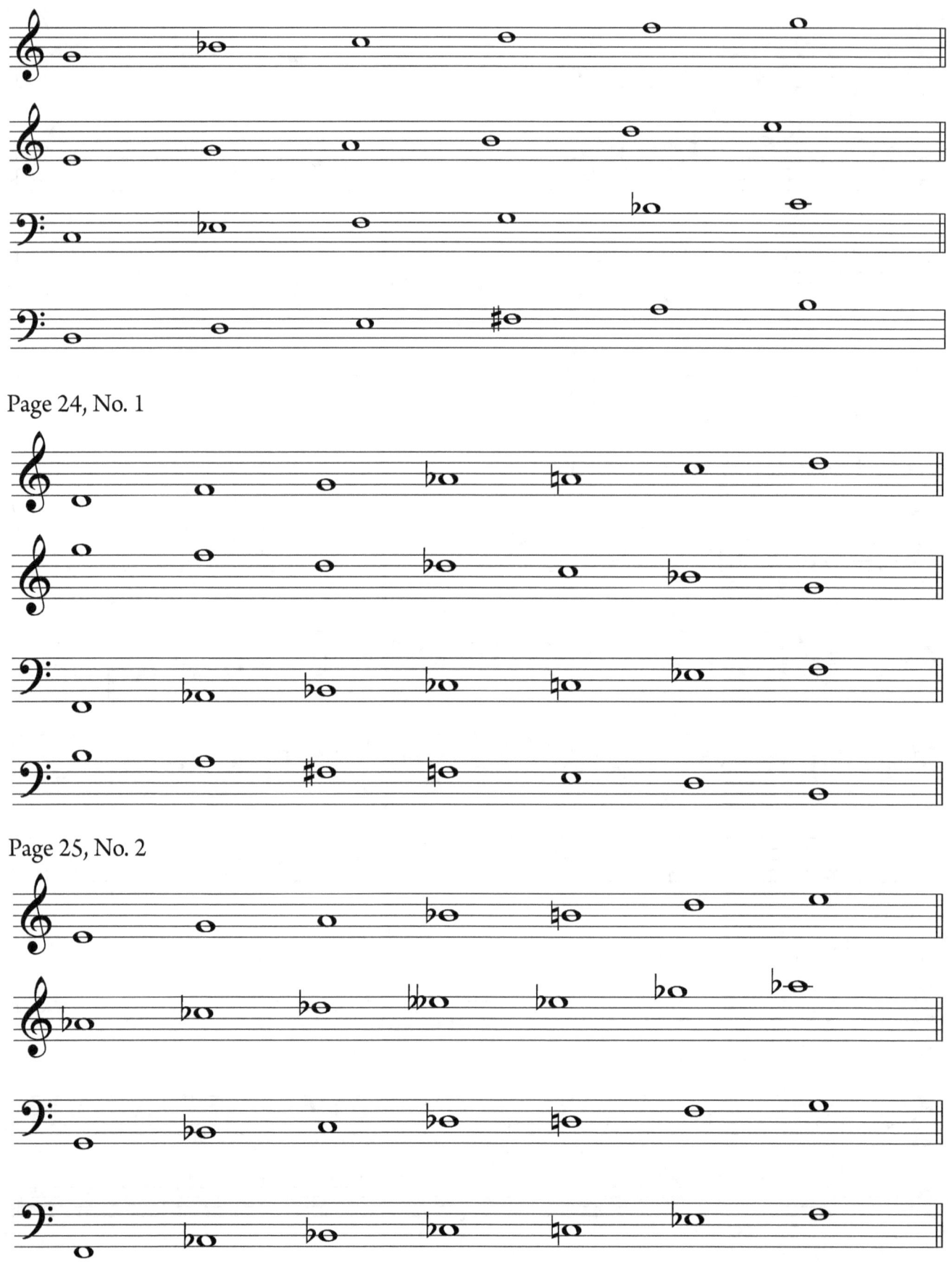

Page 25, No. 3

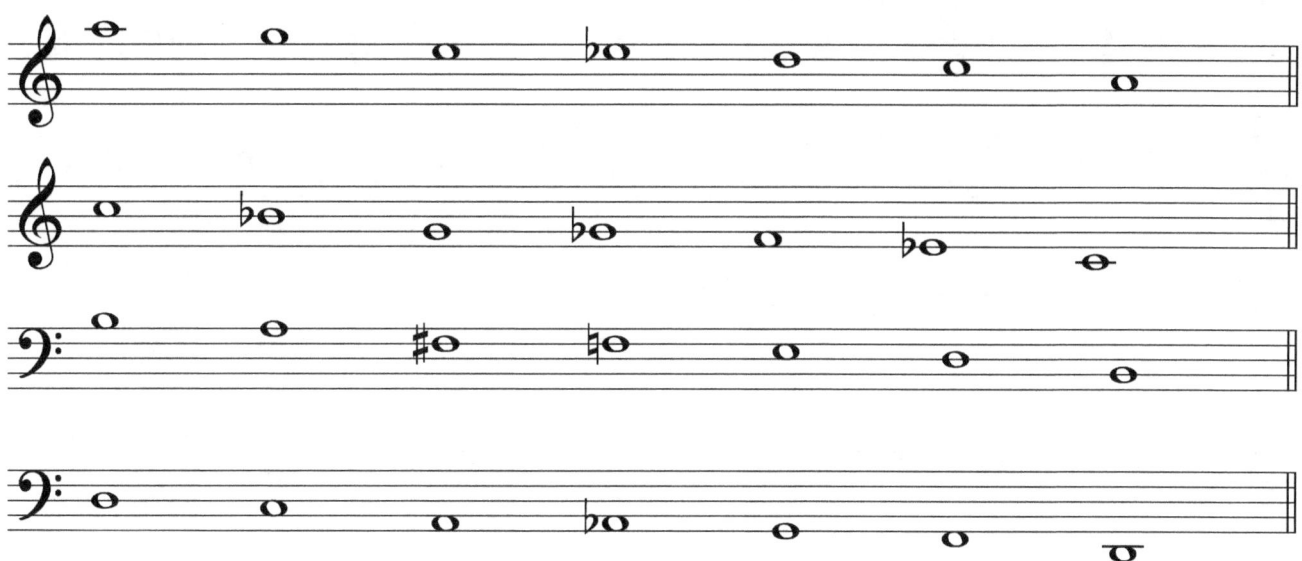

Page 26, No. 4

A♭ major
B melodic minor
E major pentatonic
C octatonic
D whole tone
F chromatic
D natural minor
A minor pentatonic

Page 32, No. 1 **Review 1**

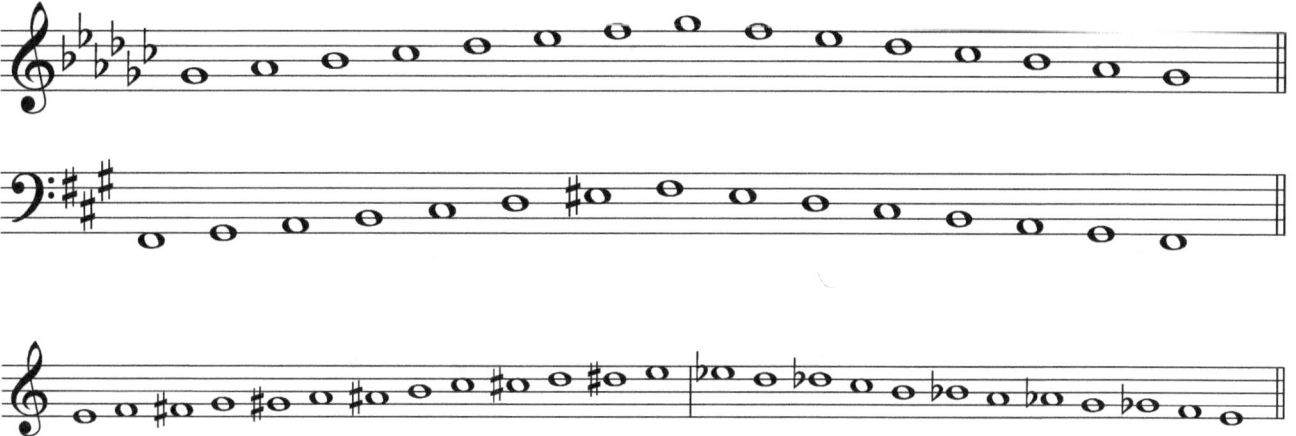

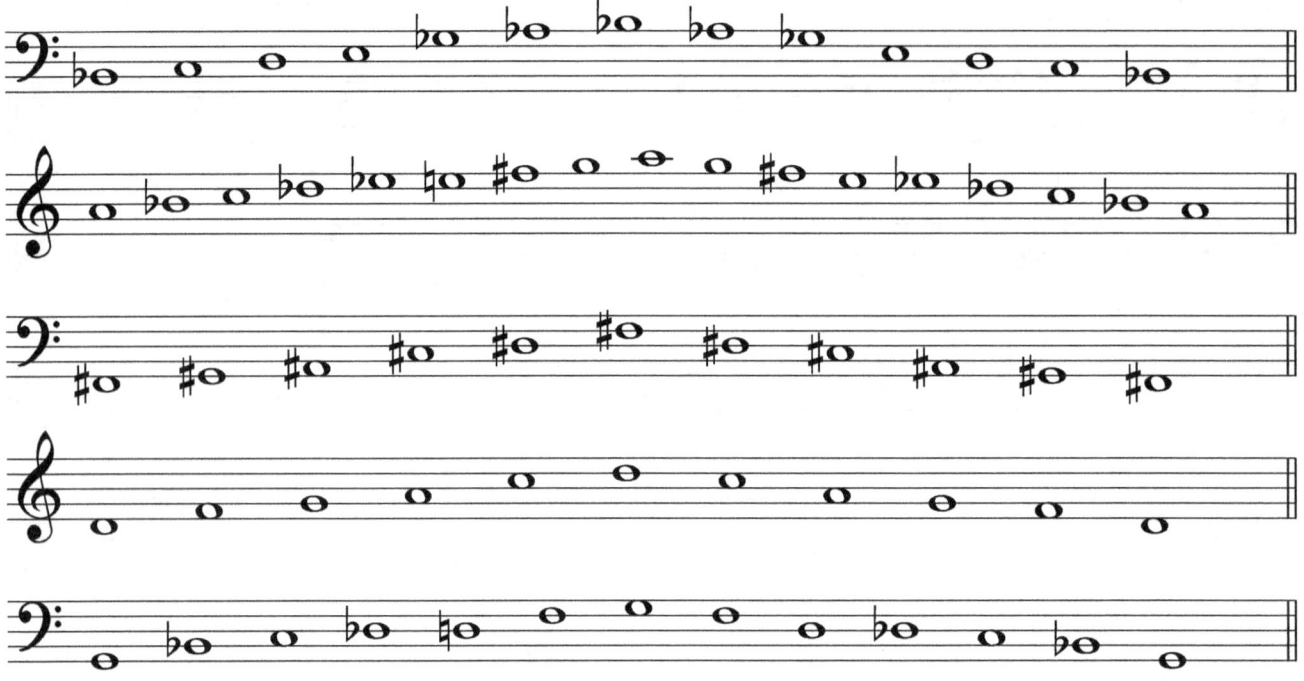

Page 33

2. When did the Romantic era occur? **1825 - 1900**

3. Music that has a literary or pictorial association is called **program music**

4. Name two Romantic period composers. **Franz Schubert, Frédéric Chopin, Franz Liszt, Robert Schumann, Johannes Brahms, Felix Mendelssohn, Edvard Grieg, Piotr Ilyich Tchaikovsky, Guisseppe Verdi, Georges Bizet**

5. Where was Felix Mendelssohn born? **Germany**

6. Whose music did Mendelssohn help revive? **J.S. Bach's**

7. What genre is Overture to a Midsummer Nights Dream? **Concert overture**

8. What author wrote the play that this work is based upon? **Shakespeare**

9. What is the form of Overture to a Midsummer Nights Dream? **Sonata form**

10. Name the three main sections in this form. **Exposition, Development, Recapitulation**

Page 33, No. 11

h, d, f, b, g, c, e, a

Page 35, No. 1

aug 5	min 6	per 5	maj 2	aug 3	aug 4
maj 3	per 8	dim 6	dim 5	dim 2	per 1

Page 36, No. 1

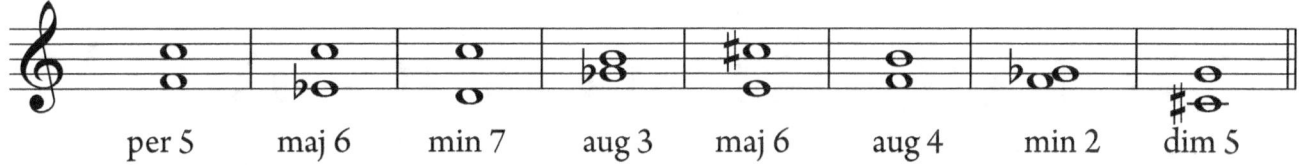

Page 38, No. 1

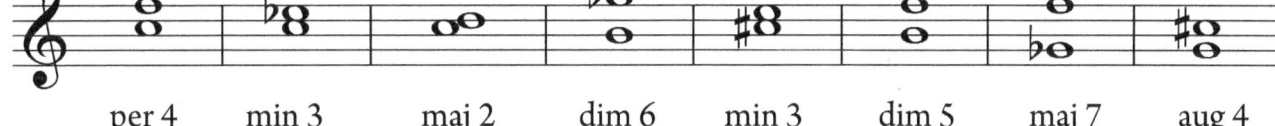

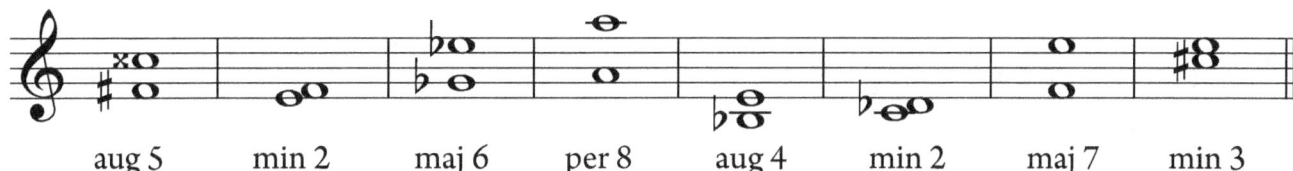

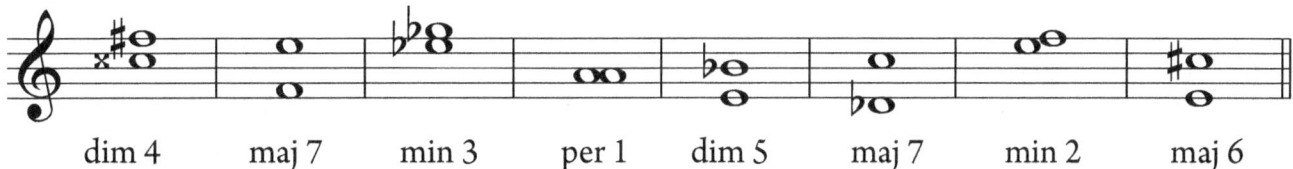

Page 38, No. 2

dim 6   min 3   per 5   dim 4   aug 1   min 7   aug 8   min 6
maj 2   maj 7   maj 3   aug 8   dim 8   min 3   aug 4   min 7

Page 39, No. 3

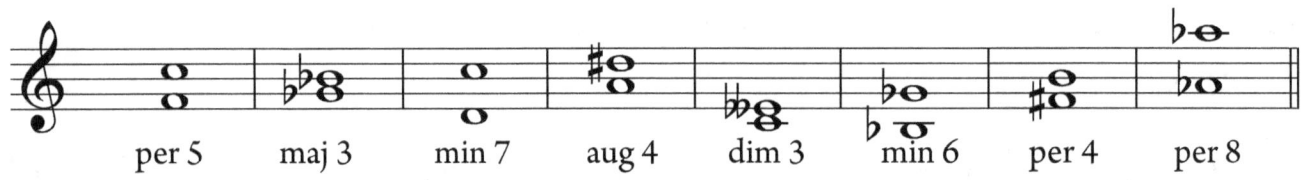

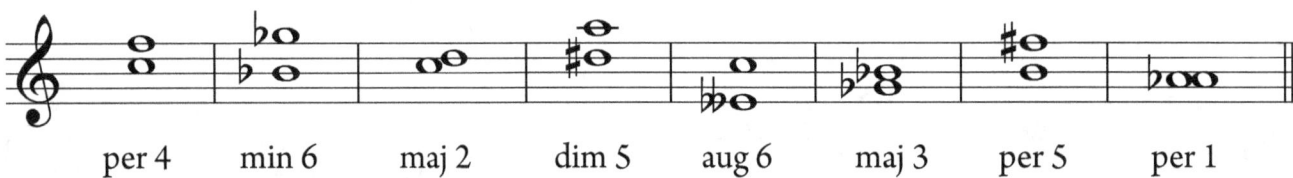

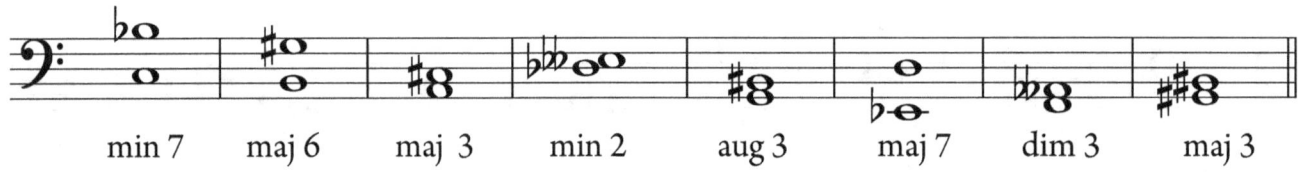

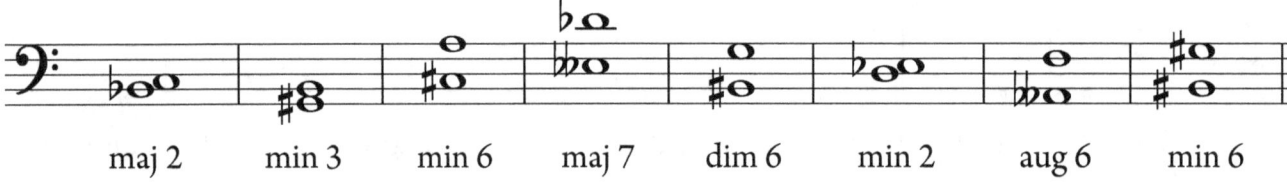

Page 39, No. 4

maj 2   dim 4   per 5   per 8   maj 3   min 2   min 3   maj 2

Page 40, No. 1

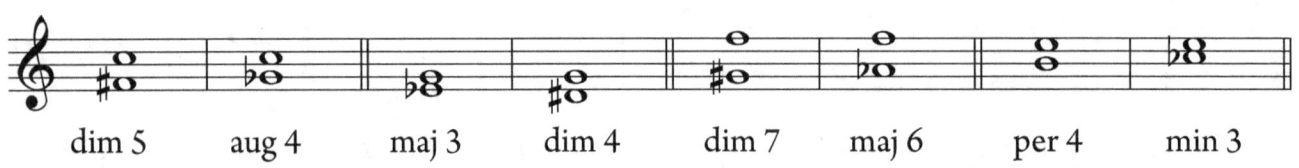

Page 40, No. 2

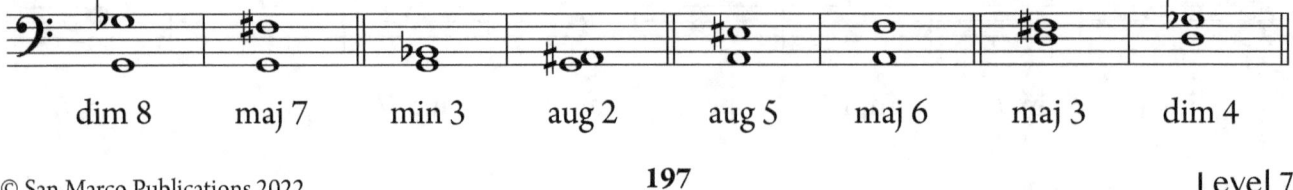

Page 43, No. 1

2, 3, 3, 3, 6, 7, 7, 7

Page 43, No. 2 and 3

Page 45, No. 1

Page 46, No. 2

12/8, 3/8, 9/4, 3/2, 6/16, 4/2, 6/8

Page 48, No. 1

Page 49 - 50, No. 1

Frédéric Chopin
Etude, Op. 10, No. 9

Frédéric Chopin
Waltz, Op. 69, No.1

Giacomo Puccini
Madam Butterfly (One Fine Day)

Lili Boulanger
Nocturne

Page 52, No. 1

Page 54, No. 1

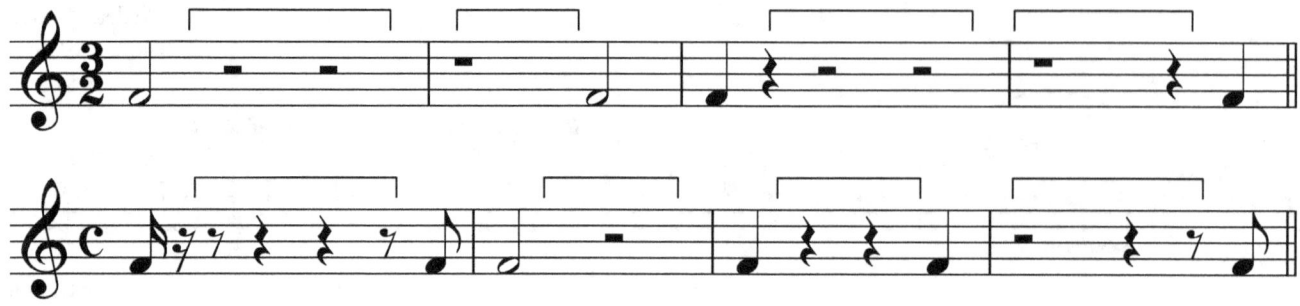

Page 55

Page 55, No. 2

Page 57, No. 1

| F | E♭m | Ddim | Caug | B♭ | Am |

| G♭aug | F♯m | C | G♯ | Adim | D♭aug |

| Em | Gm | Bdim | D | A♭ | Baug |

Page 57, No. 2

Page 57, No. 3

Page 57, No. 4

augmented   major   diminished   augmented   diminished   minor

Page 59, No. 1

F	C#	A	E♭	D	B
major	minor	diminished	major	augmented	diminished
2nd inv	root pos	1st inv	2nd inv	root pos	1st inv
G	F#	E♭	B	A	D♭
major	minor	minor	major	minor	major
root pos	2nd inv	2nd inv	root pos	1st inv	2nd inv
C	D	C	F#	B♭	E
diminished	minor	major	major	major	minor
root pos	2nd inv	1st inv	root pos	2nd inv	root pos

Page 59, No. 2

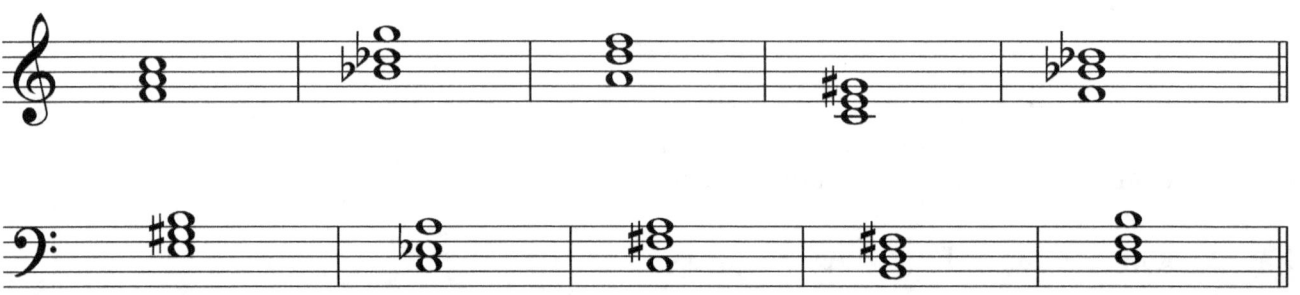

Page 60, No. 1

Symbol:	C/E	D♭aug	Am/C	G	Fdim/C	D
Root:	C	D♭	A	G	F	D
Quality:	major	augmented	minor	major	diminished	major
Position:	1st inv	root pos	1st inv	root pos	2nd inv	root pos

Symbol:	Bdim/F	Gm/D	A♭dim	F#/A#	Am	G#aug
Root:	B	G	A♭	F#	E	G#
Quality:	diminished	minor	diminished	major	minor	augmented
Position:	2nd inv	2nd inv	root pos	1st inv	root pos	root pos

Page 62, No. 1

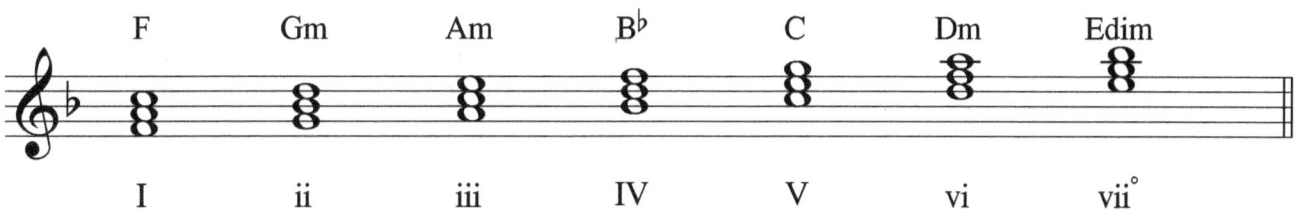

Page 62, No. 2

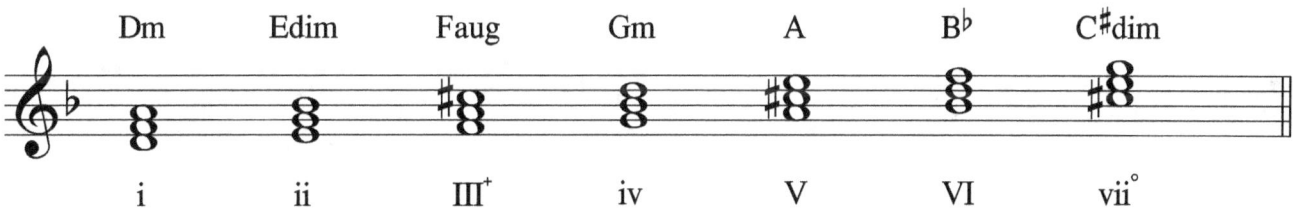

Page 63, No. 3

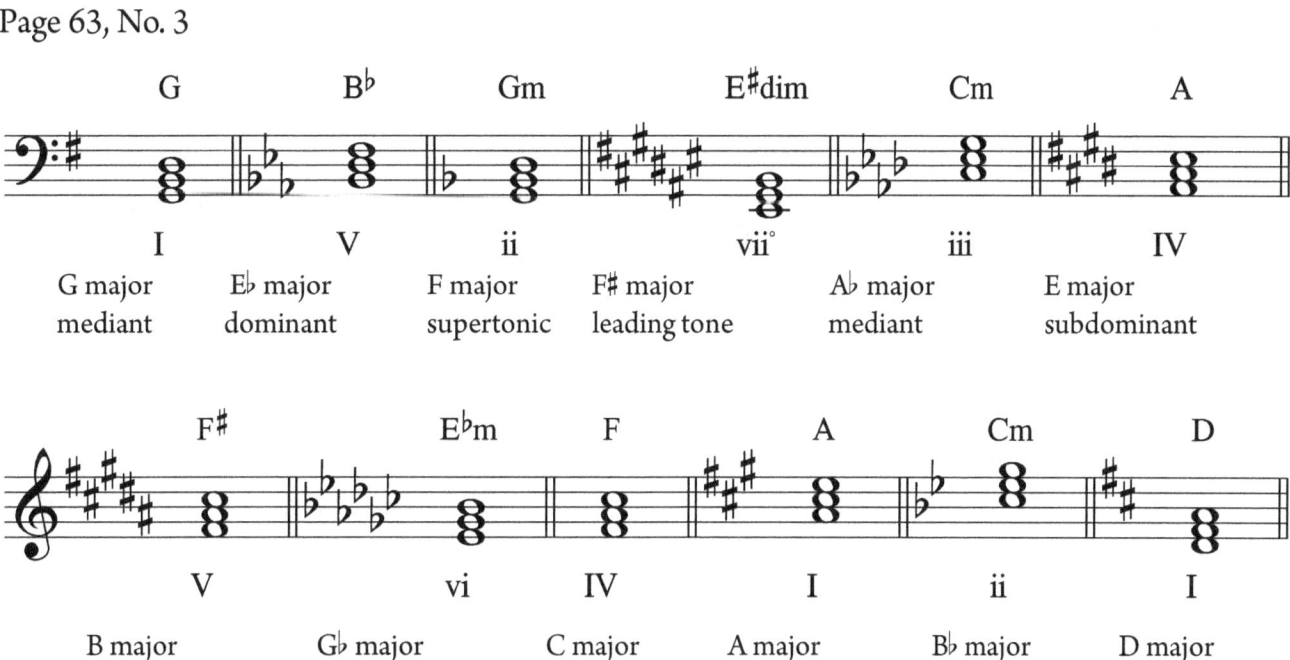

Page 63, No. 4

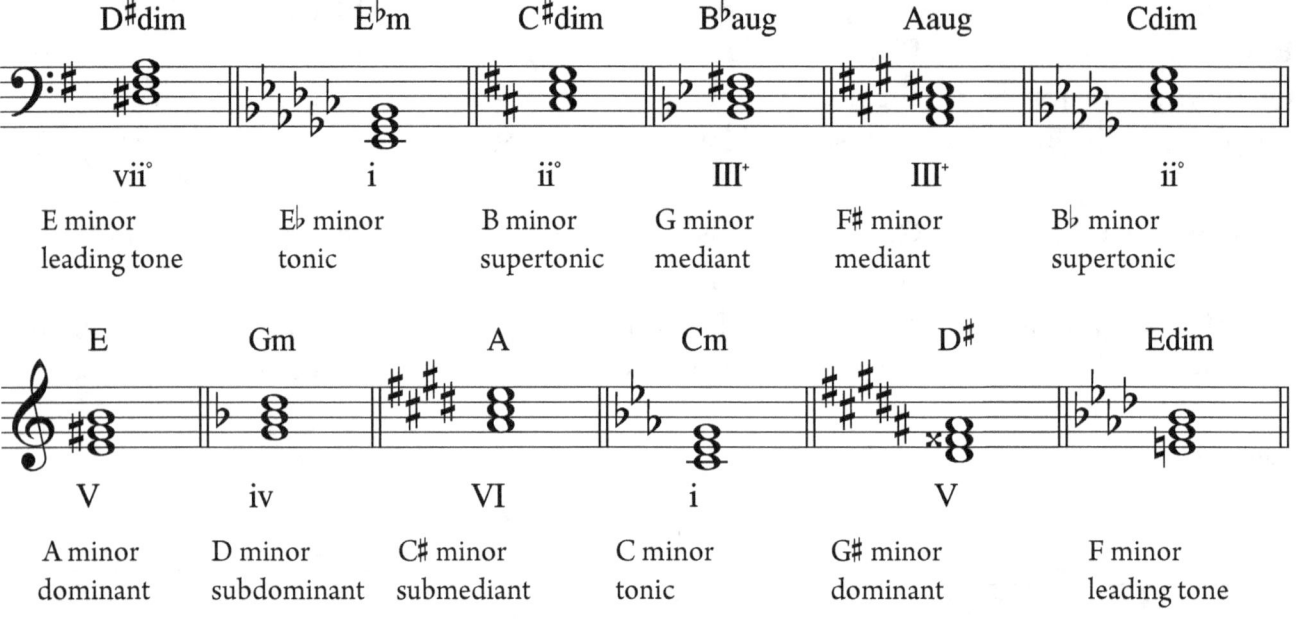

Page 64, No. 5

i.   ii.   iii.   iv.   v.   vi.

Page 64, No. 6

i.   ii.   iii.   iv.   v.   vi.

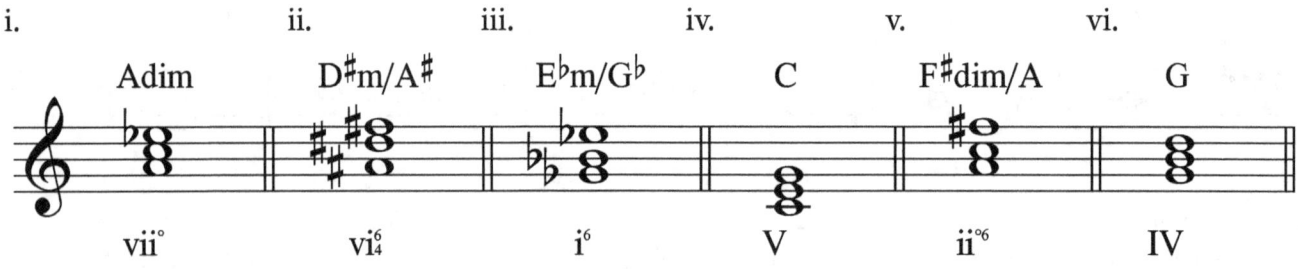

Page 64, No. 7

i.   ii.   iii.   iv.   v.   vi.

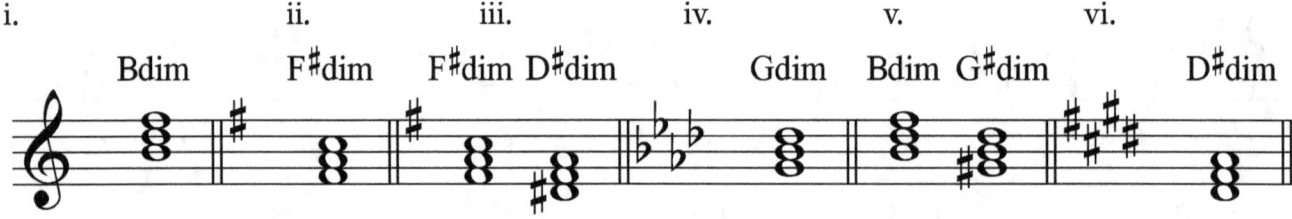

Page 70, No. 1

Key:	G minor	A major	B minor	F major
Root/quality:	D^7	E^7	$F\#^7$	C^7
Functional:	V^7	V^7	V^7	V^7

Key:	E major	F minor	B major	G major
Root/quality:	B^7	C^7	$F\#^7$	D^7
Functional:	V^7	V^7	V^7	V^7

Key:	E♭ major	D major	A minor	B♭ minor
Root/quality:	$B♭^7$	A^7	E^7	F^7
Functional:	V^7	V^7	V^7	V^7

Page 72, No. 1

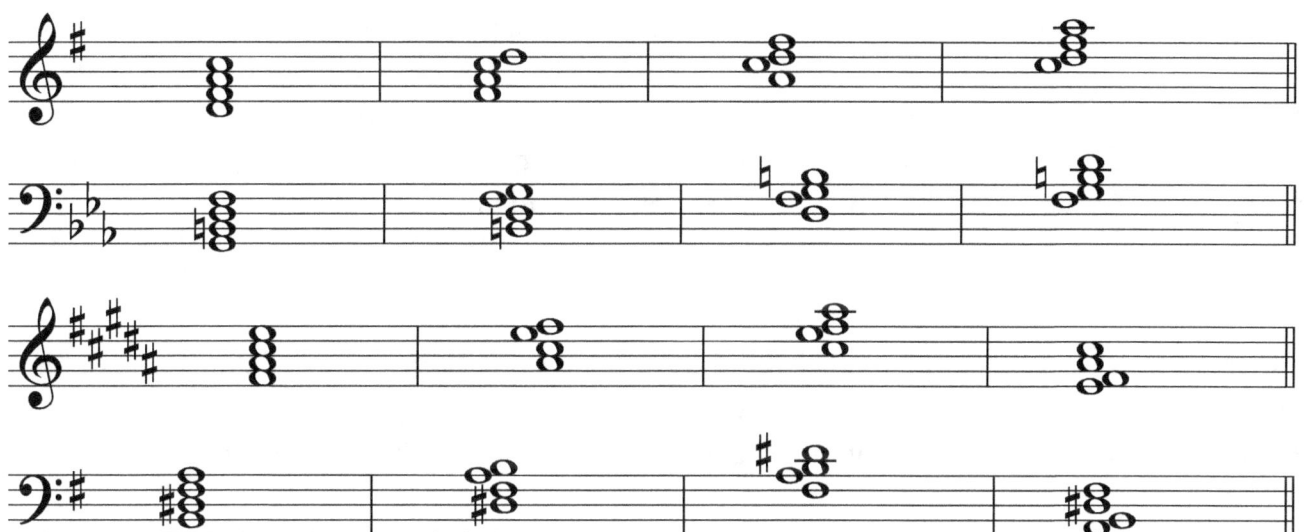

Page 72-73, No. 2

A♭	G	F	D	E	D♭
D♭ major	C major	B♭ major	G major	A major	G♭ major
D♭ minor	C minor	B♭ minor	G minor	A minor	G♭ minor
root pos	2nd inv	1st inv	3rd inv	1st inv	2nd inv

F#	A♭	C	A	G♭	B♭
B major	D♭ major	F major	D major	C♭ major	E♭ major
B minor	D♭ minor	F minor	D minor	C♭ minor	E♭ minor
root pos	1st inv	3rd inv	1st inv	root pos	1st inv

Page 73, No. 3 (other answers are possible)

F major   G major   C major   E♭ major   E major   A major

F♯ major   B♭ major   E♭ major   A♭ major   G♭ major   D major

Page 73-74, No. 4

D	C	G	B	F♯	E♭
G major	F major	C minor	E major	B minor	A♭ major
root pos	1st inv	1st inv	2nd inv	root pos	3rd inv

F♯	B	D	F	A	A
B major	E minor	G minor	B♭ minor	D major	D minor
root pos	2nd inv	2nd inv	root pos	2nd inv	1st inv

Page 75, No. 1

D♯dim⁷	F♯dim⁷	E♯dim⁷	C♯dim	Bdim⁷	F×dim⁷
vii°⁷	vii°⁷	vii°⁷	vii°⁷	vii°⁷	vii°⁷
E minor	G minor	F♯ minor	D minor	C minor	G♯ minor

Page 75, No. 2

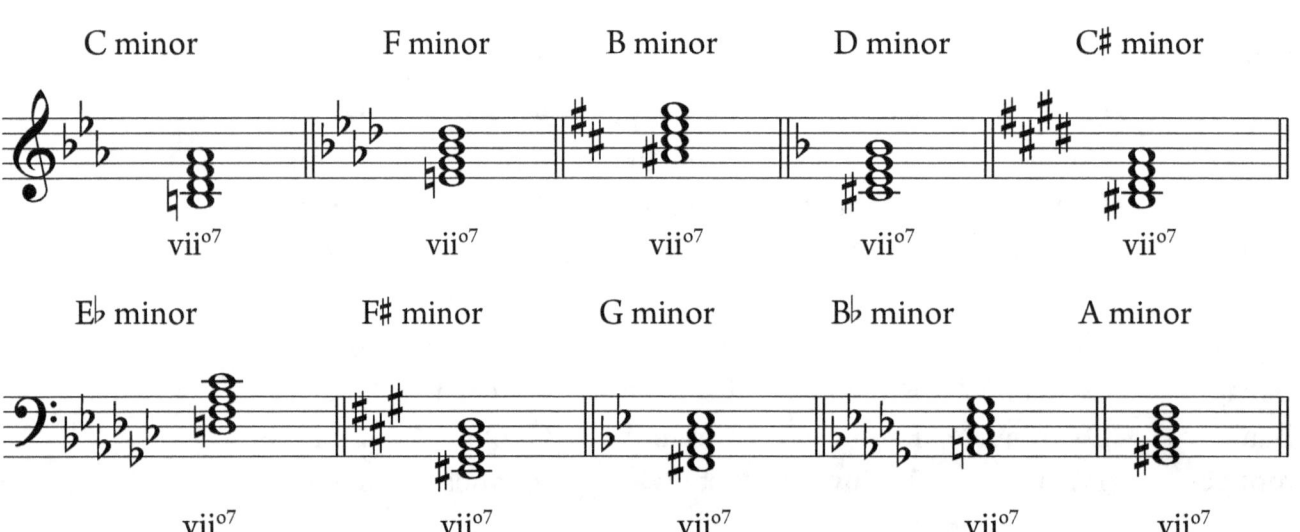

Page 76, No. 1 **Review 2**

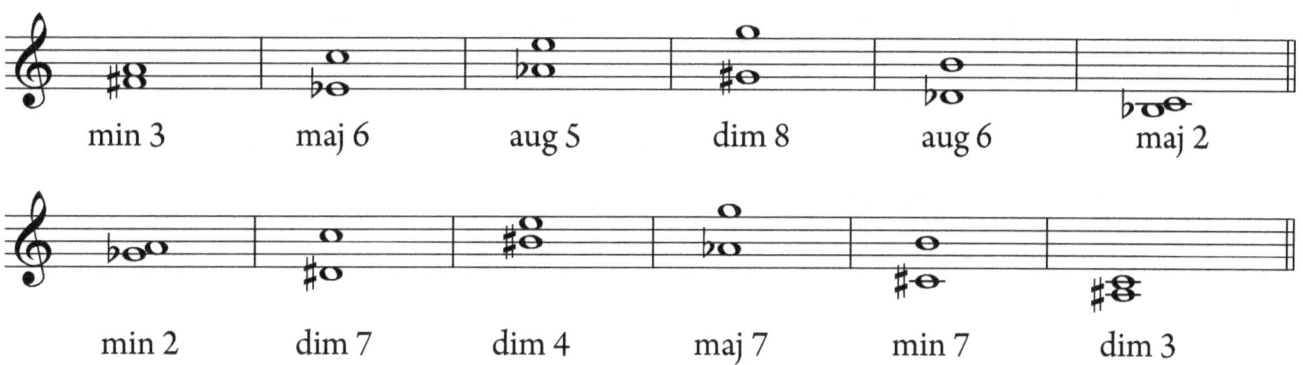

Page 76, No. 2

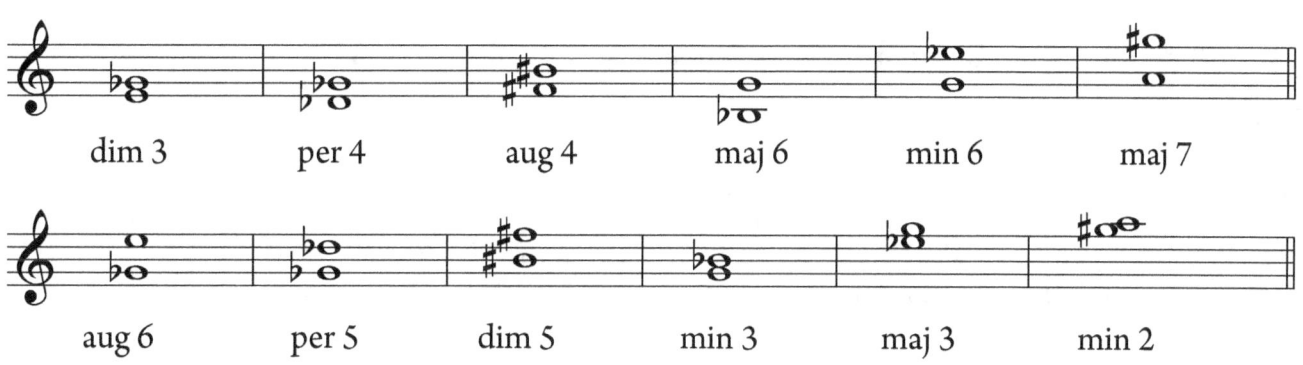

Page 76, No. 3

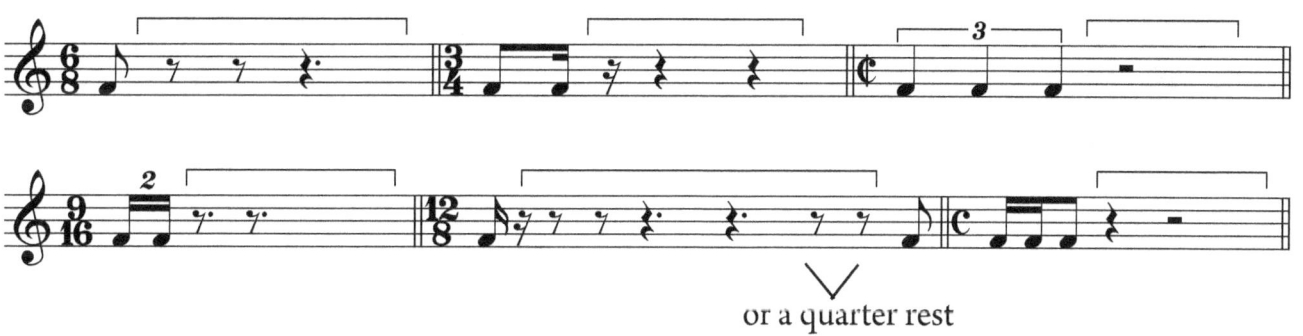

or a quarter rest

Page 76, No. 4

martellato   strongly accented or hammered

morendo   dying away

pesante   heavy

scherzando   playful

Page 77, No. 5

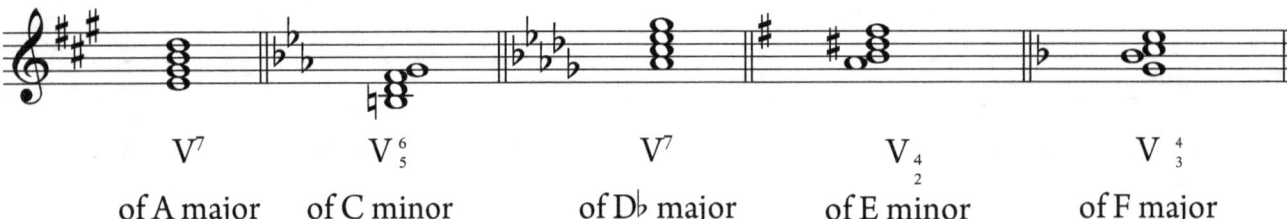

V^7 of A major V^6_5 of C minor V^7 of D♭ major V^4_2 of E minor V^4_3 of F major

Page 77, No. 6

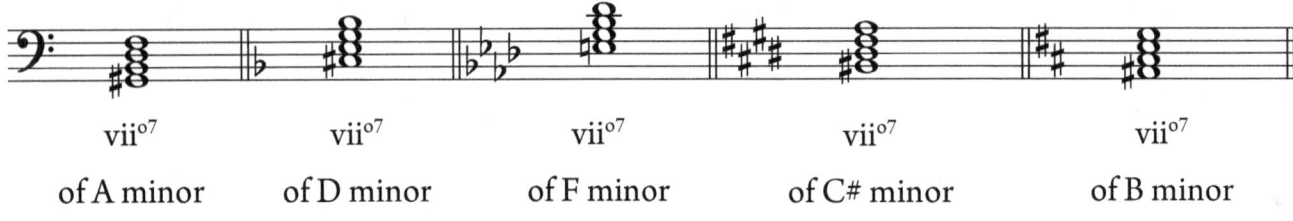

vii°7 of A minor   vii°7 of D minor   vii°7 of F minor   vii°7 of C# minor   vii°7 of B minor

Page 77, No. 7

F#	G	A	B	G	E
augmented	minor	major	diminished	augmented	diminished
root pos	1st inv	2nd inv	root pos	1st inv	2nd inv

Page 77, No. 8

F, F, T, T, F, F, T, T

Page 81, No. 1

G major: D   G   C minor: Cm   G
            V   I   i   V
            perfect authentic   half

D minor: A   Dm   A♭ major: D♭   E♭
            V   i   IV   V
            imperfect authentic   half

B minor: F# Bm   A major: E   A
            V   i   V   I
            perfect authentic   perfect authentic

A minor: Am E   D♭ major: A♭   D♭
            i   V   V   I
            half   perfect authentic

Page 85, No. 1 (other answers are possible)

Page 85, No. 2 (other answers are possible)

Page 85, No. 3 (other answers are possible)

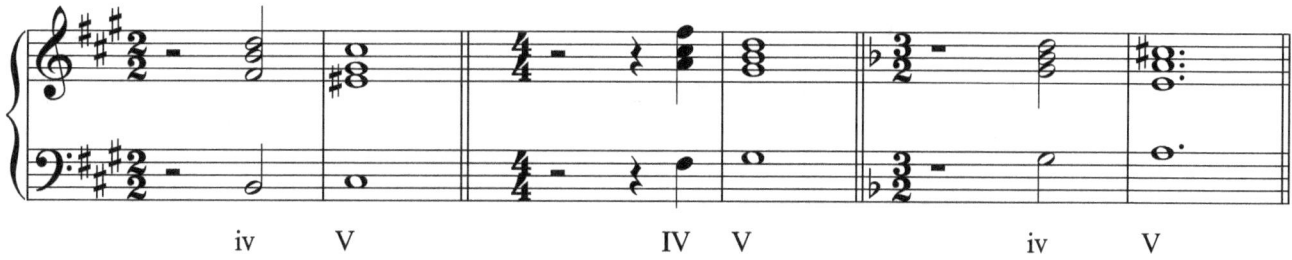

© San Marco Publications 2022   Level 7

Page 88, No. 1 (other answers are possible)

Page 89 (other answers are possible)

Page 90, No. 2 (other answers are possible)

Page 92, No. 1

Page 93, No. 2

Original key: E♭ major

Page 95, No. 1

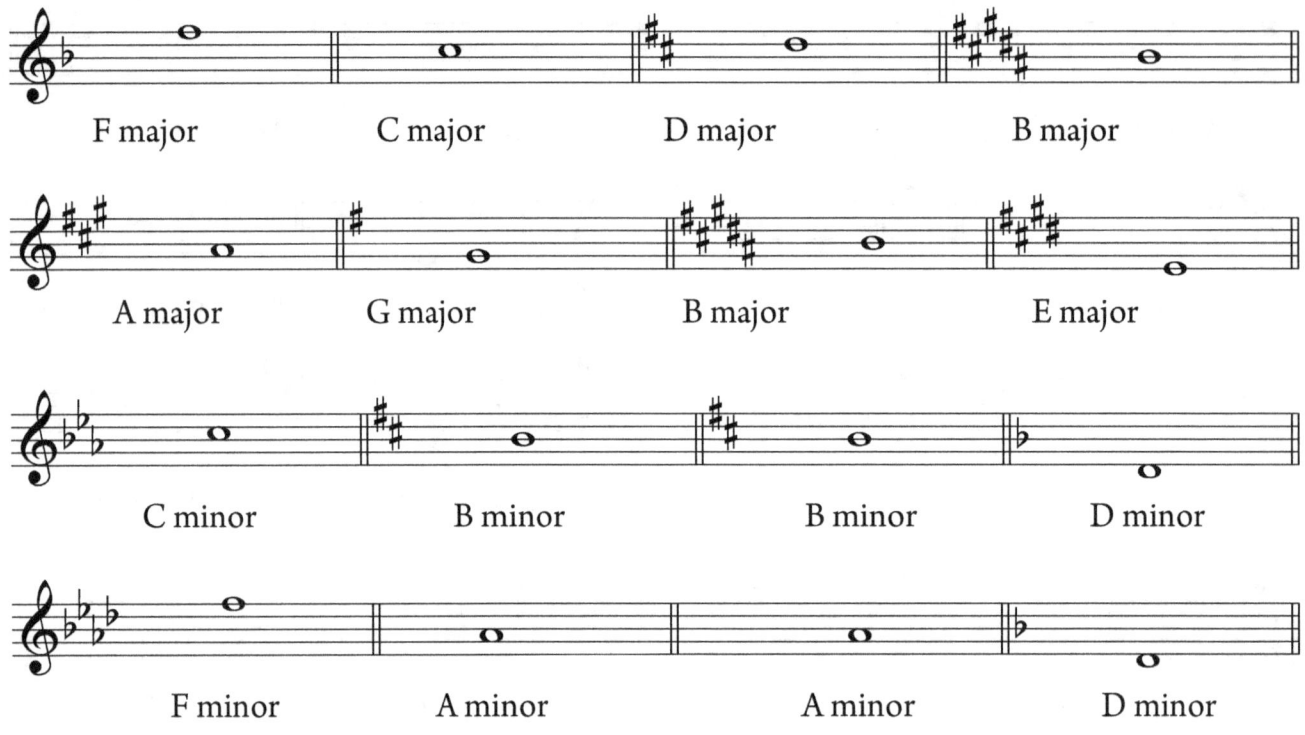

Page 96, No. 2

Original key: F major

Anton Diabelli
Sonatina, Op. 168, No. 1

Moderato

E♭ major

Anton Diabelli
Sonatina, Op. 168, No. 1

Moderato

C major

Anton Diabelli
Sonatina, Op. 168, No. 1

Moderato

D major

© San Marco Publications 2022

Level 7

Page 98, No. 1

Original key: G major

Andante maestoso

Ludwig van Beethoven
Symphony No. 9, IV

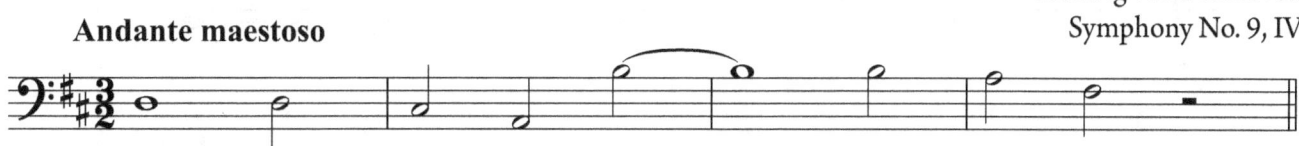

Interval of transposition: per 4

Andante maestoso

Ludwig van Beethoven
Symphony No. 9, IV

Interval of transposition: maj 3

Andante maestoso

Ludwig van Beethoven
Symphony No. 9, IV

Interval of transposition: min 6

Andante maestoso

Ludwig van Beethoven
Symphony No. 9, IV

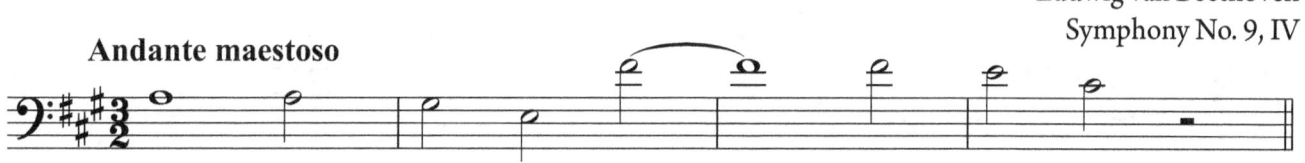

Interval of transposition: maj 2

Page 100, No. 1

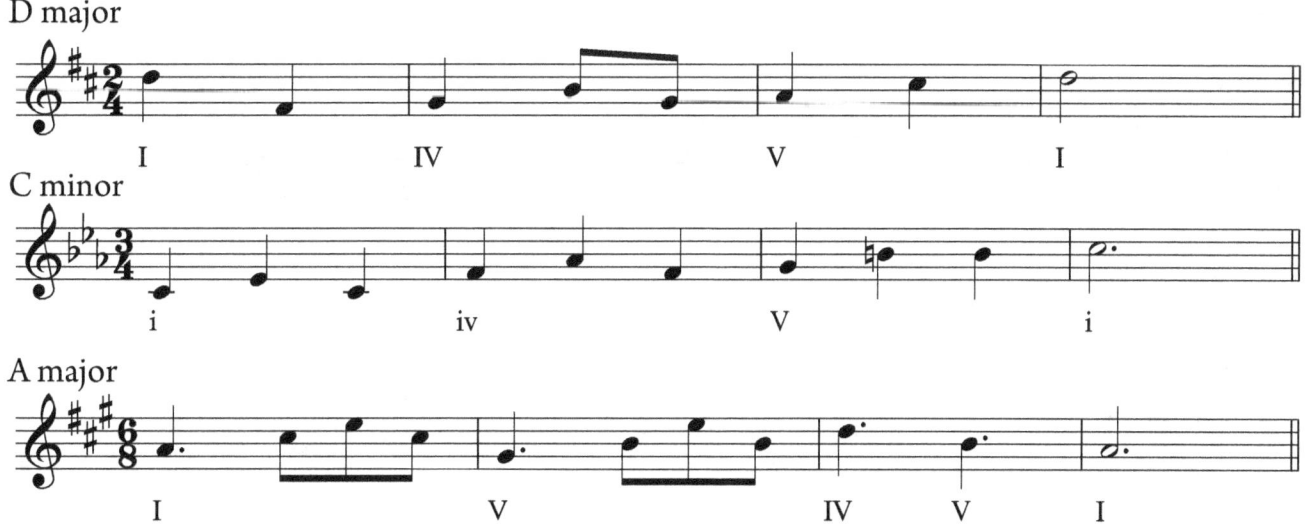

E minor

F major

Page 102, No. 1

Page 103, No. 2 (other answers are possible)

G major

B♭ major

I IV V I

D minor

i iv V i

E minor

i iv V i

Page 107, No. 1 (other answers are possible)

a

F major half

b

perfect authentic

a

D major half

b

perfect authentic

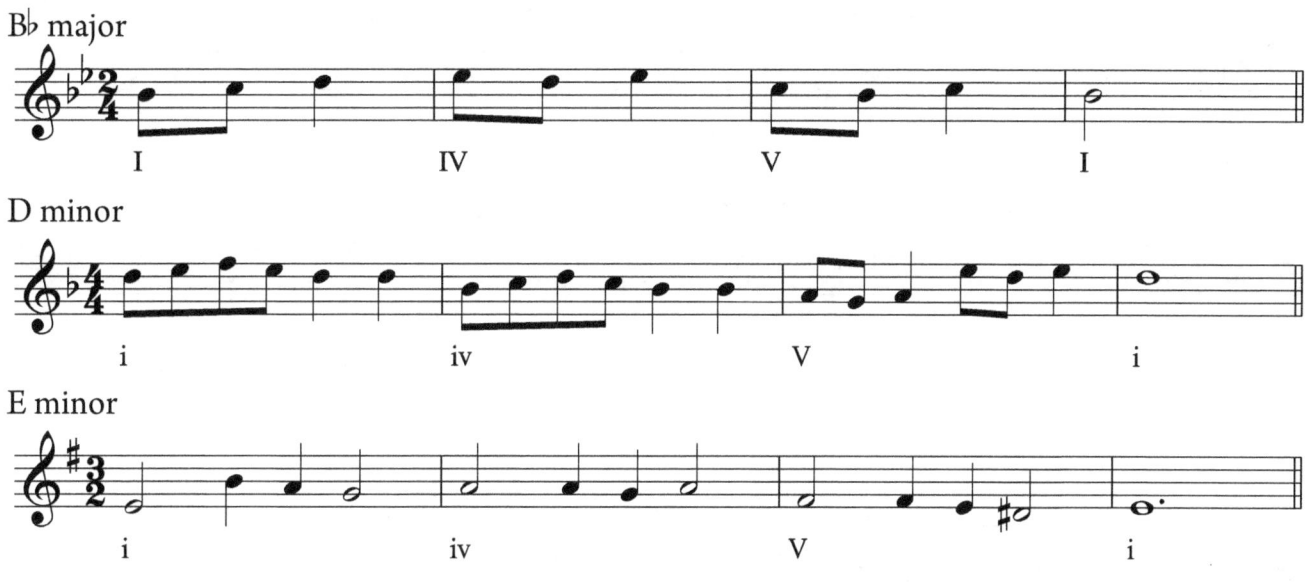

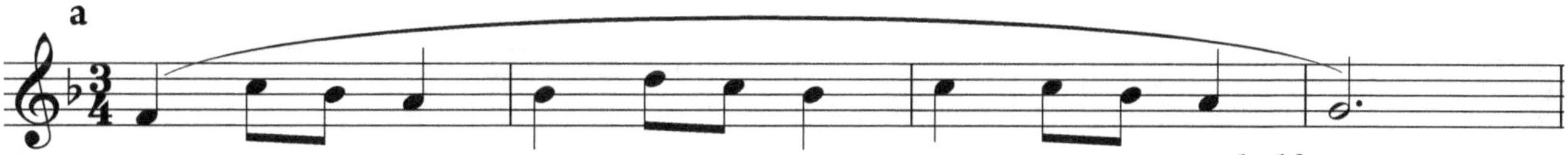

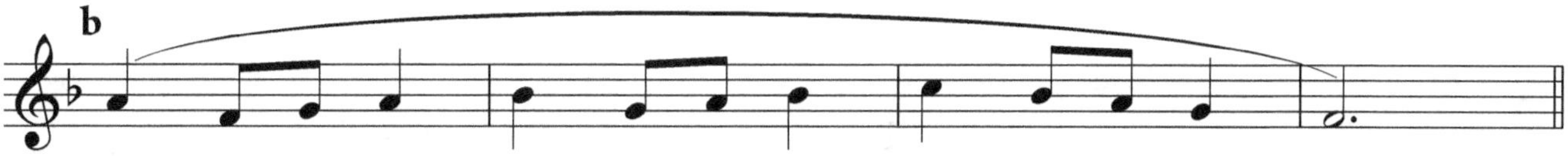

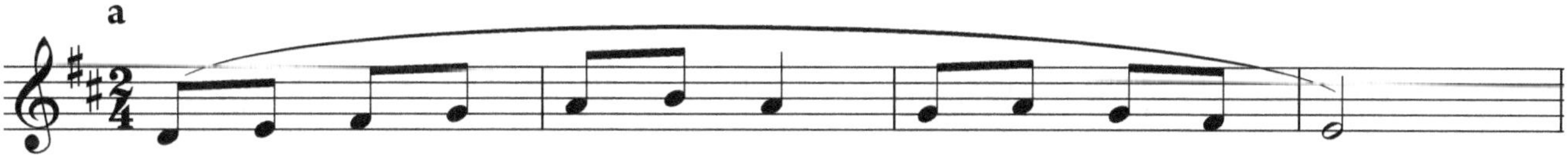

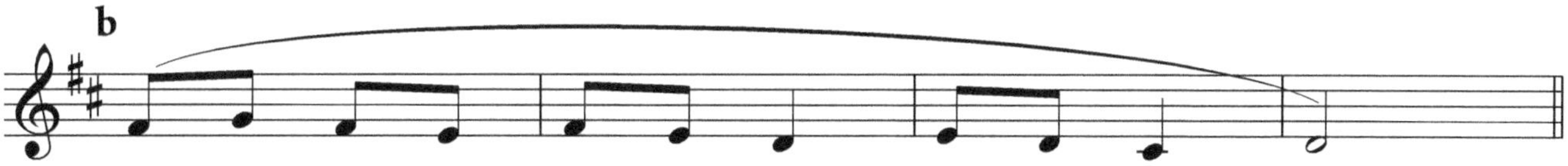

Page 117, No. 1 **Review 3** (other answers are possible)

Page 118, No. 2

Original key: F minor

Johann Sebastian Bach
WTC Bk. 1. No. 12

C minor

Original key: B minor

Pyotr Tchaikovsky
Symphony No. 6

G minor

Page 118, No. 3

Petrushka
Composer: Igor Stravinsky Genre: Ballet

Koko
Composer: Duke Ellington Genre: 12 bar blues

Dripsody
Composer: Hugh LeCaine Genre: electronic music

Etude Op. 10, No. 12 'Revolutionary'
Composer: Frédéric Chopin   Genre: solo piano piece

Overture to a Midsummer Nights Dream
Composer: Felix Mendelssohn   Genre: concert overture

Page 119, No. 4

f, u, t, v, w, a, b, r, k, s, i, x, l, o, q, p, d, t, j, c

Page 122, No. 1

E minor:	V iv V i	B minor:	iv V i
F major:	I IV V	A minor:	iv V i
D minor:	iv V i	E major:	I IV V I
G♭ major:	I IV V I	G♯ minor:	i V i

Page 122, No. 2

1. tonic   2. dominant   3. subdominant   4. tonic

Page 123, No. 1

A major: I V V
C minor: i V iv

Page 124

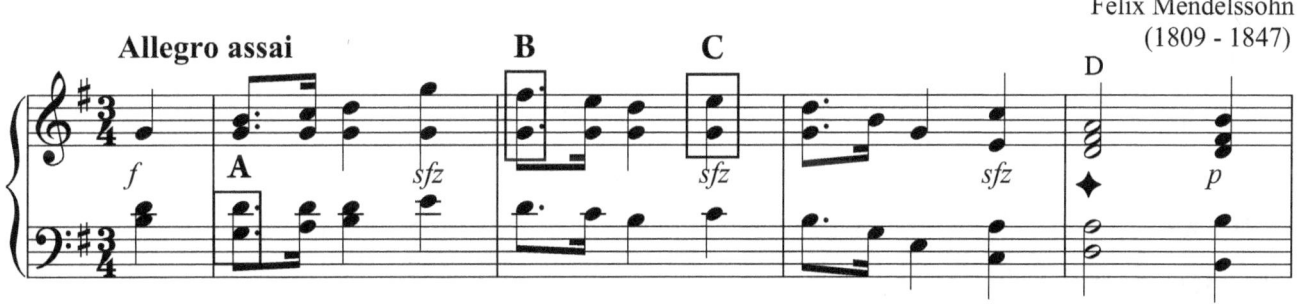

1. Felix Mendelssohn
2. Overture to a Midsummer Nights dream
3. Romantic era
4. 8
5. G major
8. per 5, maj 7, maj 6, aug 4
9. very fast
10. sforzando, sudden strong accent
11. perfect authentic
12. Because the piece begins with an incomplete measure or anacrusis.

© San Marco Publications 2022 — Level 7

Page 125

1. Romantic era
2. A♭ major
3. 3/4
4. D♭ major
5. subdominant chord
6. E♭ major
7. dominant chord
8. C: neighbor tones   D: passing tones
9. fairly fast, a little slower than allegro
10. fortepiano, loud than suddenly soft
11. stable

Page 126

George Frideric Handel
(1685 - 1759)

1. George Frideric Handel

2. Messiah

3. Baroque era

4. D minor

5. 3/2

6. simple triple time

7. tonic chord

8. dominant chord

9. subdominant chord

10. 4

11. D: min 3rd   E: min 3rd   F: min 3rd

12. 4

13. 7

© San Marco Publications 2022   226   Level 7

1. E♭ major

2. 3/4

3. homophonic texture

4. Romantic era

5. Frédéric Chopin, Felix Mendelssohn, Robert Schumann, Pyotr Tchaikovsky, Franz Liszt

7. min 3

8. maj 3

9. dim 5

Page 135, No. 1 **Exam**

G♭ chromatic
D♭ whole tone
C♯ octatonic
E blues
F melodic minor

Page 135, No. 2

Page 136, No. 3

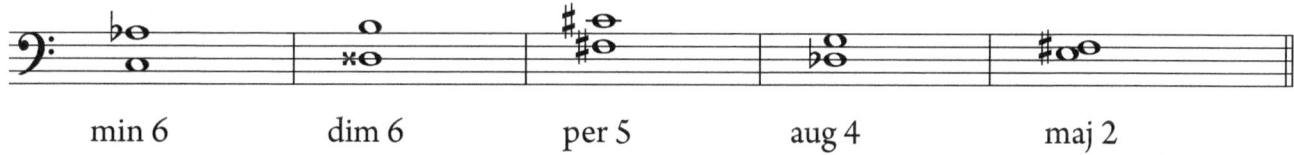

Page 136, No. 4

Page 136, No. 5

original key: G major

Johannes Brahms
Sextet op. 36

C major

Page 137, No. 6

Page 137, No. 7

d, c, a, e, b

Page 137, No. 8

D minor:	V i		B♭ major:	I V
	perfect authentic			half
C minor:	V i		E major:	IV V
	imperfect authentic			half

Page 138, No. 9

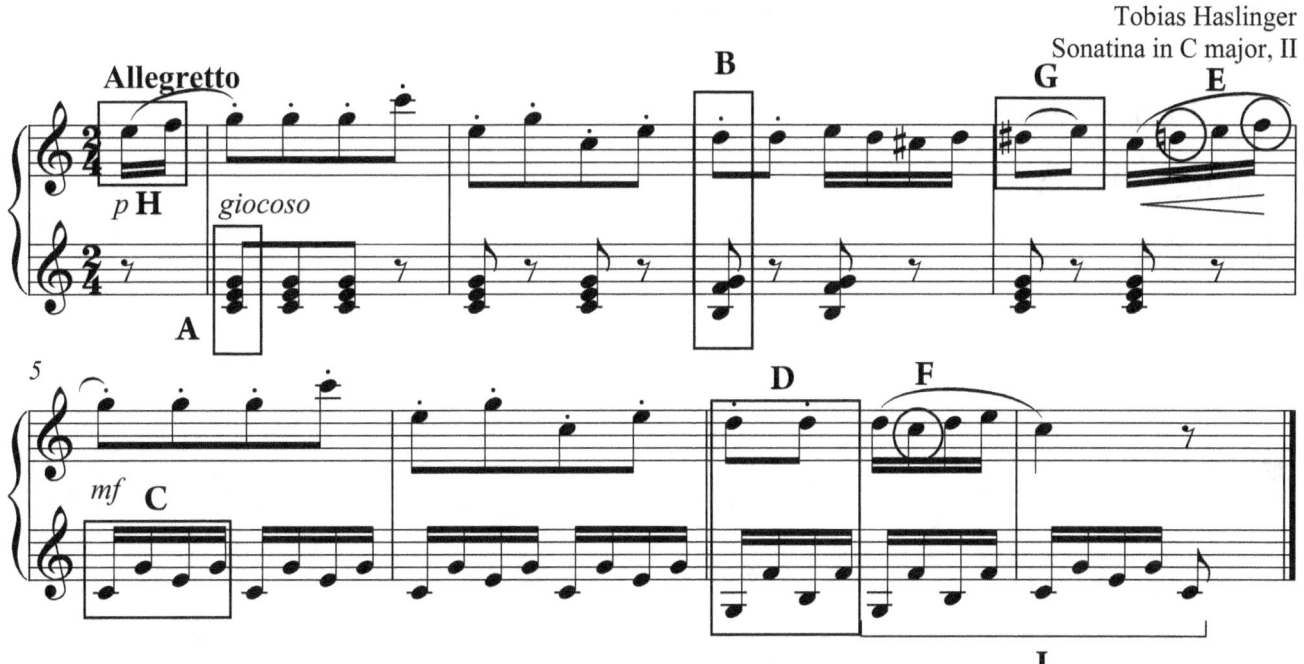

a) C major
b) 2/4
c) C   major   root pos.
d) G   dominant 7th   1st inv.
e) C   major   root pos.
f) G   dominant 7th   root pos.
g) E: passing tones   F: neighbor tone
h) min 2
i) anacrusis or pick up
j) humorous, joyful
k) perfect authentic

Page 138, No. 10

Hugh Le Caine   Modern

Frédéric Chopin   Romantic

Duke Ellington   Modern

Felix Mendelssohn   Romantic

Igor Stravinsky   Modern

Level 8

Page 3, No. 1

E A B F G C G F D

E B A E D D C G F

Page 3, No. 2

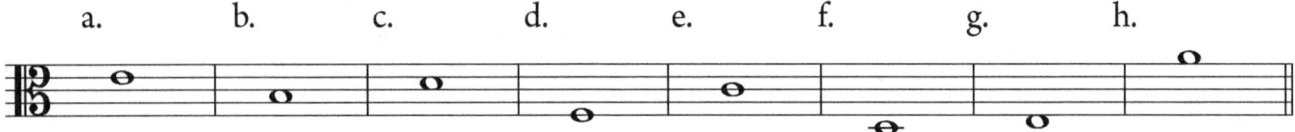

Page 3, No. 3

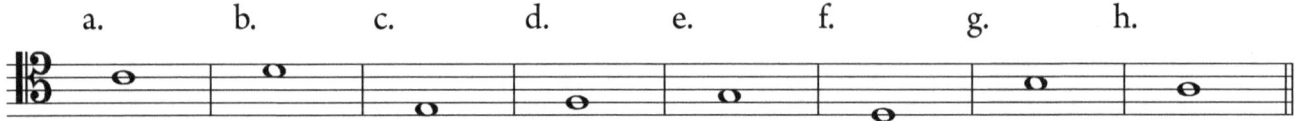

Page 4, No. 4

Wolfgang Amadeus Mozart
Cosi fan tutte

Page 4, No. 5

Gabriel Faure
Elegie, Op. 24

Page 8, No. 1

Page 12, No. 1

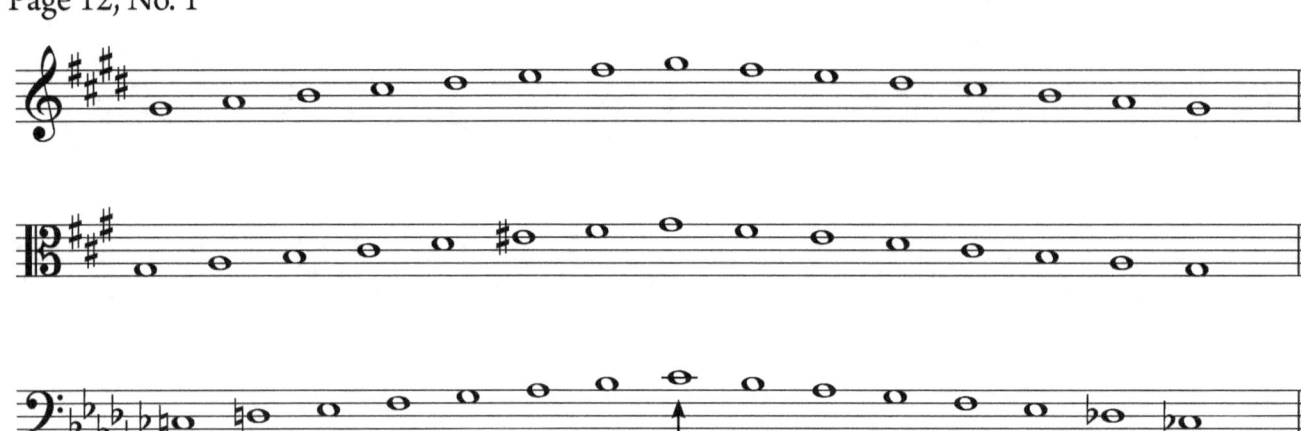

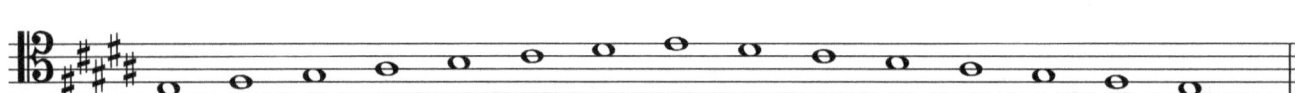
C♮ or C♭ either is correct

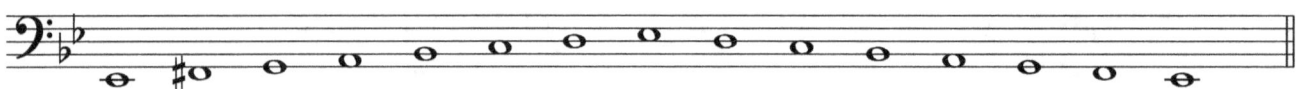

Page 13, No. 2

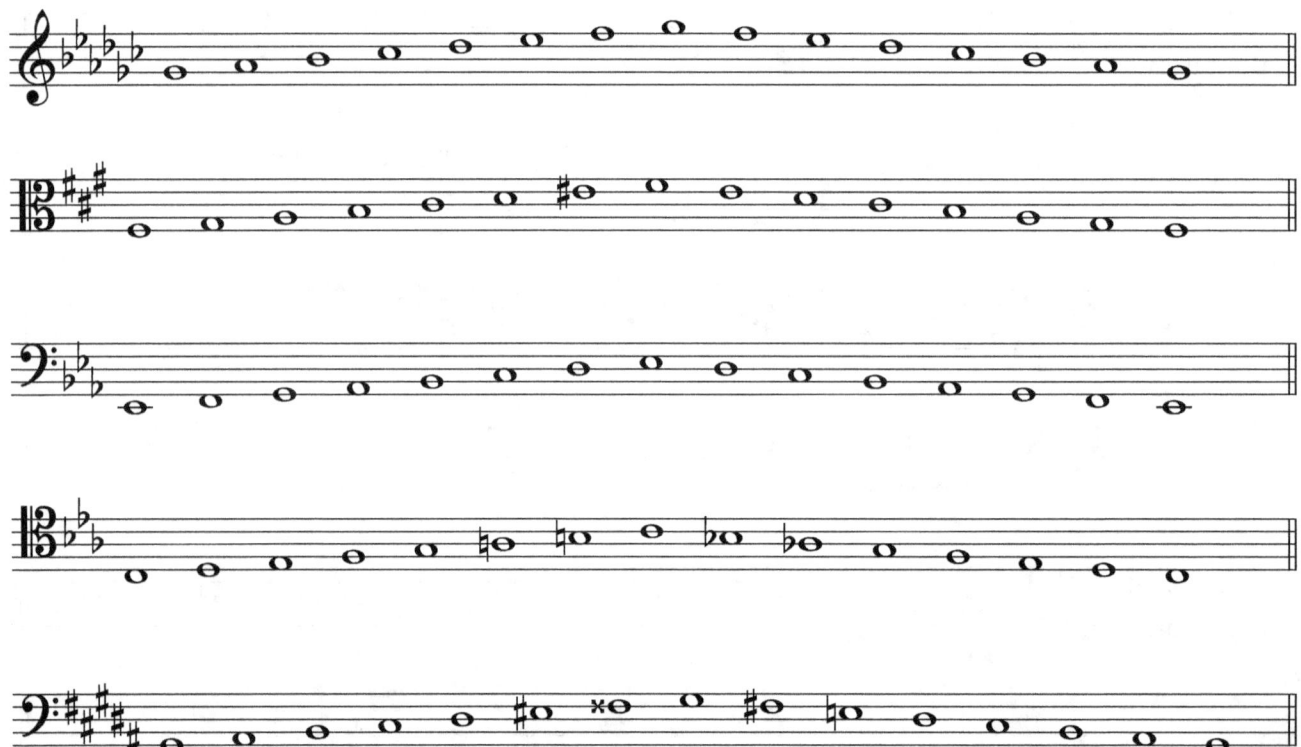

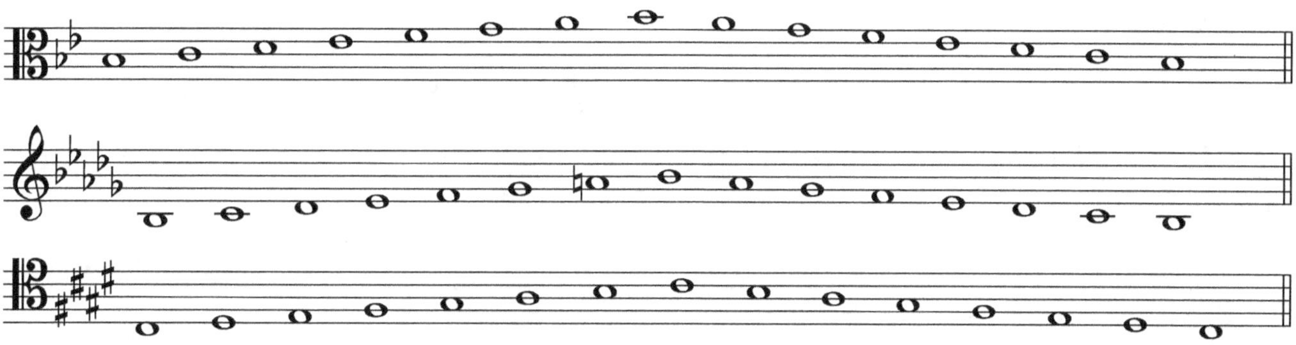

Page 18, No. 1

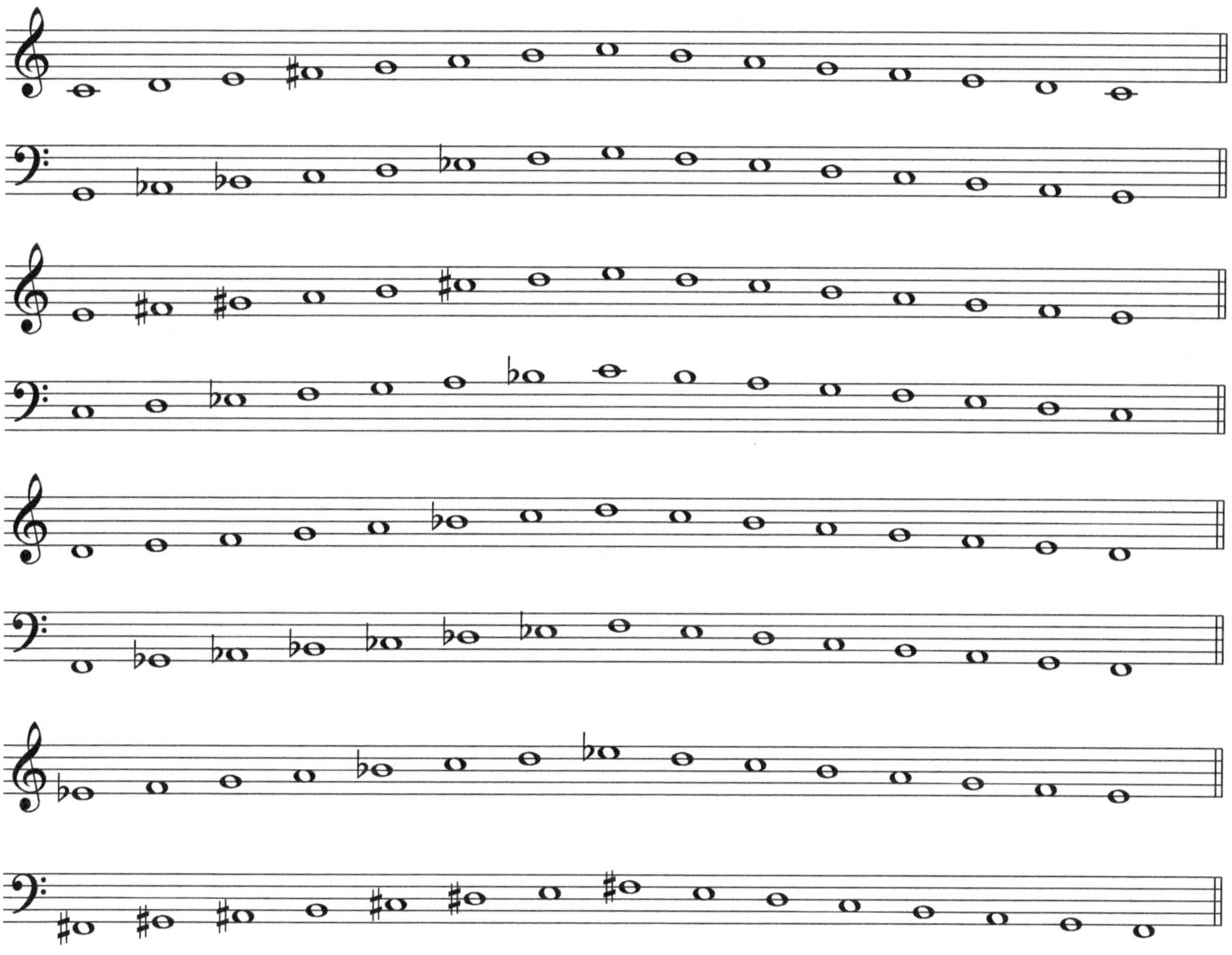

Page 19, No. 1

F dorian   B♭ mixolydian
G lydian   D aeolian
A locrian   F♯ dorian
E♭ mixolydian   B lydian
G phrygian

Page 25, No. 1

Page 26, No. 1

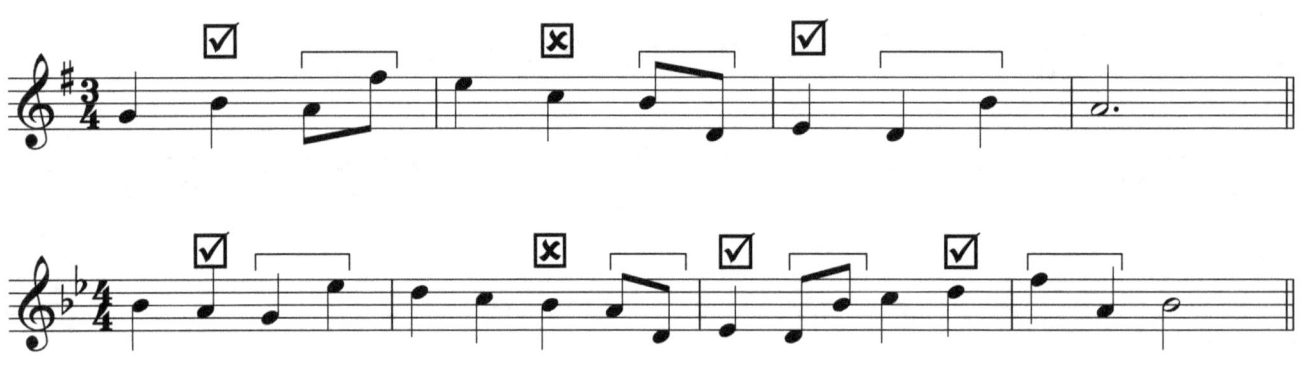

Page 27, No. 1

Page 32, No. 1 **Review 1**

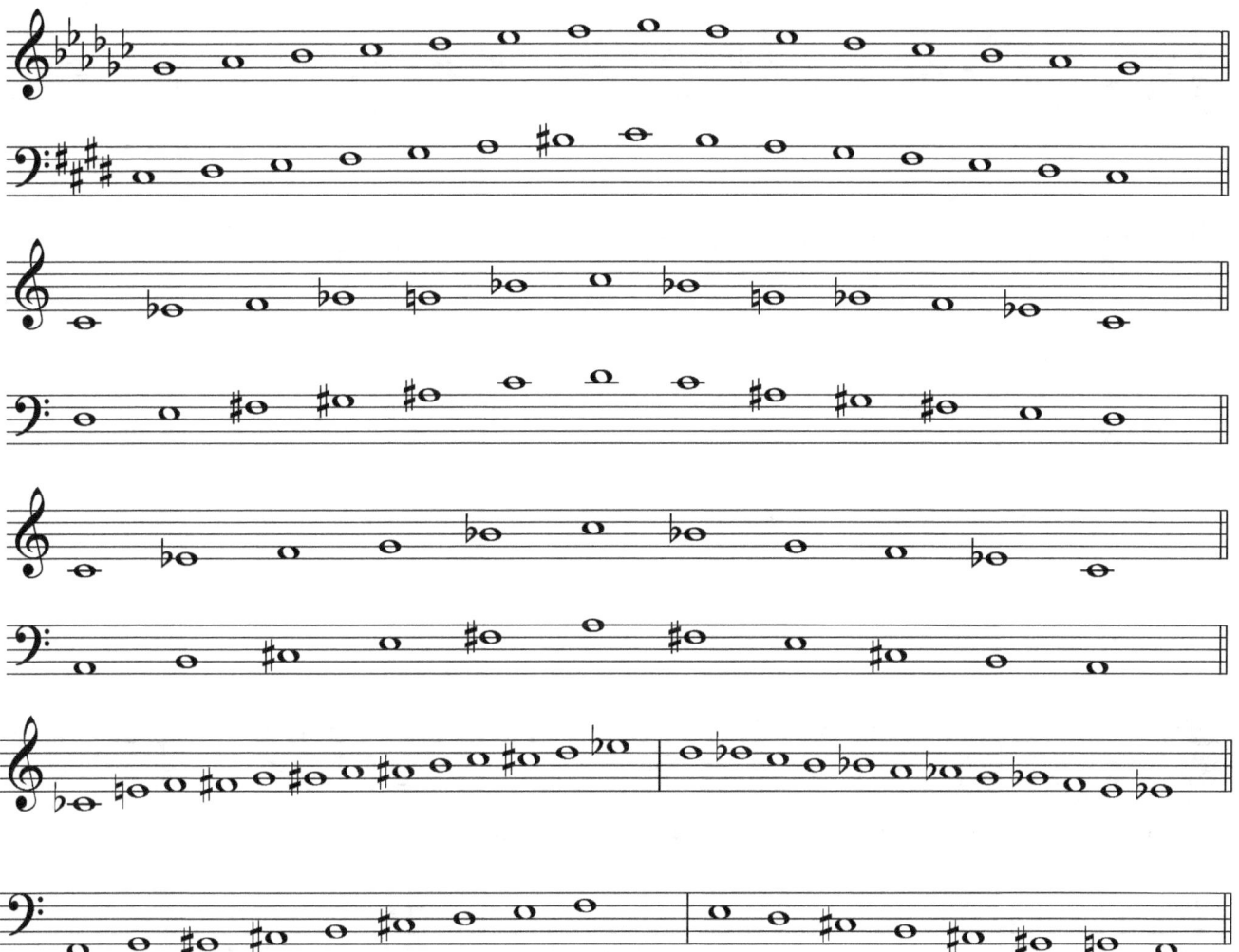

Page 33, No. 2

A phrygian
F lydian
E mixolydian
G locrian
C dorian
D lydian

Page 33, No. 3

f, e, d, c, b, a

Page 34, No. 4

G major

B♭ major

Page 34, No. 5

a. F   b. T   c. T   d. T   e. F   f. T   g. T   h. F   i. F   j. F   k. T   l. T   m. T

Page 37, No. 1

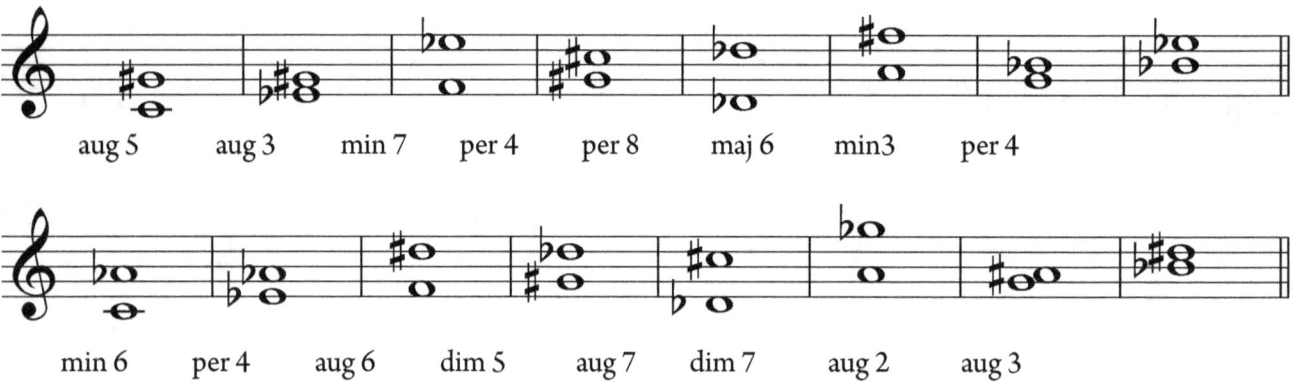

Page 38, No. 2

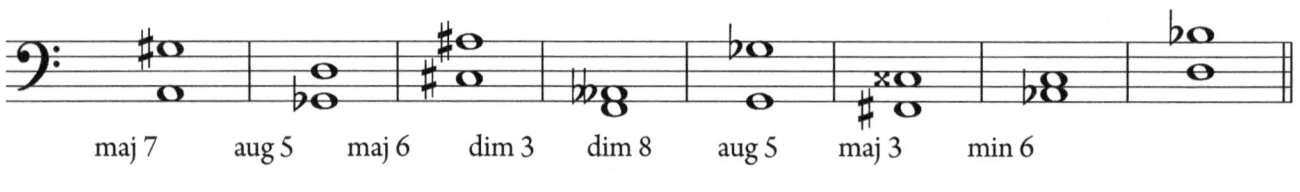

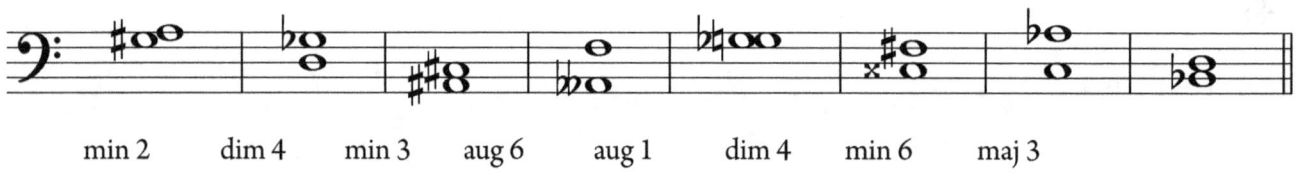

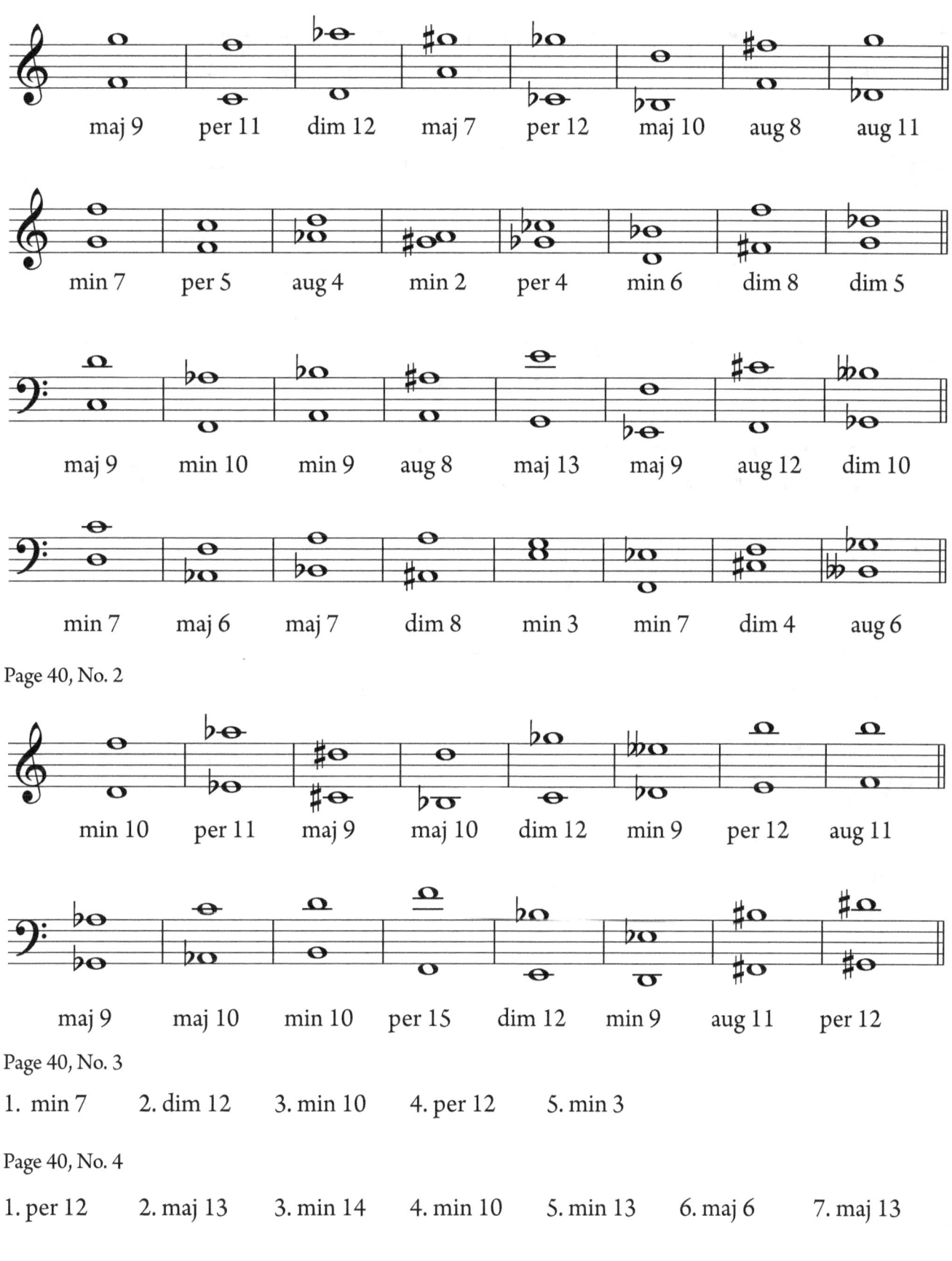

Page 42, No. 1

Page 43, No. 1

Stephen Heller
Op. 119, No. 30

Pyotr Tchaikovsky
Nutcracker Suite, Danse Arabe

Page 46, No. 1

Page 49, No. 1

Page 50, No. 2

Page 50, No. 3

Page 53, No. 1 (other answers are possible)

© San Marco Publications 2018   Level 8

Page 57, No. 1

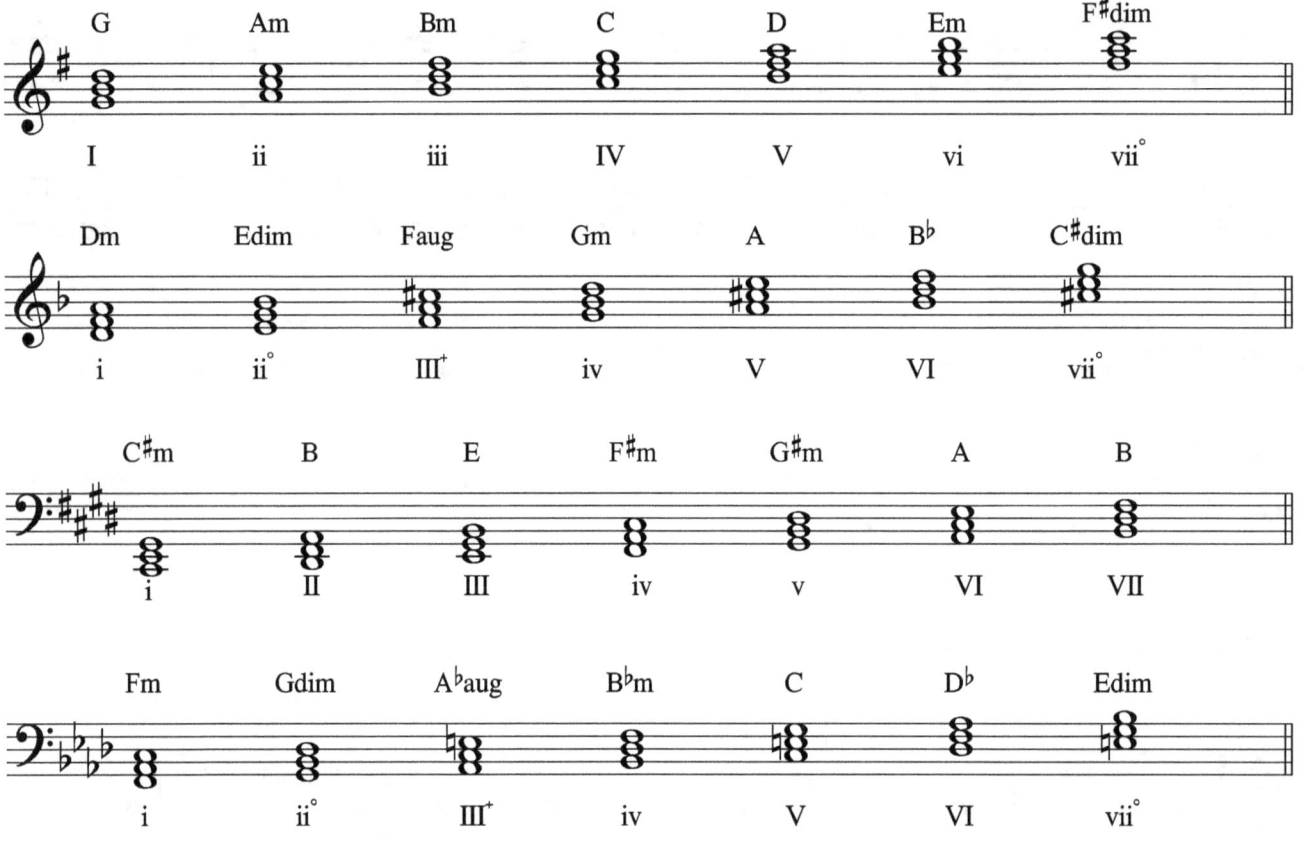

Page 57, No. 2

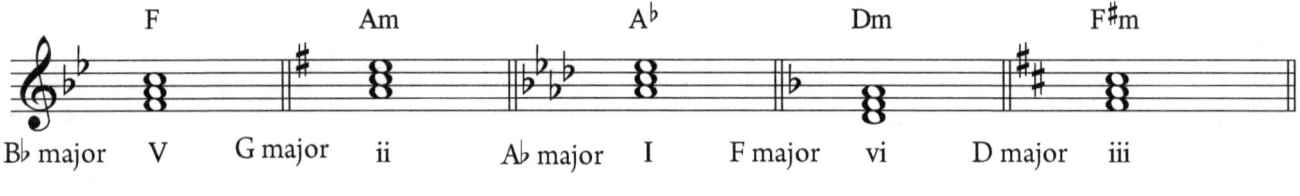

Page 58, No. 3

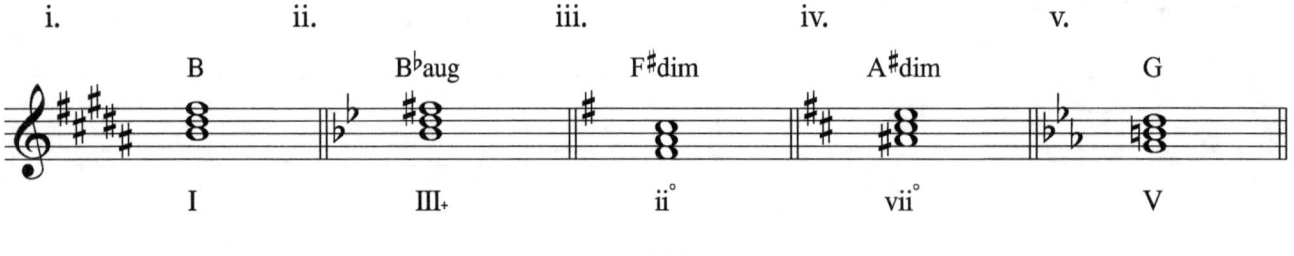

Page 58, No. 4

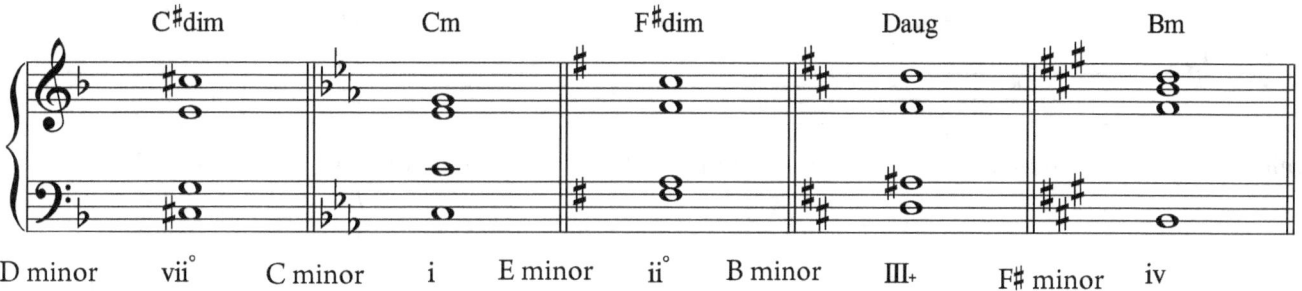

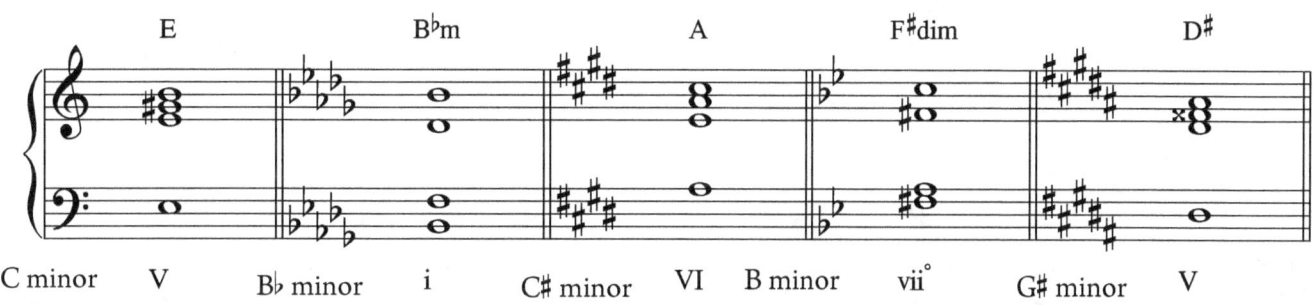

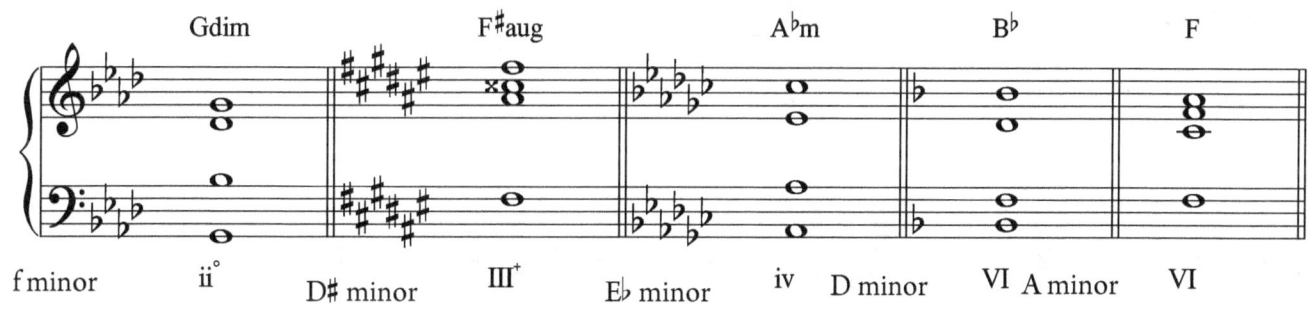

Page 60, No. 1

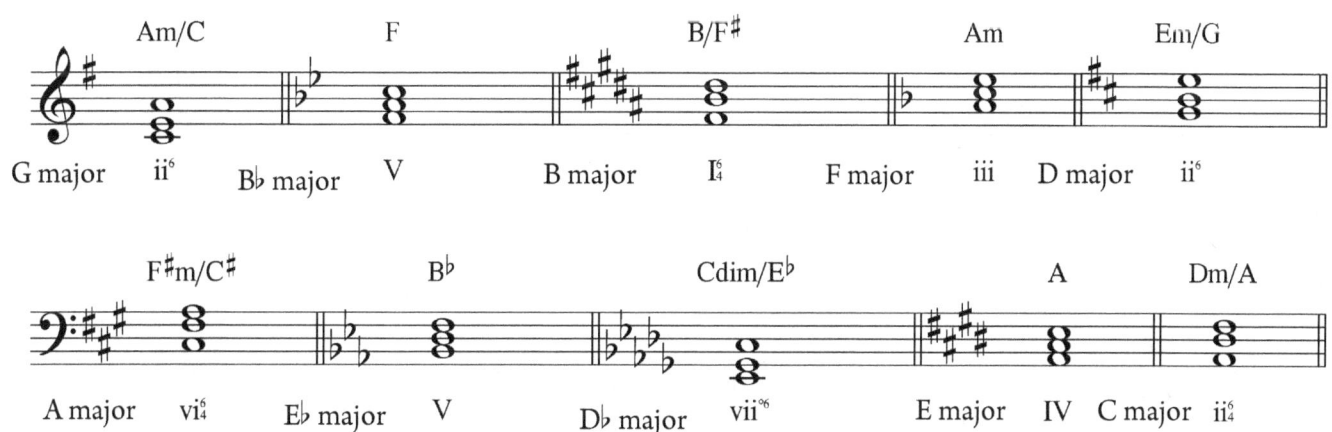

Page 60, No. 2

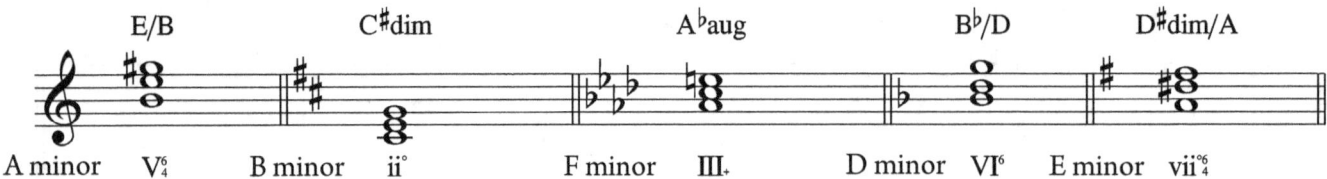

Page 61, No. 3

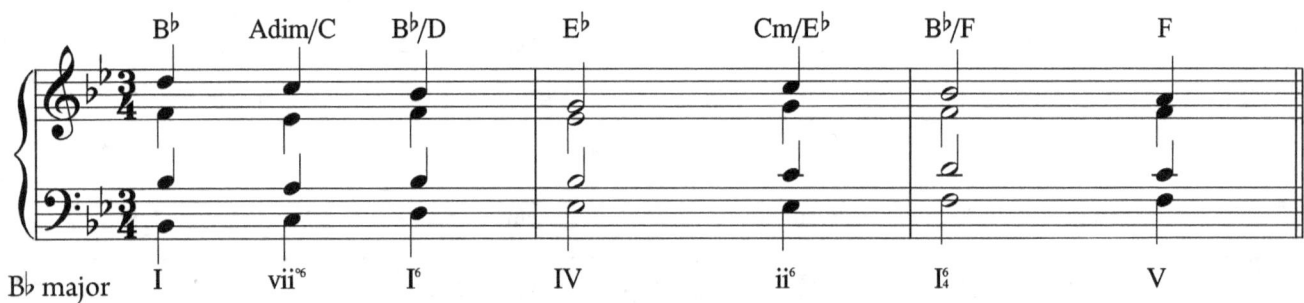

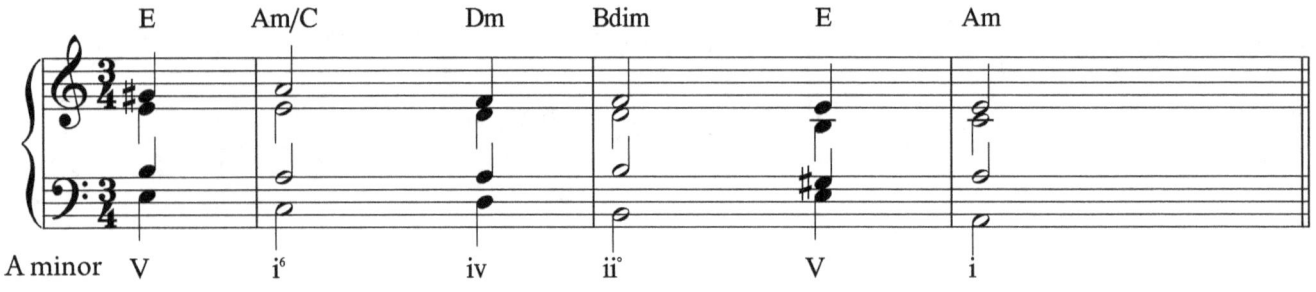

Page 63, No. 1

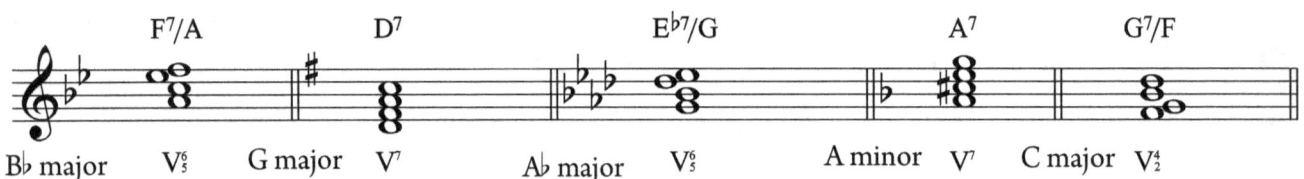

Page 64, No. 1

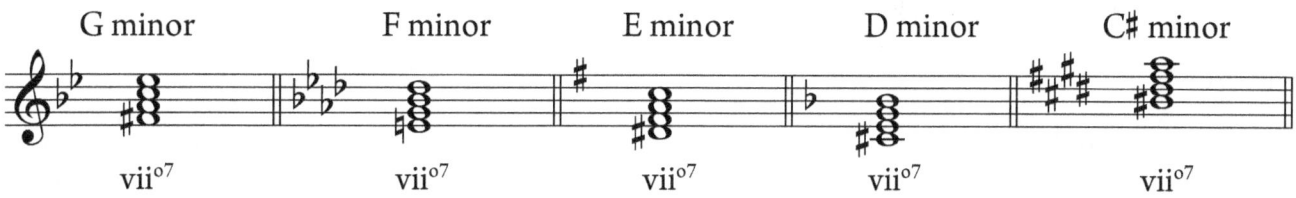

Page 64, No. 2

D	A	F#	G	C	Db
minor	major	dim7	dom7	aug	major
root	1st	root	3rd	root	1st

B	F#	D	C	Bb	Eb
dim7	dim	dom7	minor	major	dim
root	root	root	1st	1st	root

C	C#	Gb	E	F	Bb
dom7	dim7	major	minor	dim	dom7
2nd	root	root	root	1st	1st

Page 65, No. 3

Page 65, No. 4

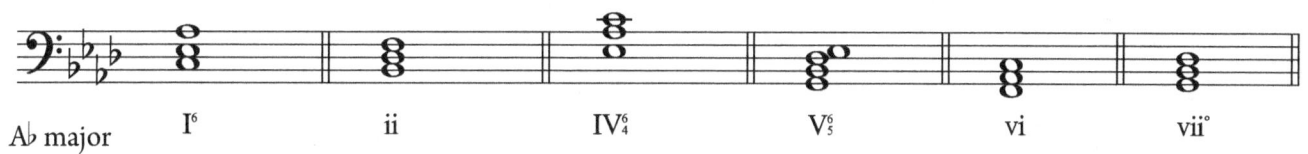

Page 67, No. 1

e. d. a. h. f. b. c. g.

Page 70, No. 1

Page 71-72, No. 1

	Gm Dm		F B♭
	iv i		V I
D minor:	plagal	B♭ major:	perfect authentic

	A E		Fm Cm
	IV I		iv i
E major:	plagal	C minor:	plagal

	Am E		E♭m B♭m
	i V		iv i
A minor:	half	B♭ minor:	plagal

	A D		Cm G
	V I		i V
D major:	imperfect authentic	C minor:	half

	E B		Bm C#
	IV I		iv V
B major:	plagal	F# minor:	half

	F G		D Gm
	IV V		V i
C major:	half	G minor:	perfect authentic

Page 74, No. 1 (other answers are possible)

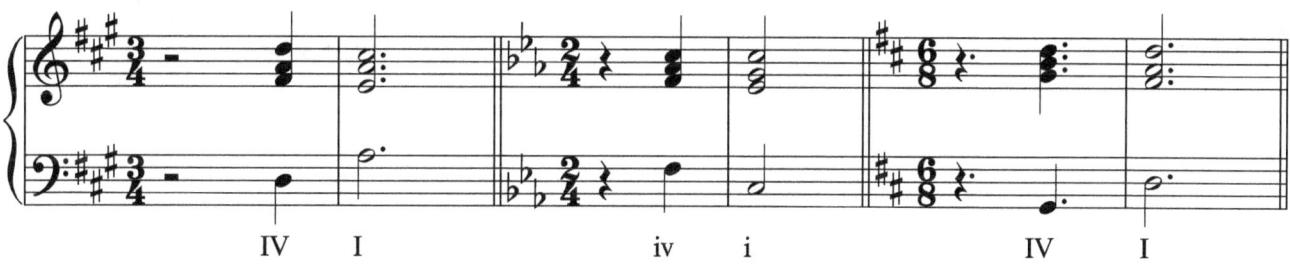

Page 78, No. 1 (other answers are possible)

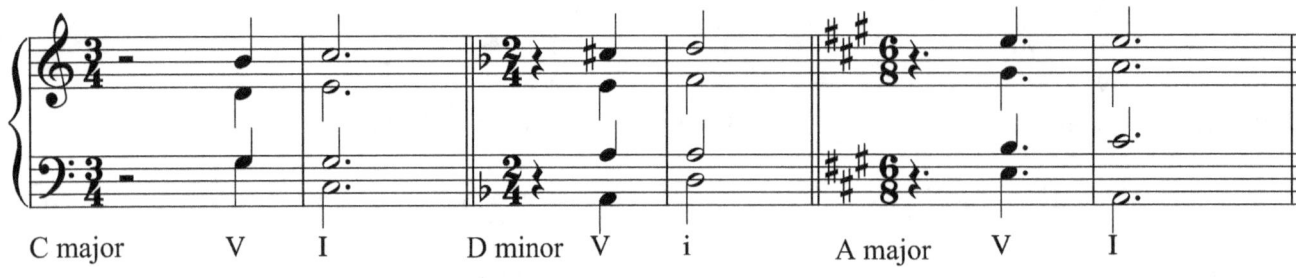

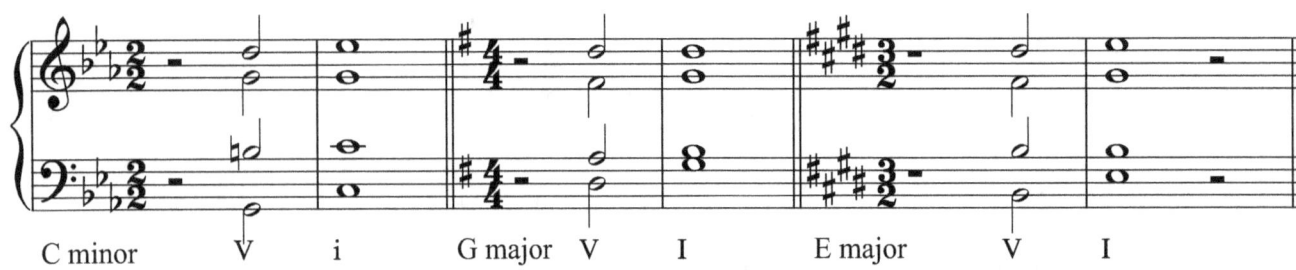

Page 78, No. 2 (other answers are possible)

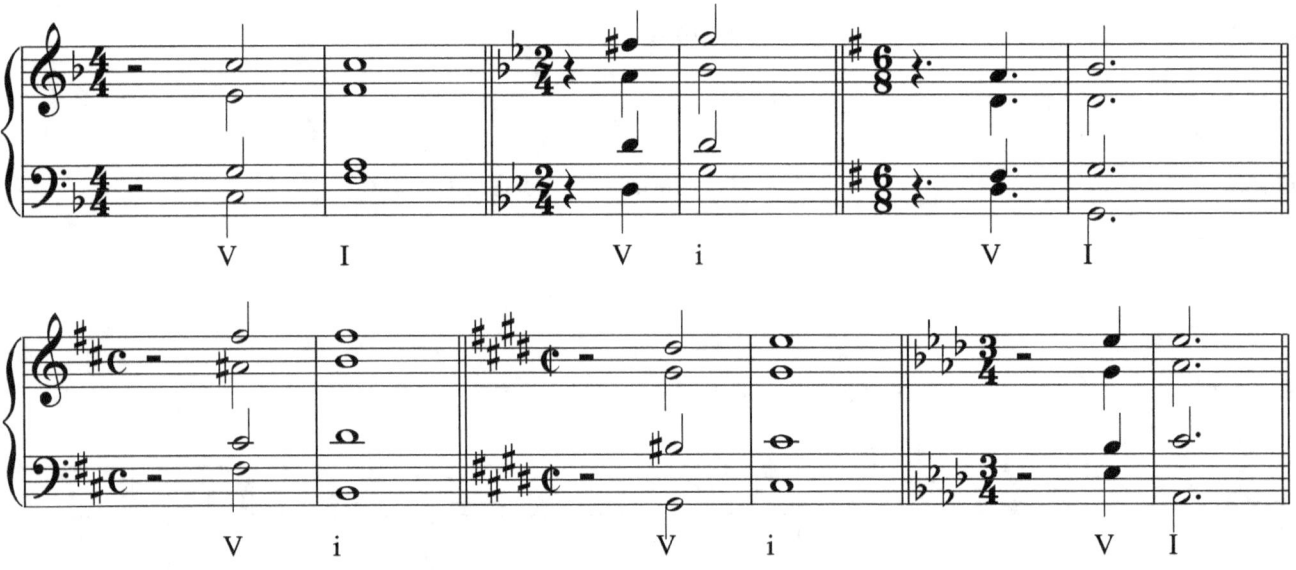

Page 80, No. 1 (other answers are possible)

© San Marco Publications 2018 — Level 8

Page 81, No. 2

Page 82, No. 3

Lentement
D minor
i
V
half

5
V
i
perfect authentic

Page 84, No. 1

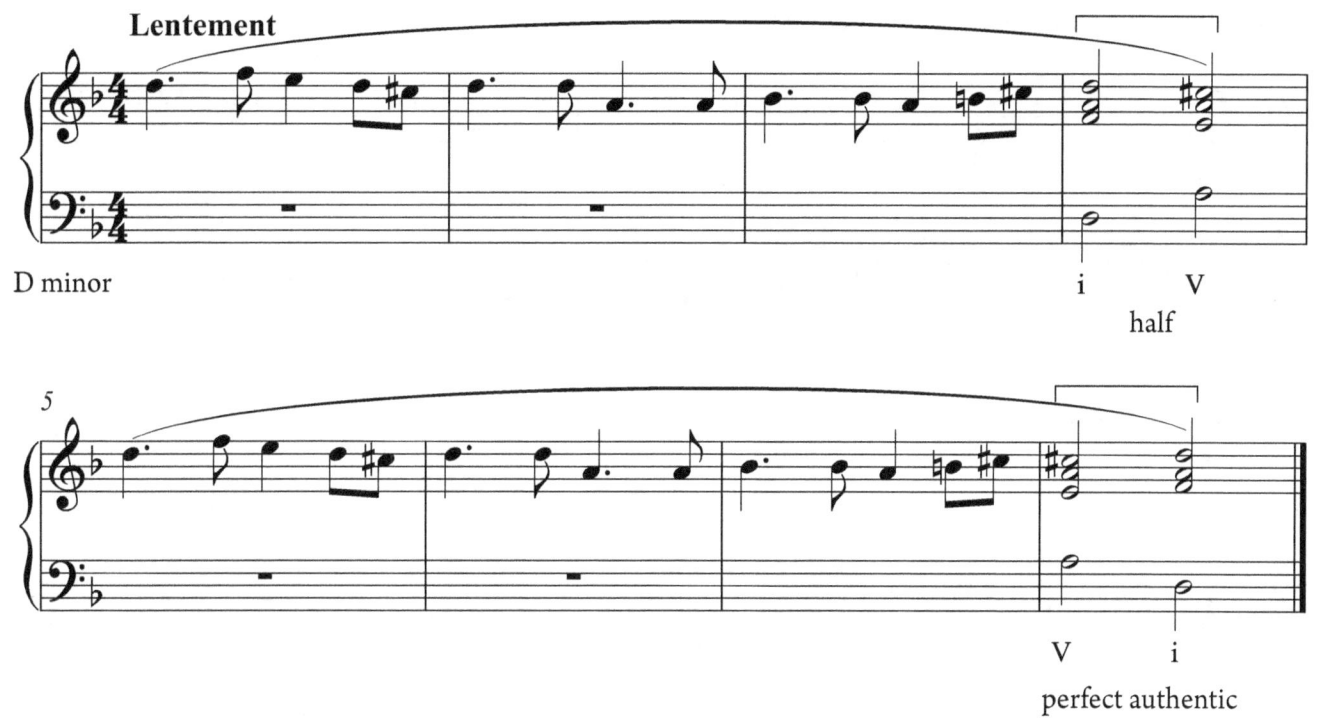

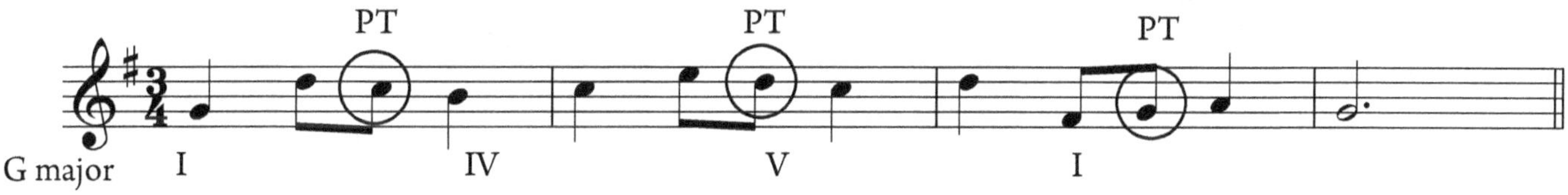
PT
PT
PT
G major
I
IV
V
I

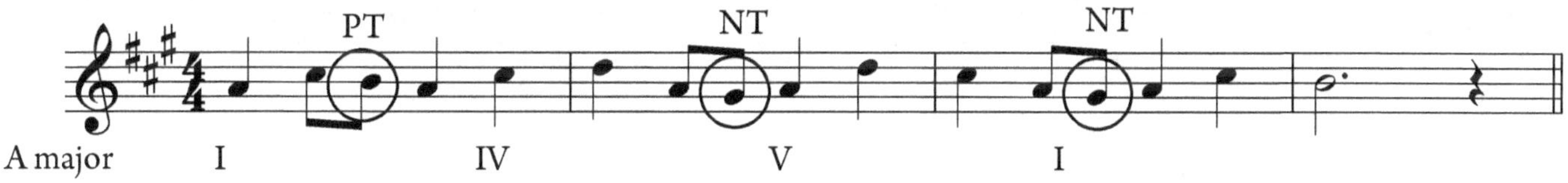
PT
NT
NT
A major
I
IV
V
I

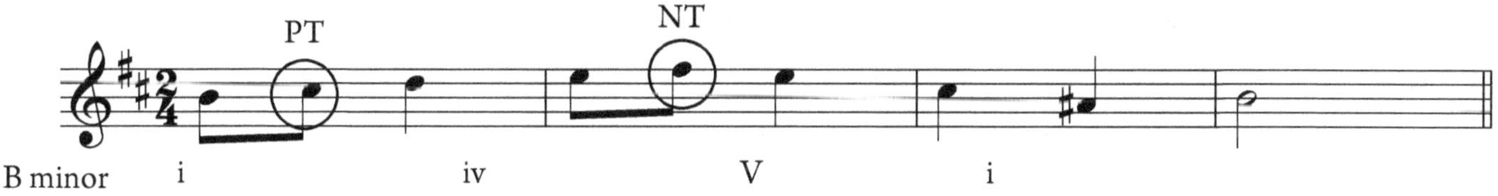
PT
NT
B minor
i
iv
V
i

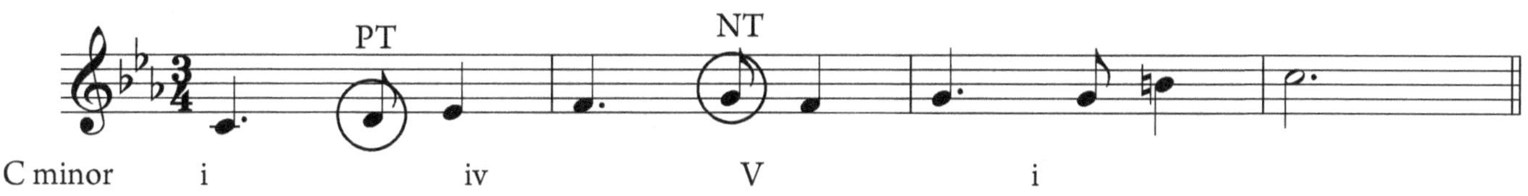
PT
NT
C minor
i
iv
V
i

Page 87, No. 2 (other answers are possible)

Page 90, No. 1 **Review 2**

Page 90, No. 3

Page 91, No. 4

Page 91, No. 5

a. the dominant 7th of D major in root position   **A⁷**

b. the supertonic triad of B♭ major in root position   **Cm**

c. the mediant triad of A major in root position   **C♯m**

d. the leading tone triad of F major in 1st inversion   **Edim/G**

e. the diminished 7th of B harmonic minor   **A♯dim⁷**

Page 91, No. 6

sehr	very
mit Ausdruck	with expression
mässig	moderately
langsam	slowly
schnell	fast
bewegt	with movement, agitated

Page 92, No. 7

C minor

E minor

Page 92, No. 8

a, c, a, b, b, c, c, a, c, a, c, a, c, c, b

Page 95, No. 1

F minor

Johann Sebastian Bach
WTC Bk. I, No. 12

A minor

B♭ major

Wolfgang Amadeus Mozart
Divertimento K.229, No. 2

F major

B minor

Pyotr Tchaikowsky
Symphony No. 6

Page 97, No. 1

C major

Allegro

Wolfgang Amadeus Mozart
Clarinet Concerto, K. 622

B♭ major

Page 98, No. 2

E♭ major

Allegro

Johann Nepomuk Hummel
Trumpet Concerto, III

F major

Page 98, No. 3

A minor

Allegretto

Wolfgang Amadeus Mozart
Symphony No. 40, Minuet

G minor

Page 99, No. 1

B♭ major

Allegro

Wolfgang Amadeus Mozart
Concerto for Horn, K.447, III

E♭ major

Page 100, No. 2

G minor

Allegro

Wolfgang Amadeus Mozart
Allegro, K.312

A minor

Wolfgang Amadeus Mozart
Allegro, K.312

D minor

C# minor

Antono Vivaldi
The Four Seasons, Spring

G# minor

Antono Vivaldi
The Four Seasons, Spring

D# minor

Page 109, No. 1

Johann Sebastian Bach
Chorale no. 67: Freu'dich sehr, o meine Seele

© San Marco Publications 2018   258   Level 8

Page 110, No. 2

Johann Sebastian Bach
Das walt' mein gott

Page 111, No. 3

Ludwig van Beethoven
String Quartet Op 18, No. 1

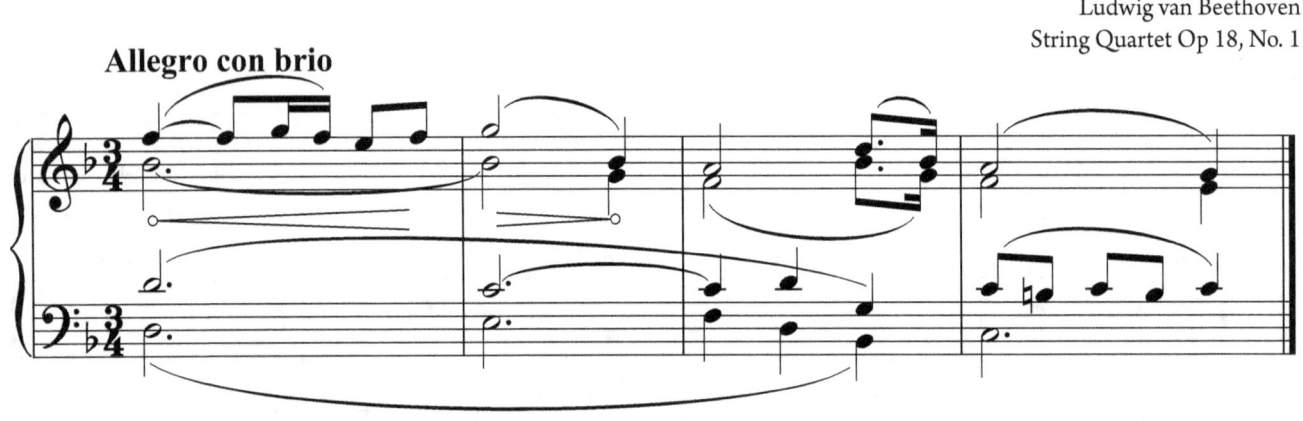

Page 112, No. 4

Franz Joseph Haydn
String Quartet Op 76, No. 3

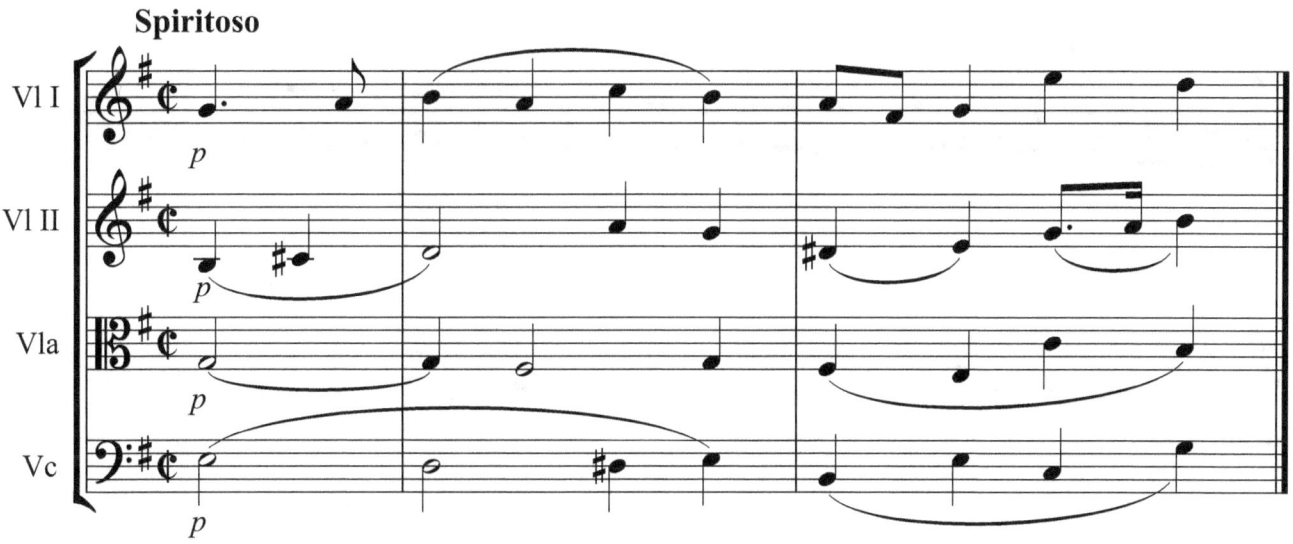

Page 113, No. 5

Johann Sebastian Bach
O Haupt Voll und Wunden

Page 116, No. 1 (other answers are possible)

Page 117, No. 2 (other answers are possible)

B minor   i   iv   i   V

i   iv   V   i

Page 121, No. 1 **Review 3**

B♭ major

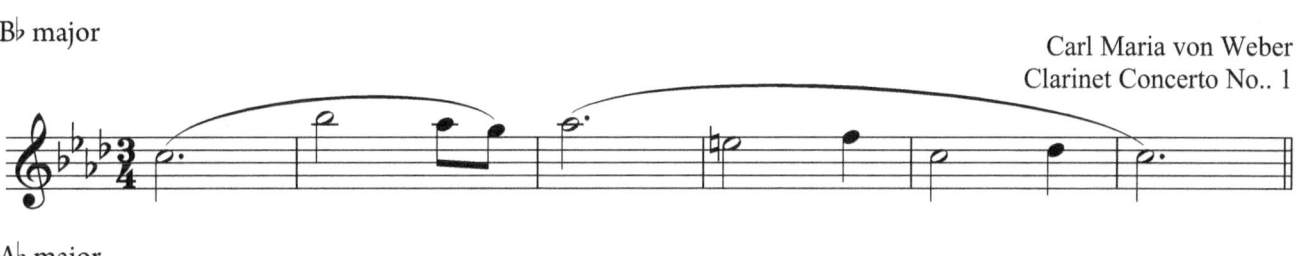

Carl Maria von Weber
Clarinet Concerto No.. 1

A♭ major

C major

Wolfgang Amadeus Mozart
Adagio for 2 Horns and Bassoon

F major

F minor

Wolfgang Amadeus Mozart
Concerto for Horn and Orchestra

C minor

Page 122, No. 3

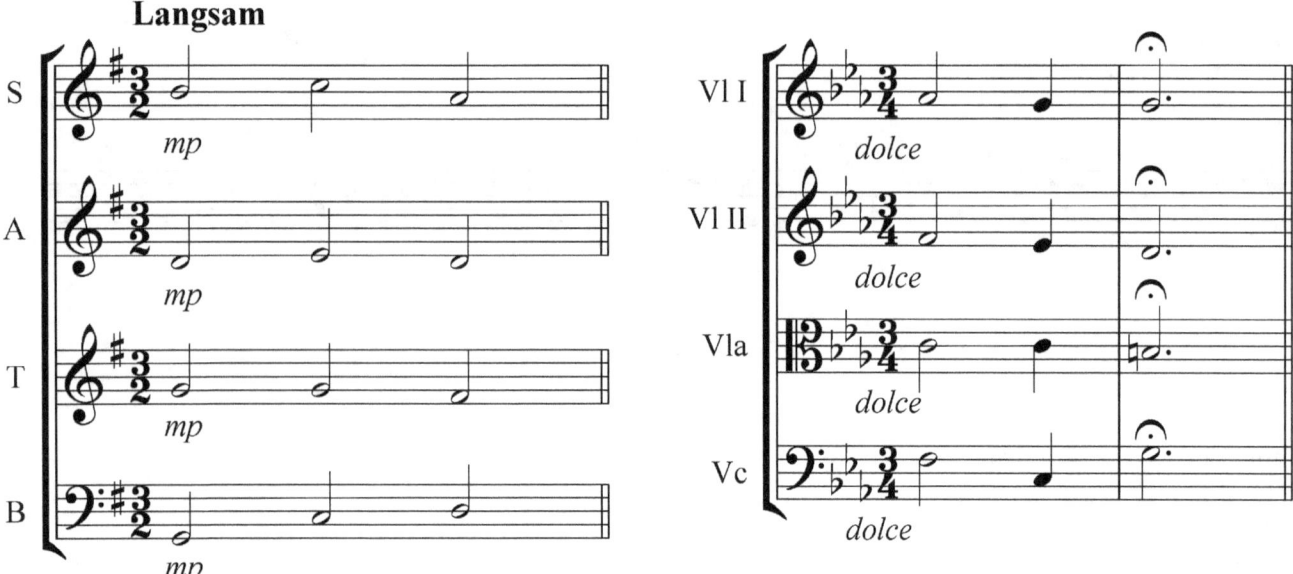

Page 122, No. 4

pizzicato
comodo
stringendo
arco
con sordino
ritenuto

Page 123, No. 5

Page 123, No. 6

a. ***gamelan*** orchestra made up of several types of mallet instruments, or keyboard-style instruments struck with mallets or hammers, as well as different drums, flutes, and occasionally stringed instruments or vocalists.

b. ***metallaphone*** a xylophone-like instrument with metal bars struck by mallets.

c. ***raga*** a mode (scale) found in Indian classical music and used in improvised performances.

d. ***microtone*** smaller intervals than those found in Western music.

e. ***tabla*** a pair of drums that are tuned to work with the notes of the raga.

f. ***tala*** a regular rhythmic cycle found in the raga.

Page 124, No. 1

a. Name the key of this piece. **F major**
b. Write the time signature directly on the score. **6/8**
c. In what musical period was this piece composed? **Classical**
d. Mark the phrases directly on the score.
e. Is this an example of a: ☑parallel period ☐contrasting period
f. Mark the form on the score using the letters **a**, **a¹**, or **b**.
g. State the implied harmony using functional and root/quality chord symbols.
h. Circle and identify any non-chord tones.

Page 125, No. 2

a. Name the key of this piece. **D major**
b. Write the time signature directly on the score. **6/8**
c. In what musical period was this piece composed? **Classical**
d. Mark the phrases directly on the score.
e. Is this an example of a: ☑parallel period ☐contrasting period
f. Mark the form on the score using the letters **a**, **a¹**, or **b**.
g. State the implied harmony using functional and root/quality chord symbols.
h. Circle and identify any non-chord tones.
i. Write the name of the cadences at the end of each phrase in the place provided on the score.

Page 127, No. 1

contrary   oblique   parallel   similar

oblique   parallel   contrary   parallel

similar   oblique   contrary   oblique

Page 128, No. 1

Page 128, No. 2

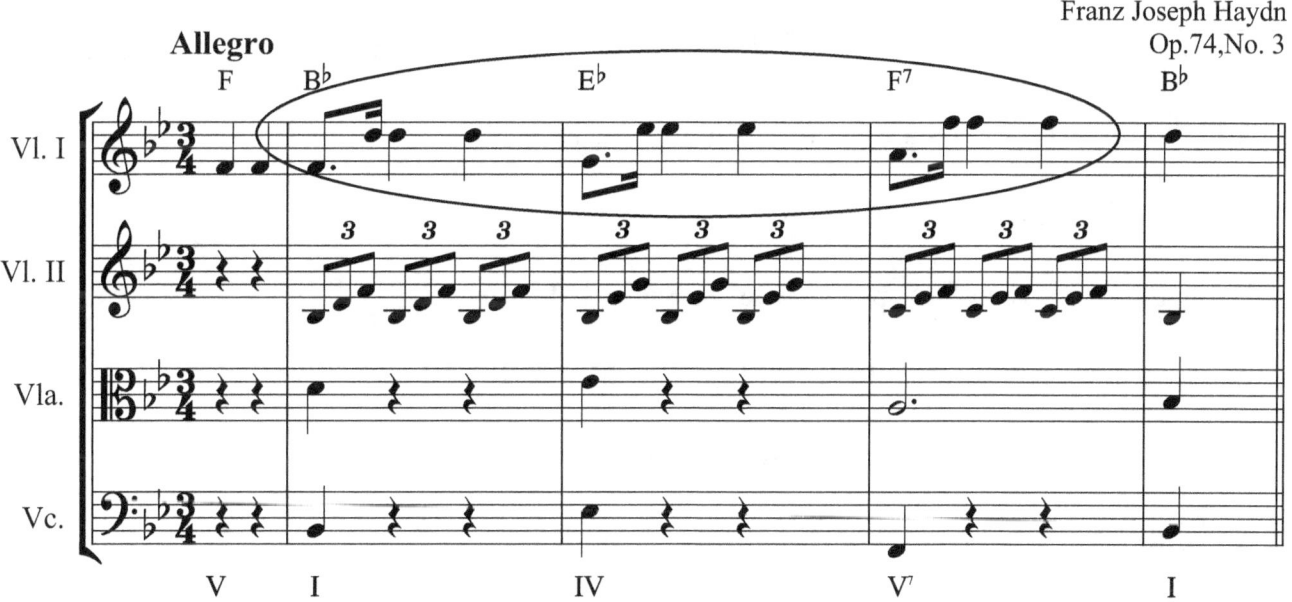

a. Name the key of this phrase. **B♭ major**

b. Write the time signature directly on the score. **3/4**

c. In what musical period was this piece composed? **Classical**

d. What open score is this written for? **String quartet**

e. State the implied harmony using functional and root/quality chord symbols on the score.

f. Find and circle a melodic sequence.

g. Name the cadence at the end of this phrase. **Imperfect authentic**

Passepied

George Frideric Handel
(1685-1759)

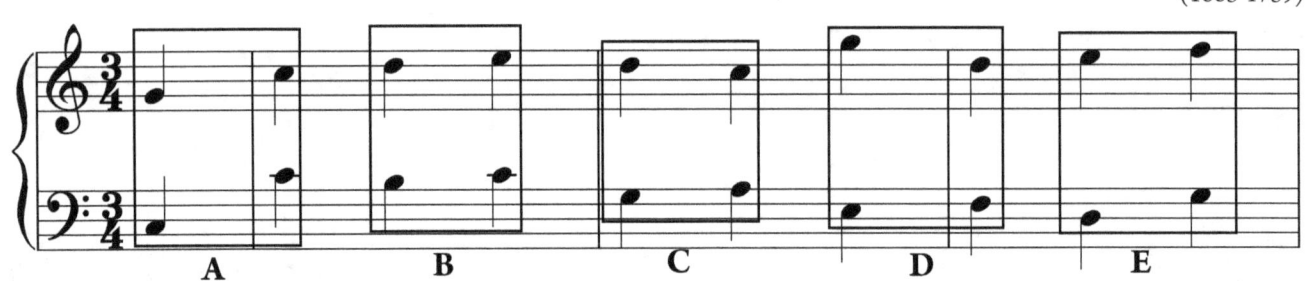

a. Add the correct time signature directly on the music. **3/4**

b. Name the key of this piece. **C major**

c. Name the composer of this piece. **George Frideric Handel**

d. Name another composition by this composer. **Messiah**

d. In what musical era was this composed? **Baroque**

e. This piece is: ☐ monophonic ☑ polyphonic

f. Identify the motion at:

	contrary	parallel	similar	oblique
A:	☐	☐	☑	☐
B:	☐	☑	☐	☐
C:	☑	☐	☐	☐
D:	☑	☐	☐	☐
E:	☐	☐	☑	☐
F:	☐	☐	☐	☑

Page 138, No. 1 **Exam**

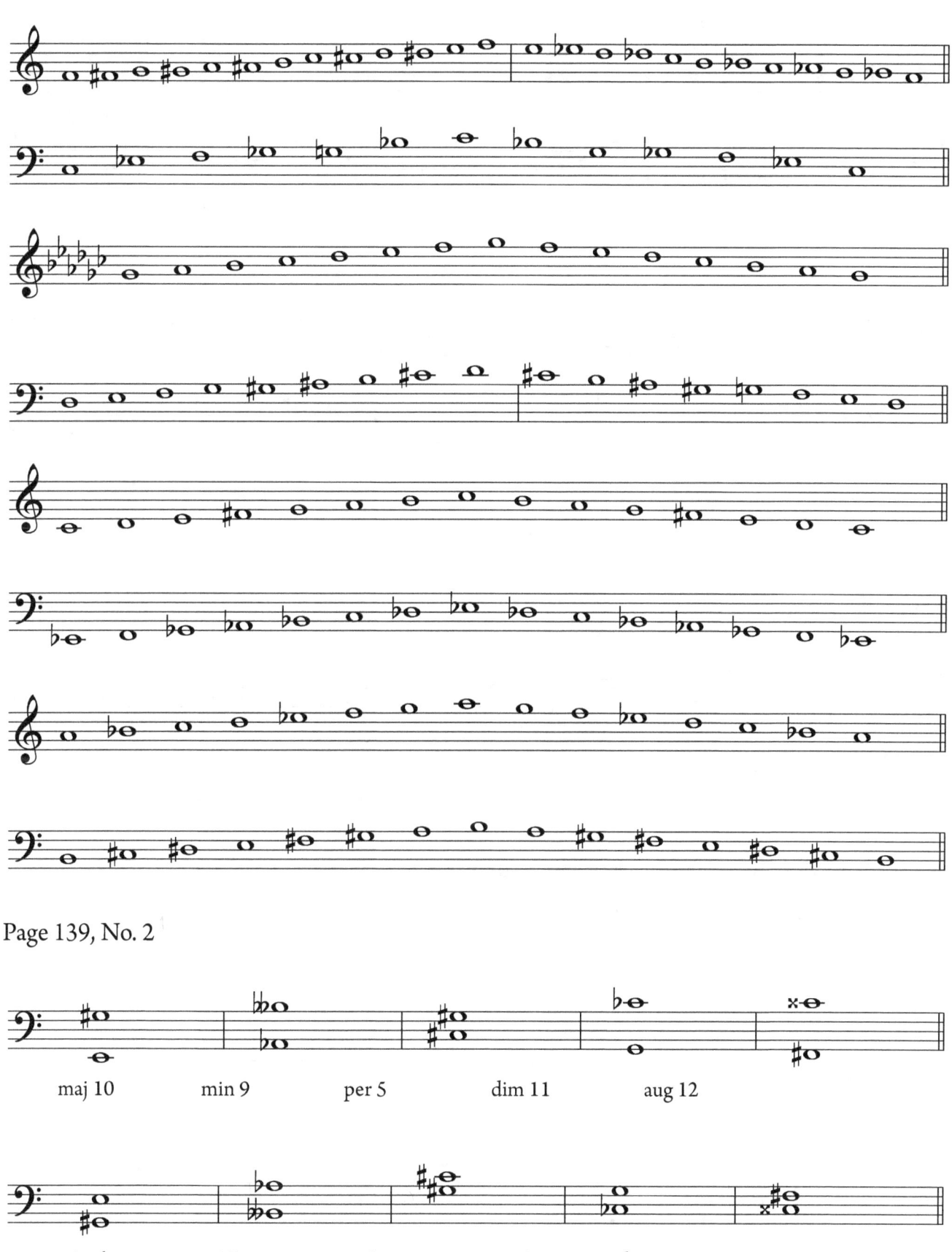

Page 139, No. 2

Level 8

Page 139, No. 3

Page 139, No. 4

Db major

Antonin Dvorak
Scherzo Capriccioso

Gb major

Page 140, No. 5

minor triad   dominant 7th   quartal chord   diminished 7th
polychord   tone cluster   major triad   diminished triad

Page 140, No. 6

Page 141, No. 7

Page 141, No. 8

Giovanni Croce
Is it Nothing to You?

Page 142, No. 9

a. ritenuto
b. gamelon
c. con sordino
d. raga
e. Josquin des Prez
f. schnell
g. monophony
h. homorhythmic
i. leger
j. Renaissance
k. Hildegard von Bingen
l. polyphony
m. sitar
n. frottola
o. langsam
p. a capella
q. ostinato
r. Medieval
s. tala
t. plainchant

Page 143, No. 10

Ludwig van Beethoven
String Quartet No.16

Lento assai

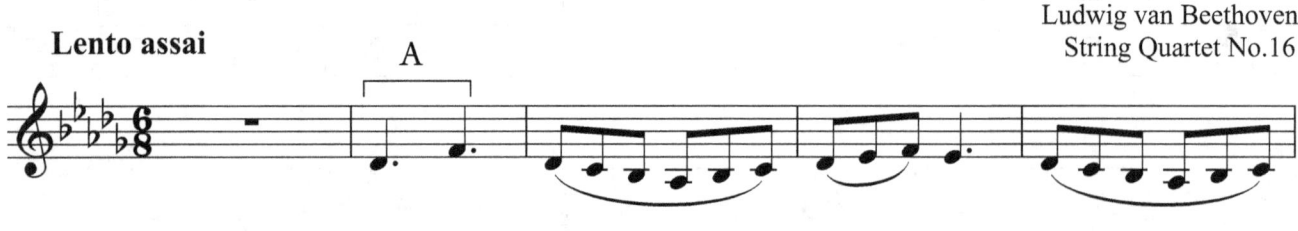

a) Name the key of this piece. **D flat major**

b) Name the enharmonic tonic minor for this key. **C sharp minor**

c) Write the time signature directly on the score. **6/8**

d) Check two words that describe this time signature:

❑simple ☑duple ☑compound ❑triple ❑quadruple

e) Name the intervals at A: **maj 3** B: **per 4** C: **per 4**

f) Define **Lento assai: very slow**

g) How are mm.7, 8, and 9 related? **They are part of a melodic sequence**

h) This is an excerpt from a string quartet. What instument is it written for? **violin**

i) Name the four instruments of the string quartet.

Violin I   Violin II   Viola   Cello

Level 8

www.ingramcontent.com/pod-product-compliance
Lightning Source LLC
Chambersburg PA
CBHW081614100526
44590CB00021B/3439